OUR ORIGIN
AND
DESTINY

Leo,
With Love & Light,
Kathy L. Callahan

OUR ORIGIN AND DESTINY

An Evolutionary Perspective on the New Millennium

Kathy L. Callahan, Ph.D.

ARE PRESS

**ASSOCIATION FOR
RESEARCH AND
ENLIGHTENMENT**

A.R.E. Press • Virginia Beach • Virginia

A.R.E. Press
215 67th Street
Virginia Beach, VA 23451-2061

Library of Congress Cataloging-in-Publication Data
  Callahan, Kathy L. (Kathy Lynn), 1953-
  Our origin and destiny : an evolutionary perspective on the
new milennium / Kathy L. Callahan.
      p. cm.
  Includes bibliographical references.
  ISBN 0-87604-368-6
  1. Prophecies (Occultism). 2. Creation—Miscellanea. 3.
Human evolution—Miscellanea. 4. Cayce, Edgar, 1877-1945.
Edgar Cayce readings. I. Title
BF1791.C34 1996
133.3-dc20   96-44801

Biblical references are to the King James Version
unless otherwise specified.

Cover design by Lightbourne Images

Dedication

This book is dedicated to the great teachers, whose visionary insight echoes still across the span of recorded history, gently awakening within us the truth of our spiritual being; and to the countless "unnamed" others, who, despite ridicule, persecution, and disbelief, dared to believe that we are more than we appear to be.

Contents

List of Tables and Figures

Acknowledgments

I wish to thank my husband, Tino Aragon, and my daughter, Deirdre Aragon, not only for their love and support during the arduous process of writing this book, but for their insights and counsel into many of the topics contained herein.

A special thank you to my sister, Darcie Callahan, and the members of the Search for God Study Groups I have been blessed to be a part of, particularly Jerry Lekstrom, Barbara Lekstrom, Bill Kirklin, Dot Kirklin, Sharon Riley, Brenda Umholtz, Rita Baliunas, John Baliunas, Jeannie Riley, Jack Reed, and Mary Harrington. Our many discussions over the years made a significant contribution to the development of the ideas contained in this book.

I would like to thank my editor, Jon Robertson, for his advice and guidance, and also thank the publishers of the A.R.E. Press for their support.

Finally, as always, a most humble thank you to the Christ Presence, which guides my steps along the path.

Foreword

MY MAIN purpose for writing this book was to address some of the questions which have been raised regarding humanity's future as a new millennium approaches. As an anthropologist, I knew that history shows that all life is predicated upon that which has gone before. The universe operates according to natural, orderly laws. Nothing happens by chance or without reason. I therefore felt it was necessary to take an evolutionary perspective and examine humankind's origins and nature before speculating about the future. In seeking to answer questions about our destiny, I found that I first had to address questions which have long haunted humanity, namely

assumption

questions on the how and why of our creation, our purpose for existence, and the true nature of our being.

I have long accepted the concept that humans are complex beings who exist on three distinct, yet interrelated levels—physical, mental, and spiritual. We are, in effect, comprised of three components—a corporeal body, a mental faculty called mind, and an etheric life-force known as the soul. I therefore felt it was necessary to address our origins, nature, purpose, and destiny in terms of each aspect of our being, so that we might more thoroughly understand the complexities of humankind.

Faith Versus Reason: Bridging the Gap

In seeking to address these issues, I was faced with the prospect of choosing from one of two traditional sources of knowledge—religion or science. Religion seeks to explain all phenomena as the result of a divine intelligence who wills all things into existence. No concrete proof exists to demonstrate the existence of this divine intelligence, and such beliefs must be accepted on the basis of faith alone. Science, on the other hand, seeks to explain physical phenomena in terms of objective, verifiable observation, which can be repeated by any independent observer, and from these observations derives physical laws as the means to explain physical phenomena. Science deals only with tangible physical experience which can be observed, measured, and recorded.

Rather than choose one source of knowledge to the exclusion of the other, however, I decided to seek a middle ground between the two. While some may consider this a radical approach, it is a method which is rapidly growing in favor. Recent years have seen an increasing blend of science, spirituality, and religion on many fronts as people realize that faith and reason are not mutually exclusive. This is perhaps most evident in medical science, where physicians such as Larry Dossey, Bernie Siegel, Herbert Benson, and Deepak Chopra, have paved the way to an acceptance of holistic medicine.

Perhaps it is because I am an anthropologist that this approach seemed not only the most comprehensive, but the most natural to me, for I believe that only by considering reason, faith, and spiritual principle can we truly understand ourselves as physical, mental, and spiritual beings. Anthropologists have traditionally taken a holistic approach in their study of the human species and its behavior, acknowledging that all aspects of human existence—biological, psychological, social, and cultural—contribute toward the understanding of humanity as a whole. The richness of human variation makes evaluation through any particular religious manifesto inadequate, and analysis by scientific models impractical. Human behavior cannot be reduced to a formula—there are as many variables as there are individuals within the species.

Anthropologists have also observed that there are aspects of human existence such as shamanism, which defy current scientific explanation. In fact, one of the best-known anthropologists in the United States today is Carlos Castenda, who has authored several bestselling books based on his mystic experiences under the tutelage of a Yaqui shaman.

It is perhaps where I seek that middle ground between religion and science that gives this book a somewhat unique perspective, and will also be its most controversial feature. For I choose to look for a common point of understanding between religion and science within the realm of metaphysics.[1] A working definition of metaphysics I have adapted is "the cause-and-effect relationship between spirit or energy and the physical or material." Metaphysical principles can thus bridge the gap between religion, which seeks to understand the spiritual, and science, which seeks to understand the physical.

Metaphysical beliefs are based on the premise that all physical phenomena are manifestations of spirit or energy. Energy, be it human thought and idea, the physical forces of nature, or divine will, is the cause, while the physical condition is the effect. Metaphysics thus acknowledges the physical laws which govern the universe but seeks to find the spiritual meaning behind those laws, or the reasons for which they were brought into existence by the universal Creative Force. The philosophy of metaphysics extends back thousands of years, transcending time, religion, and culture, and is evident within many Eastern religions, the writings of Western philosophers, and even within the Judeo-Christian tradition.

The material presented in this book is thus a synthesis of traditional religious belief, scientific findings, and metaphysical principle. Religious material was drawn from a cross-cultural sample of religious doctrine, including Judeo-Christian biblical scriptures, ancient Mayan texts, sacred Hopi teachings, and the Polynesian philosophy of *huna*. Scientific material includes the scientific cosmology of the creation of the universe, the latest discoveries in paleoanthropology and human prehistory, recorded history, ethnographic studies, current theories in cognitive psychology and perceptual studies, linguistics, quantum physics, geophysics and paleogeology, and recent controversial theories regarding the origin of the Egyptian pyramids. The primary source for metaphysical material comes from what is perhaps the most thoroughly documented and consistently reliable source of metaphysical teachings, namely the Edgar Cayce psychic readings. Other metaphysical sources include *A Course in Miracles*,[2] Sanskrit teachings, shamanic studies, and the prophecies of Nostradamus, a fourteenth-century seer. Given their use as the primary source of metaphysical information, a brief description of the Cayce readings follows.

The Edgar Cayce Readings

Edgar Cayce, often called the "sleeping prophet," is perhaps America's best-known psychic. Born in Hopkinsville, Kentucky, in 1877, he displayed psychic abilities at an early age, including the ability to read auras. A devout Christian who read the Bible once through for each year of his life, he was guided by one principle—to be of service to others. Until his death in 1945, he used his unique talents to achieve that end.

His ability to enter a self-induced, semiconscious state and connect with the Universal Consciousness[3] came to light in 1901, when, during hypnosis, he diagnosed the cause of and cure for his own chronic laryngitis. Although encouraged by family and friends, Cayce was at first reluctant to pursue this talent, wondering why God would "pick an uneducated country boy like me." He was also concerned that the information which came through this "sleep" state might inadvertently harm someone. His wife Gertrude, however, pointed out that this might be what he had been seeking for so long—a way to help others. So began the legacy of the Cayce readings.

In the following years, Cayce continued to give "physical readings" which diagnosed the cause of and recommended treatment for hundreds of ailments. Then in 1923, a visit from a man seeking not medical information, but the answers to questions on life, death, and the meaning of everything in between, was to add a new aspect to the readings. During a reading given in response this request, Cayce surprised everyone with the words, "He was once a monk," thereby raising the possibility of reincarnation. The words threw Cayce and his family into a turmoil. As a Presbyterian Sunday school teacher, Cayce hardly believed in the concept of reincarnation. He began to doubt the source of his own information and seriously considered stopping the readings altogether. Following extensive prayer and meditation, and the encouragement of others, however, Cayce continued. Over the years, his continued study of the Bible led him to accept that reincarnation was not contrary to Christianity, but a long-forgotten tenet of that faith. From this start came what would later be known as the "life readings," where Cayce addressed questions from people on issues other than health, often relating the circumstances of this lifetime to experiences in past lives.

Cayce's life was not an easy one. He certainly did not become a rich man, because he solicited no fee for the readings. A photographer by trade, he balanced the time he devoted to giving readings with the time he needed to support his family. There were occasions when he barely had enough money to make the monthly rent payment. Despite the success of the physical readings, and the testimony of the thousands he had helped, he was still subject to scorn, ridicule, and disbelief. Still, he had the constant support of his devoted wife Gertrude, sons Hugh Lynn and Edgar Evans, and Gladys Davis Turner, who served as secretary and stenographer. Those who came to discredit Cayce and expose him as a fraud ended up becoming stalwart supporters. The principal biography of Cayce, *There Is a River*, written by Thomas Sugrue, was first published in 1942;[4] it has never been out of print. Over 300 other books have been written on his work.

Throughout his life, Cayce gave more than 14,000 psychic readings, of which over 9,000 are physical readings, nearly 2,000 life readings, and the remainder being given on various topics. Each reading is numbered, the first sequence identifying the person for whom the reading was given (to protect identity), and the second sequence indicating, in chronological order, the number of the reading given for that person. Today they comprise one of the most comprehensive and well-documented records of psychic perception. They have been cross-indexed under thousands of subject headings, computerized, and made available for study through the Association for Research and Enlightenment, Inc. (A.R.E.). The A.R.E. is a nonprofit, open membership organization founded in 1931 by Cayce and his supporters. Its headquarters in Virginia Beach, Virginia, boasts one of the largest libraries on metaphysical subjects in the country. The organization is committed to spiritual growth, holistic healing, psychical research, parapsychology, and metaphysical studies.

Edgar Cayce left behind a legacy of information on more than 10,000 different subjects. The accuracy of his physical readings continue to amaze the medical professionals who come to study them. The consistency within 14,000 readings, spanning over forty years, attests to their authenticity. In the words of Abraham Lincoln, "No man has a good enough memory to be a successful liar." It is for these reasons that I chose the Edgar Cayce readings as the primary source of information for metaphysical explanations of human creation, purpose, and destiny.

The Mosaic of Human Experience

I acknowledge that there will be those who will be uncomfortable with the approach I have taken in this book. Hard-core scientists will reject it outright as being subjective speculation based on unverifiable myth, legend, and psychic nonsense. I would remind them that "one generation's miracle may be another's scientific fact."[5] Orthodox religious purists will reject it as being contrary to the word of God as recorded in scripture. I ask them not to denounce something they have never really examined nor taken the time to understand. Science is not the tool of the devil; it is the product of human reason seeking to understand the world around us.

Yet I believe that a synthesized approach to the study of humankind is necessary, for I believe that each body of knowledge—religion, science, and metaphysics—addresses certain aspects of our being. Any one individually does not encompass the whole of who we are, how we came to be, why we are here, and where we are going. Yet take the pieces of each and blend them together, and you have a magnificent mosaic which encompasses all aspects of the human experience.

> *"I see science and mysticism as two complementary manifestations of the human mind, of its rational and intuitive faculties. The two approaches are entirely different . . . However, they are 'complimentary,' as we have learned to say in physics. Both of them are necessary, supplementing one another for a fuller understanding of the world."*[6]

As the quotation of physicist Fritjof Capra demonstrates, the time is ripe for acceptance of a methodology which considers religion, science, and spiritual principle. Medical science is the first area to demonstrate the effects of this quiet revolution, which first began with discoveries in quantum physics which showed support for ancient metaphysical principles concerning the unitive nature of the universe.

The greatest minds throughout history recognized the physical, mental, and spiritual dimensions of human existence. The Greek philosophers Socrates and Plato, the Stoics Seneca and Marcus Aurelius, the religious innovators such as Buddha, Jesus, and St. Thomas Aquinas, and the modern-day scientists such as Leonardo da Vinci, Albert Schweitzer, and Albert Einstein, all knew that the human experience was much greater than that taught by religious tradition or observed through scientific measure. They did not allow themselves to be limited by the narrowly defined beliefs of their day, but sought to rise above their contemporaries, understanding that there were times when religion and science could join hands and learn from one another.

As we look to the new millennium and the opportunities it may bring, isn't it time to put aside restrictive, outmoded ways of thinking, embrace the totality of the human experience, and join with the great teachers who tried to show us that we are more than we appear to be? I think it is, and I invite you to do so with me, as we explore the questions of humanity's origins, nature, purpose, and destiny.

Preface

A New Millennium

As THIS book nears publication, the year 1996 is drawing to a close. In three years, we will be approaching not only the advent of a new century, but the beginning of a new millennium, a millennium which many people believe will be characterized by profound change and transformation. The year 2000 draws near, and numerous books and articles advocate diverse and sometimes contradictory views as to what this new millennium may bring.

There are a number of people who regard the coming millennium with a sense of eagerness and anticipation. They envision a world replete with even greater scientific advances which will cure disease, solve world problems, and create an idealistic society. Others, however, face the end of this century with a sense of fear and dread, believing that the new millennium will bring devastating earth changes and cataclysmic upheavals which will drastically alter the global surface. There are still others who view this time with a sense of moral contemplation, believing that the hour is near when the unrighteous will be chastised for their errant ways, and the righteous will inherit their due in a "new kingdom." There are even groups of people who enthusiastically believe that they, along with other "enlightened souls," will be carried away by alien beings to superior worlds, while the rest of humanity is left to deal with the chaos that will envelop the earth.

It should come as no surprise that the advent of a new millennium should generate such discussion. Anyone familiar with history knows that such ideas, especially those advocating "end of the world" themes, often gain prominence as a century draws to a close. In fact, in medieval Europe, the beginning of this millennium was preceded by dire predictions that God was going to destroy the "wicked" cities and their inhabitants. These predictions caused riots and panic, and resulted in mass migrations of people from urban centers to rural areas.

It seems that each generation since the Book of Revelation was first written, has believed that predictions concerning the end of the world would come true in its day. Even Christ's own disciples believed that they would witness the end of the world, and subsequent generations have been quick to echo that belief. Why is it that we seem to forget Christ's own admonition that "of that day and hour knoweth no man, no, not the angels of heaven, but my Father only" (Matthew 24:36)?

A review of history will show that cultural epochs do

not begin at the start of a given century. Recognized cultural periods, such as the Renaissance, the Age of Exploration, or the Golden Age of Greece, are the result of interrelated developments in such areas as religion, philosophical thought, politics, economics, and science. It is only through the advantage hindsight provides that we can recognize these cultural divisions, and arbitrarily assign a general time period to each.

Considering what we know of human history, and the fact that it has always progressed in an orderly and consistent manner, why, then, are we still so fascinated as to what this next millennium may bring? One would think that we would have outgrown such ideas during the last thousand years, particularly when one considers that science has replaced magic, and reason has supposedly replaced superstition. Why are we still susceptible to the idea that the end of the millennium means the end of the world? Perhaps it is human nature to look forward to the future. In fact, the ability to envision the future is probably a characteristic that has helped us adapt to change and make the most of what the world offers up to us. Then again, perhaps, this time, there might be some truth underlying the myriad of speculation.

It's interesting to note that there are a number of sources, both ancient and modern, which agree that the coming millennium will be a time of significant change and transformation. For example, according to the Mayan calendar, the year 2012 A.D. marks the end of our present age of the Fifth Sun, followed by a shift or movement that will create a new world order. One need only point to the establishment of Israel as an independent nation to realize that this is but one of the many biblical prophecies that was to precede the "end of the world," that has come true in this generation. Further, according to the Hopi prophecies, many events which are to signal the end of this, the Fourth World, and the subsequent Purification Day, have occurred in the last one hundred years. The Hopi belief in their prophecies is so fervent, that they sent delegations to the United Nations in 1948 and 1973, seeking to share this knowledge with other nations.

In addition to these so-called ancient prophecies, modern prophecies, such as the quatrains of Nostradamus, the Edgar Cayce psychic readings, and the Marian revelations, to name only a few, all indicate that the next ten years will be a time of major world change and transformation. Modern interpretations of the Great Pyramid of Gizeh have proposed the idea that it was built as a "chronogram," whose time line indicates that major changes will occur in the next few years. Finally, in terms of astrological cycles, which are determined by the constellation in which the sun rises on the vernal (spring) equinox, our sun is about to move out of the constellation of Pisces, which it entered 2,000 years ago, and into the constellation of Aquarius.

After reviewing the information contained in these and other sources, I must confess that I belong to the growing group of people who believe that the coming millennium will be a time of change. But I do not believe that the changes we will experience will be instantaneous or magical. The changes we will face are actually the culmination of thousands, if not millions, of years of natural and orderly development on this planet. As a part of God's divine order and plan, they are a result of the natural evolutionary process we experience on the physical, mental, and spiritual levels. The changes we will encounter should not be feared, but viewed as stepping stones, albeit major ones, on the path back to oneness with our spiritual source.

The Changes Ahead

While the dawn of the next millennium may bring change in many areas, I believe that the changes we will encounter fall under the purview of three separate yet interrelated areas. Specifically, these are: a change in the sensory perception of the human species, a change in human cognition or consciousness, and geophysical earth changes on a global level. The first two developments fall within the sphere of microcosmic (species) evolution, while earth changes can be considered as evolution on the macrocosmic (global) level. The microcosmic changes we are even now experiencing have been happening so gradually as to be almost imperceptible. The geophysical changes, however, will be apparent to everyone, and while they may seem sudden, are actually the result of choices made and actions taken in times past.

As regards the change in our sensory perception, I believe that the human species is in the midst of a transitory period wherein we are changing from a five-sensory species to a multisensory species, an idea first proposed by Gary Zukav.[1] There are increasing indications that in addition to our senses of sight, hearing, smell, touch, and taste, humans are developing and experiencing a sixth and perhaps even seventh sense. While our first five senses are capable of interpreting stimuli received from the physical world of matter, these new senses are capable of perceiving phenomena which manifest as thought or energy. This development has been in progress for generations, but it has been such a gradual process that we have not been aware of it until recently.

All that we know of human development shows that it has been a slow and gradual process. Evolutionary changes within a species or population are subtle and undetectable at first, and it is only through retrospection that we can point to structural and morphological changes within a population and proclaim that certain specimens belong to one species or another. The fossil record of well-documented species clearly demonstrates that you don't have a population belonging to one species one day, and a totally new species the next. In fact, the record indicates that in some cases, there may be a "transitory period," when a population contains individual forms which are difficult to assign to one species or the other, or individuals which may possess traits characteristic of two distinct species.[2]

It is no different with this development, for the manifestations of the sixth sense and seventh sense have been ongoing for many generations. It is quite possible that the experiences of so-called seers and mystics, who heard voices or saw visions, were the first documentations of this new sensory ability. This honored group includes Socrates and Plato, the Buddha, Christian mystics such as Joan of Arc, Jacob Böhme, Meister Eckhardt, Teilhard de Chardin, and the Jewish seers Martin Buber and Nostradamus.[3] Their ability to perceive input from nonphysical stimuli was not understood, and could not be explained in the terminology of their day. I further believe that the recent rise in the number of psychic or intuitive experiences being reported by people today could very well be evidence that increasing numbers of humans are now manifesting this new sensory ability which will one day be attained by all.

I realize, however, that not everyone accepts this idea. There are those who will continue to think that persons displaying such intuitive abilities are a little bit off-center, react with emotion rather than logic, and are subject to delusions and flights of fancy. But, when we encounter such opinions, it is important to remember that it is difficult to understand something you cannot experience for yourself. Any woman who has given birth knows that you cannot fully comprehend the labor process until you have experienced it. Despite photographs I had seen, I never really fathomed the beauty and vibrance of a mountain until I actually saw the Colorado Rockies. Just as it is difficult to explain sight to a person born blind, so is it difficult to explain an intuitive sense to a physical-sensory person. Yet with time, as more and more people manifest this ability, I believe that it will become an accepted and acknowledged part of the human experience.

While the change in sensory perception is a physical adaptation, the evolutionary process is not limited to biological change alone; mental processes also evolve over time. Human cognition, or the way we perceive and analyze the world around us, is just such a mental process. Human cognition is intricately linked to what is commonly referred to as human consciousness, which includes those universal beliefs, values, and attitudes, which the human species, as a whole, holds to be true. As human cognition changes, so does human consciousness, and it is often changes in this area which have had the most profound effects upon society and culture. We need only consider the development of symbolic thought (language) to realize that the impact of such change is often immeasurable.

I believe that the development of new sensory perception will result in a change in human consciousness, as we move beyond the limited paradigms of "divergence" which have kept us separate from one another, and embrace the paradigm of "oneness" or "unity," which sees beyond surface differences and acknowledges our true identity as spiritual beings.

If you have any doubt that we are about to experience

a shift in human consciousness, you need only review history to realize that humanity has been making steady, forward progress in this respect. For thousands of years, power belonged to the strong, wealth was reserved for the few, slavery or serfdom was commonplace, human rights were nonexistent, and life for the "commoner" held little hope or promise. Yet gradually, we made a little progress here and there, and saw positive change in many areas. Brutal laws which once exacted physical punishment or death for minor crimes were gradually replaced by a more equitable "tooth for a tooth" mentality, and these laws were eventually replaced with codified laws specifying more humane punishments for crimes committed. In many countries today, the law has evolved into a system of justice which guarantees the accused certain rights with respect to arrest, trial, and conviction. Power no longer belongs only to the strong. While it is true that in some countries we still see a disparity between rich and poor, overall the standard of living for the "common man" has shown steady improvement over time. In many countries, slavery has been abolished, and certain human rights are not only acknowledged, but also guaranteed and protected by law.

If you still doubt that there is a change occurring in human consciousness, consider the fall of the U.S.S.R. and the Soviet bloc countries. As a young child, I remember hearing about the building of the Berlin Wall, a wall designed to keep people in and freedom out. I prefer to think of myself as an optimist, yet I never believed that I would see that wall come down in my lifetime. The very thought was almost inconceivable. Yet the wall did come down! But it didn't come down through military might. It came down, literally brick by brick, through the will of the people, who would no longer accept the beliefs of the old world order. Who of us, in this generation, ever believed that this would happen in our lifetime?

I acknowledge that despite great progress, there are still areas of the world which are held in the grip of the old divergent paradigms that bring about war and destruction. But I believe that those who still hold those views are now in the minority, and will continue to diminish in number as more and more people begin to perceive the world through the paradigm of unity. For according to metaphysical principles, when one person moves forward, it has the resultant effect of lifting all of humanity a little bit higher as well.

The scientific principle of critical mass also states that it doesn't require a one hundred percent shift in force to change the tilt of a fulcrum; it only takes fifty-one percent. I believe that we are rapidly approaching that critical fifty-one percent. It is also quite likely that as we reach that fifty-one percent, we will experience the "hundredth monkey" effect. This means that when the fulcrum tips, all of humanity will be drawn with it, and propelled at an even faster rate toward acceptance of a new perception of the world.

Finally, as our species experiences biological and cognitive change, I believe that we are about to experience certain geophysical or earth changes as well. It is these changes which will cause the most fear and panic, primarily because they may cause much destruction. Still, if we can understand the why of these changes, we may be better able to deal with and accept them as a part of the natural order.

In actuality, the global world without will be reflecting the physical and cognitive changes humankind is experiencing within, as expressed in the concept "as above, so below," or "as within, so without," a metaphysical axiom dating back thousands of years. It has been echoed in many cultures, traditions, and religions. Even the

"Lord's Prayer," taught by Jesus of Nazareth, reflects this thought in the words "on earth as it is in heaven." Two thousand years later, medical science acknowledges the truth of this statement as the link between mental attitude and emotions, to the state of physical health. Negative attitudes and emotions, such as fear, anger, jealousy, resentment, and hate (within), can be manifested in the body as "dis-ease" (without). Carrying this idea a step further, we see that as humanity changes, so does the physical planet.

The earth changes we face, however, are more than reflections of ourselves. I maintain that they are also the result or consequence of our choices and actions in times past. On the whole, we have badly mistreated Mother Earth, and it may be time to reap the seed we have sown. For this reason, some of the changes may be inevitable, for their cause was set in motion hundreds of years ago. We are merely reaping the effect of those causes enacted in the past.

Yet, it is true that many of us have realized the error of our ways and have tried desperately to correct the damage that was done. Recycling programs, conservation efforts, and legislation designed to protect the environment are some of the steps taken to ensure that humanity's mistreatment of our planet will not continue. We have learned the lesson. We have changed! Why can't prophecy be changed also? I believe that it can.

While some earth changes may be inevitable, I believe that the manner in which many of these changes manifest, can and is being modified. If it is true that we are constantly creating our world, then it must follow that our future is not set in stone; it is fluid and variable. The shape and form of our future not only depend upon the choices and decisions of the past, but those we make in the present moment as well. Prophecy is based on conditions as they are at the time the prophecy is given, and the prediction made is based on the continuation of those conditions. Change the conditions, and you change the prophecy. I call this principle the "Nineveh Factor." Love, prayer, and positive thought are the most powerful forces in the world, and if we apply them, as many have already been doing, we can influence the way these changes will manifest. It's possible that some predictions may be avoided entirely, while others which must be met as the effect of prior causes set in motion, will be tempered with mercy and grace.

Greeting the Changes to Come

If we accept the premise that the coming millennium is going to bring change, we then must decide how we will greet those changes. We can either fight and resist them, seeing them as destroyers of the familiar and comfortable, or we can accept them as harbingers of transformation which will open new doors and opportunities for spiritual growth.

We can choose to regard the coming changes with an "end-of-the-world" mentality, viewing them with distrust and suspicion in the belief that they pose a threat to the safe and familiar world we know. Resisting the changes ahead will be self-defeating, however, for they will come regardless of whether or not they are welcomed. Resistance will only reinforce negative thought patterns and deplete our energy, adversely affecting both physical and mental health. Further, by reacting with resistance, we are in effect denying the truth of divine order, and acknowledging that we are susceptible to the chaotic whims of an impartial universe.

Or, we can choose to view the coming changes as evidence of *transformation* rather than destruction, remembering that these changes are actually steps in a natural and orderly process that has been unfolding for a long, long time. By understanding the meaning behind the changes, we can begin to see them as opportunities for learning and growth, which will lead us to a closer oneness with the Creative Force. By reacting with acceptance, we acknowledge the truth of divine order, and greet the changes to come as stepping stones on our spiritual path.

It's true that certain changes, such as the shift in human consciousness, will be easier to accept than others, for we can see that some changes hold the promise of a better way. The geophysical changes, on the other hand, will be the most difficult to accept, for they are certain to be accompanied by death and destruction, and it is hard to understand that there is any good which can come from this path. Still, we must strive to look beyond the surface disruptions the changes may bring and keep our eyes on the prize they will lead us to, and the transformation they will bring. For while there will be aspects to these changes which may be unpleasant and even painful, we need to remember that it is often through the meeting and overcoming of adversity that we experience the greatest growth.

About This Book

The premise of this book is that humankind is standing at the threshold of a new millennium which will bring change and transformation in terms of both physical, cognitive, and spiritual development, as well as geophysical change on a global level. It takes an evolutionary perspective by proposing that these changes, rather than being sudden or unexpected, are actually the result of millions of years of preparation on the physical, mental, and spiritual levels of our being. The purpose of this book is not only to describe what those changes may be, but to explore the reasons as to why they will occur, so that we can better understand and accept them.

In order to understand the why behind the change, we must first understand that the future, even of our planet, is always predicated upon our past actions and choices. Science acknowledges this as "causation." Albert Einstein expressed it thus: "The scientist is possessed by the sense of universal causation. The future, to him, is every whit as necessary and determined as the past."[4] Metaphysical sources refer to this as the universal Law of Cause and Effect, which states that the future is the effect of causes previously set in motion; nothing happens by chance. This concept was repeatedly emphasized in the Cayce readings: "For each entity in the earth is what it is because of what it has been! And each moment is dependent upon another moment."[5]

Both science and metaphysics thus agree that to understand the future, we must first understand the past. In addition to examining the past, we must also consider the present, for the future is also affected by choices and actions made in the present moment. Once we, as individuals and as a species, understand this concept, we can perhaps make wiser decisions and choices, knowing that our actions today will shape our tomorrow.

To achieve this end, the book is divided into three sections. Part One, "Understanding Our Past," examines our origins, beginning with the spiritual creation of the soul as described in the biblical account and the metaphysical data of the Cayce readings. Next, the physical creation of the human body is explored through a comparison of the Cayce readings with the scientific fossil record. Part One concludes with a discussion of the development of human consciousness as based on the

Cayce readings and the prehistoric record of human history. Part Two, "Embracing Our Present," addresses the nature of humankind today, taking a microcosmic look at the nature of the human species as body, mind, and soul, and a macrocosmic look at the current state of human culture. Speculations on the future of humankind are presented in Part III, "Accepting Our Future: Coming to Terms with the New Millennium." Human evolution is discussed in terms of the development of multisensory perception, an expansion of cognitive perception or consciousness, and the acceptance of a spiritual paradigm in the next millennium. Included here is a cross-cultural look at various prophecies concerning the new millennium, a discussion of the nature of prophecy, and the presentation of a time line for anticipated change. The book concludes with the "Author's Postscript," which presents a brief summary and conclusions, and offers the author's personal view of life in the new millennium.

Making a Choice

Before continuing, however, there is one more factor we need to consider when discussing the changes the new millennium will bring. We need to begin with the premise that no man, woman, or child, is on this planet by accident. Each soul present has *chosen* to incarnate on the earth plane at this particular time. Some have returned to earth in this generation for it offers them a second chance to right old wrongs. Others have come to learn one of the many lessons this time will offer, while others have come to serve as teachers. Still others have chosen to be here simply out of love for their brethren. It will be their role to aid and comfort those who have forgotten why they are here, and view the changes through the eyes of fear rather than understanding. We must remember that we made the choice to experience all that this era will bring, for on the soul level we know that pain and suffering are but momentary illusions, and that the spiritual growth we can experience during this time will last for all eternity.

Yet, even as we stand at a critical turning point in human history, there is still one choice yet to make. We can either honor the purpose for which we entered the earth, or forget that purpose as we become entangled in the fears and doubts which all too often tempt us to leave our chosen path. We can either become lost in the anxiety and fear which comes with change, or we can look to a higher purpose, and face these changes with a sense of wonder and anticipation, knowing that we are about to take a great step forward in our journey home to God.

As I consider what lies ahead, I am reminded of a proverb of unknown origin, which goes something like this:

Two men stood on a hillside, each looking at the same night sky.
One man sighed, filled with despair, for he saw only darkness.
The other man, smiled, overwhelmed by great joy, for he saw only stars.

Which would you rather see, darkness or stars? The choice is yours to make.

Part
I

Understanding Our Past

1

Our Spiritual Origins: Creation of the Soul

Our birth is but a sleep and a forgetting:
The Soul that rises with us, our life's Star,
Hath had elsewhere its setting, and cometh from afar . . .
Trailing clouds of glory do we come from God, who is our
home.

—William Wordsworth,
from *Intimations of Immortality*

THROUGHOUT HISTORY, humankind has pondered the secrets of its origin, the truth of its nature, and its relationship to the universe. Questions such as "Who am I?" "Where do I come from?" "For what purpose am I here?" and "Where am I going?" have echoed across the generations, regardless of nationality, culture, or tradition. We have taken this ability to analyze ourselves as evidence of self-awareness, meaning that we are capable of comprehending ourselves as individuals, separate from one another and from our environment.

For many years, this faculty of self-identity was accepted as a purely human characteristic, an ability which distinguished "man"[1] from the "lower" animals. It was generally assumed that this aspect of our intelligence somehow made us superior to the other life forms with which we share this planet. Man could think and reason while the other animals could not.

In the last twenty years, however, scientific studies have slowly chipped away at the idea that humans are unique, thinking beings. The definition of man as the only toolmaker was shattered by Jane Goodall's studies of chimpanzee behavior which revealed that chimps not only use, but fashion tools. Shortly after that revelation, anthropologists began the task of teaching sign language to chimpanzees, and these studies would soon call man's "uniqueness" into question to an even greater degree.

The first chimp to master sign language was a young female named Washo. Within months, Washo had mastered a vocabulary of over 400 words and could converse freely on a number of subjects. One day, her teacher showed Washo her reflection in a mirror and asked, "Who is that?" Without hesitation, Washo signed, "Me, Washo." With that simple gesture, the young chimp demonstrated the faculty of self-identity, and challenged the idea that self-awareness was a uniquely human characteristic. Since Washo, other species such as gorillas and orangutans have also demonstrated this faculty, and have further demonstrated the capability to comprehend such abstract concepts as death, as evidenced by the gorilla Koko, who mourned following the death of her pet kitten, "All Ball."

Yet, a close look at humankind's analysis of itself will reveal that there is more to the issue of "humanness" than the concept of self-awareness. The questions we humans ask raise not only the issue of who we are, but why we are here, and whither we are going. They often take on a spiritual aspect, hinting at the idea that there may be something outside of humanity, a power greater than ourselves, which we have forgotten or no longer comprehend.

From time to time, great teachers have appeared who have tried to answer these questions. For the most part, however, humanity has ignored or misunderstood their teachings, often encasing them in symbolic ritual. At best, these teachings were interpreted to mean that we were physical beings seeking a spiritual experience. Yet no idea could have been more incorrect. A review of the great religious works of the world's cultures such as the Egyptian *Book of the Dead*, the biblical account of Genesis, the *Bhagavad Gita*, the Sermon on the Mount, the *Tao Teh Ching*, and Zen philosophy, to name only a few, each teach one simple truth: we are spiritual beings having a physical experience.[2]

The fact is that we are spiritual beings, created by God to be companions and co-creators with Him. The soul came into existence as God, in the spirit of love, extended a portion of Himself. Our true origin is not on this earth for we are not physical beings. While we sojourn on this planet, however, the soul, which is our real self, inhabits a human body, a vehicle created for the purpose of housing the soul during its experiences on earth. While the body can be destroyed, the soul is eternal. The soul's origin is divine, the result of a spiritual creation, while the body's origin is earthly, the result of a physical creation.

It is this duality of nature which has baffled humankind throughout the centuries, for we too often see only our physical selves, and do not understand our true spiritual being. It is also the reason humanity continues to question its origins, its purpose, and its destiny. In order to address the questions which humanity has long pondered, we must therefore consider both our spiritual origins *and* our physical heritage. For we cannot understand who we are, why we are here, or where we are going, until we first understand how and why we came to be. We will therefore begin by taking a look at our spiritual creation, so that we might better understand the nature of our true selves. " . . . in man's analysis and understanding of himself, it is as well to know from whence he came as to know whither he is going."[3]

The Creation of the Soul

The biblical account of creation with which people are most familiar does not come from the book of Genesis, but from the Gospel of Saint John: "In the beginning was the Word, and the Word was with God, and the Word was God." (John 1:1) This eloquent passage has long been the subject of speculation and debate. It garnered the interest of early Christian scholars who were quick to identify the "Logos" (word), interpreted from the Greek as the Christ. Some excerpts from the Edgar Cayce readings support this idea: "We have first the Son, then the other sons or celestial beings that are given their force and power."[4]

Another interpretation, however, proposes that the logos is actually a pattern of consciousness, which was imprinted upon each soul at the moment of its creation. The following excerpt from the readings seems to support this view: "For, as is given in the beginning: God moved and said, 'Let there be light,' and there was light, not the light of the sun, but rather that of which, through which, in which every soul had, has, and ever has its being."[5]

It is not so much which interpretation is correct, as it is that this pattern, whether expressed in the soul of our Elder Brother, Jesus, or as a configuration of awareness, existed at the time the soul was created. It was this pattern which was imprinted upon the spirit or life force of the soul at the moment of its creation. This pattern, sometimes called God or Christ Consciousness, refers to the state of consciousness wherein the soul acts in perfect harmony with the Creative Force.

While the Gospel of John briefly mentions the "beginning," the most complete biblical account of creation is found in the Book of Genesis. A comparison of Genesis and the material in the Cayce readings reveals that there are many parallels. Both versions make it clear that the true nature of man is spiritual, for we were first created in spirit. The spiritual creation is recalled in Genesis 1:26, "And God said, let us make man in our image, and after our likeness." Since God is Spirit or energy (force), and not a physical being, this passage refers to the fact that humankind was created in the *spiritual* image or likeness of God. It does not refer to physical attributes.

The readings further elaborate that God, in a desire for companionship and expression, extended Himself, through love, and thus souls came into being. ". . . when there was the creating, or the calling of individual entities into being, we were made to be the companions with the Father-God."[6] "Hence, as He moved, souls—portions of Himself—came into being."[7] This indicates that all souls were created in spirit at the same moment.

Our Spiritual Purpose

We were created to be more than just companions with God, however, for our Creator also gave a purpose to our existence. This purpose was for us to be His heirs, co-creators with Him. "For, we are joint heirs with that universal force we call God . . . "[8] "The soul of each individual is a portion then of the Whole, *with* the birthright of Creative Forces to become a co-creator with the Father . . . "[9] The soul, as a portion of the Creative Force, is everlasting, and possesses the ability of creative power. Through our expression of that power, we may come to know that we are one with the Father-God. The attainment of oneness with our Creator is thus our destiny. *"For in the beginning, God said, 'Let there be light.' Ye . . . are one of those sparks of light with all the ability of creation, with all the knowledge of God."*[10]

Our birthright, the purpose for which we were created, is called the First Cause. As our original purpose, it is the underlying principle which motivates all that we do. When we are in spirit form, free of bodily limitations, we possess full knowledge of the First Cause. When we enter physical form, however, the density of the matter we inhabit (the physical body) causes us to lose sight of that principle. We see only our physical form and we come to identify with it, rather than with our spiritual nature. It was Jesus of Nazareth, as the first soul to achieve Christ Consciousness and recall His spiritual purpose, who, in His parables and teachings, would call that birthright to our remembrance.

The Gift of Free Will

In addition to bringing us into existence, and giving us purpose, the Creator God bestowed a gift upon the soul, a gift that would prove to be its greatest blessing as well as its greatest burden. Once given to the soul, this attribute became an irrevocable part of our being. When used correctly, in accordance with universal law, it would allow us to express our co-creative abilities and experience companionship with the Creative Force. When used incorrectly, however, in a manner contrary to universal law, it has the ability to create great chaos.

The attribute of free will was necessary to allow the soul to experience companionship with God. God was well aware that the gift of free will could be used for purposes contrary to universal law. Yet a necessary condition of this gift was the fact that once given, God would not interfere with our choices. For the Father-God knew that we could not be true heirs and co-creators unless we possessed the same attributes as He.

As a corollary to the attribute of free will, God also imbued the soul with the faculty of development. This is the quality or ability given to the soul which enables it to learn from experience, and change or grow as it encounters new conditions.

So the universal stage was set. Born of a desire for companionship and expression, the God-Force, through an act of love, extended His own spiritual pattern to create companions, who were at once individual, and yet part of the whole. We are part of the whole of the Creative Force, for the spirit of God which divided itself, is our life force. It is that part of us which is immutable and never changing. The soul, however, is our individual nature, able to choose and learn, so that it might become a companion to its Creator. Each soul can therefore be thought of as an individualized expression of the spirit of God, one with the whole and yet the individualized sum of its unique experiences.

The Error of Separation

At the time of creation, the soul's will and God's will were one. Through the attribute of will, we were to learn from experience and express our co-creative abilities throughout the universe. Permeated with the Spirit of the God-Force, the soul began to experiment with its creative powers. What a glorious time that must have been, as the individualized expressions of God's love moved in harmony and oneness throughout the various spheres of existence. Each soul expressed the divine will and power of the Creative Force it carried within itself, and by acting in unity with universal law, extended divine love ever further into the developing universe.

At some point, however, the soul became enamored of its creative ability and power, and began to think that it, and not the God-Force, was the source of that power. As it did so, the soul began to see itself not as an individualized expression of God, but as an entity separate from God, a separate "self." It came to see God as being outside of itself, rather than the motivating force or cause within. By doing so, the soul chose to separate from the consciousness of unity with its Creator.

At the moment the soul believed itself to be separate from the God-Force, it created in its own mind a separation between itself and the Father. This error in thought has been called original sin by some, or the fall of man by others. Many believe that it refers to a time when God exiled us from His presence, as represented in the Bible by Adam and Eve's exile from the Garden of Eden.

Yet God didn't separate Himself from us. *We separated ourselves from Him.* A Course in Miracles teaches that we thought ourselves to be separate, creating an error in our perception, which we then chose to believe. The Cayce readings also support this view: "Hence the separation, and light and darkness. Darkness, that it had separated—that *a soul had separated itself* [author's italics] from the light."[11] We, through free will, made the choice to believe in separation, and deny our oneness with God. We chose self over oneness, and through this choice brought sin into existence, for all sin stems from self.

Once the soul thought itself to be separate, it came to see its own wants and desires as different from those of

God. The gift of free will gave the soul the freedom to choose to express that will according to its own wishes, even if they were contrary to those of the Creative Force. The soul then made a second choice, and chose to use its will to further its own wants, rather than follow the divine order of universal law. The soul thus rebelled against the Creative Force, and because of this rebellion in thought, began to lose sight of its original purpose.

Not only did the soul begin to apply its will for selfish purposes, but it began to do so without regard for the well-being of others. Dissension among groups and between individuals arose, and the perception of separation grew even greater. In addition to the perceived separation from God, souls soon came to perceive themselves as being separate from one another. The soul had turned away from the Creative Force, hereafter symbolized by the light, and had stepped onto the path of error, symbolized by shadow, embarking upon a path which would lead to complete loss of spiritual knowledge, symbolized by the darkness.

Yet, while we believed ourselves to be separate from God, God, being love, could not condemn us for our error, and did not desire that any soul should be lost. So great was His love, that in the moment that we created the separation, God created a plan designed to help us remember our true nature and purpose, and find the way back to God consciousness. According to the readings, that plan included the creation of time, space, and patience,[12] to be expressed in materiality, as well as the creation of the Holy Spirit, whose purpose would be to awaken us from the "dream" of separation we had created.[13]

The Material Dimension

It was evident by now that the gift of free will proved to be too great of a responsibility, or perhaps too much of a temptation, for many souls. This is not to say that all souls had rebelled and used this gift incorrectly. There were still many who had not fallen into the path of error and still honored their unity with God. Yet God loves all equally, and shows the same concern for the loss of one, as for the loss of many. In an attempt to help those souls who had chosen the path of error, God created a means or experience by which they might remember their original purpose. Since God had imbued the soul with the faculty of development, it was possible that the errant souls could learn the error they had made and chose to return to their original state of unity.

In order to understand that it had made a choice of error, however, the soul would need to understand the state of consciousness at which it now existed as opposed to that state of consciousness at the time of its creation. The vibrational rate of the soul is one of the highest frequencies in creation. This high rate of vibration made it difficult for the soul to retain the understanding necessary to comprehend the error it had made. Have you ever run through a forest or wooded area so fast that you never saw the trees alongside the path? It was as if the soul were moving through the universe so fast that it couldn't take time to "stop and smell the roses," and understand what it was actually doing.

God, therefore, provided a means to slow down that vibration so the soul might comprehend the error it had made and regain its understanding. To accomplish this, He brought the concepts of time, space, and patience into existence in the material dimension. Since time and space do not exist in spirit, which is a dimension of energy or force, these had to be expressed in the physical plane. The concepts are all attributes of the Creative Force,[14] and were created as teaching devices so that, through them, the soul would have the opportunity to recognize its error of separation, understand the nature of itself and God, and remember its original state of unity with God.

The concept of time provided the opportunity to understand that each experience has a beginning and an end. The dawn of each new day was to show that we always have the opportunity to move into another experience or state of consciousness, if we make the choice to do so. Every moment provides an opportunity to make that choice. It is never too late to start again. The popular saying, "Today is the first day of the rest of your life," holds more truth than people realize. The concept of time was designed to help the soul learn that at any moment it could make the choice to see past the erroneous thought of separation and reclaim its oneness with the Creative Force.

The concept of space provided us the opportunity to understand our true relationship with the universe. The vastness of space was to help us understand the vastness of God, or the fact that the Creative Force permeates all that exists. Just as the stars are a part of that vastness, so the individual soul is a part of the vastness that is God. The grandeur and immensity of the universe that we see when we gaze at the stars was designed to reflect the nature of God, even though it is but a pale reflection of God's true glory. When we gaze at the heavens, don't we often marvel at the magnificence of the universe? Don't we often take that a step further and marvel at the majesty of the God who created it? Somehow, in that humbleness, don't we, if only for a moment, draw nearer to our Creator?

While time and space were the teaching devices which provided us the opportunity to recall our nature and relationship with God, patience was the spiritual force through which this learning was to be expressed. Through the expression of patience, the soul was given the opportunity to demonstrate "God-like" qualities, and come to realize that these qualities are not only of God, but are the natural attributes of the soul.

Time, space, and patience, expressed in materiality, thus became the three teaching devices in the spiritual development of the soul. They, along with the Holy Spirit, the "voice of God within," call us to a remembrance of the true state of our being. "But the Comforter, which is the Holy Ghost, whom the Father will send in my name, he shall teach you all things, and bring all things to your remembrance . . . " (John 14:26) As the Cayce readings explain it: "When we begin to catch a glimpse of the fact that all space exists in time, that all time is one, that all force is one, that all Force is God, we will be getting back to the oneness of which Christ was speaking when He said that He would be in the Father and we would be in Him."[15]

So throughout the universe, time, space, and patience were expressed in the material dimension. The soul now had the opportunity to explore the worlds of materiality. Prior to this development, the soul had been in spirit form; it had not yet entered physical matter. The soul now saw before it a whole new realm of experience, and quickly moved to venture into these new worlds.

The Scientific View of Creation

Before we discuss the soul's entry into matter, let's take a brief look at the scientific view of creation, also known as the study of cosmology. While it's true that religious and scientific thought systems operate from different paradigms,[16] they are not mutually exclusive. In fact, many scientists express a belief in God, Albert Einstein being among the most famous. Many simply accept the fact that a Supreme Being initially created the universe and put into place certain laws, such as the laws of physics or evolution, as a means of bringing order to the universe; and they seek to understand the universe as it operates under those laws.

When considering scientific explanations, we need to recognize that science deals with material phenomena only. The purpose of any scientific theory is to take the existing observable evidence and use that as a framework to explain how and why a certain phenomenon occurs. It does not mention the existence of a Supreme Being because that is not an area of its concern.

Once we accept the fact that science and religion employ different methodologies, we can move on to examine what these different methodologies reveal about our origins. We may even discover that their perceived differences are nothing more than using different words to convey the same concept.

The Big Bang Theory.   The most widely accepted scientific theory of creation is the "Big Bang Theory," a term first coined by George Gamow, in 1946, as a name for the initial cataclysmic creation event.[17] Simply stated, the Big Bang Theory assumes that the universe originated from a singular state of infinite density, which, due to a high-temperature state, expanded in an explosive moment of creation. The current estimate for the age of the universe ranges from 14 billion to 18 billion years. New discoveries within the last twenty years have consistently pushed this date further back in time.

The Big Bang Theory was elaborated upon by Alan H. Guth, who, in the early 1980s proposed the "Inflationary

Theory," which used particle physics to account for the physical events taking place in the first moments of the creation explosion. It should be noted that this theory also makes predictions as to the ultimate decay of protons, which would indicate that at some point the expansion of the universe would not only halt, but collapse back in upon itself. This brings us to an interesting point concerning scientific models. They disagree as to whether the structure of the universe is open, in which case it will expand forever, or if it is closed, in which case expansion will cease and space will contract in upon itself.

Now, while this theory may sound very dissimilar to the biblical creation account, a closer look might show otherwise. The scientific view states that the universe originated from a singular state of density. Doesn't this singular state sound similar to a state of unity, wherein all was one? Isn't this similar to the state of God prior to His act of creation, when all was one? Might it possibly correlate to the "void" mentioned in Genesis? Then, due to a condition of high-temperature, an explosive moment occurred, resulting in the creation of diverse elements which began to expand outward. Isn't this similar to the moment of creation wherein God extended Himself, and brought free-willed souls into being, thus creating diversity within the Creative Force? Might this correlate with the statement "Let there be light," for light and heat are both forms of energy? Then, following the big bang, the elements of the universe continued to expand outward, away from the center. Haven't we, since the moment of our creation, drawn further and further away from our spiritual source? Further, if we consider the concept of a closed structure universe, we must contend that at some point, the universe will cease to expand and collapse in upon itself, thus returning to a singular state. Isn't this similar to the state of unity, or oneness with the Creative Force to which we are all striving to return?

Supposition perhaps, but isn't it possible that scientific cosmology and religious creation simply use different terminology to explain the same process as to how the universe came to be? Whichever interpretation you prefer, the end result is the same. Somehow, the physical universe, and later biological life, came into existence.

The Descent into Matter

Once materiality had been brought into expression, the soul was free to experience any of the material worlds which had been created. While not all planets were capable of sustaining biological life, the Cayce readings make it clear that there are other planets within other solar systems that represent the third dimension of matter as the earth does within this system. As the souls began to move into material expression, not all came to the earth plane, as some chose to experience material existence on other worlds.

God intended that the soul's entry into matter be a learning experience, an opportunity for the soul to regain a sense of its relationship as co-creator with God. Through time, space, and patience, the soul was to use its individual will to express its co-creative abilities in harmony with universal law.

While God intended that the soul should *experience* the opportunities materiality offered, it was not intended that the soul permanently assume the characteristics of matter. The soul was to enter the earth plane in spirit form, and be "in the world," but not "of the world."

(Refer to Table 1, *The Devolution of the Soul*, for a comparison of the various expressions of the soul in the earth plane.)

Table 1. THE DEVOLUTION OF THE SOUL		
The original state of the soul in the spiritual realm: Spirit/Soul, an individualized expression of God's Love/State of Unity. The soul entered the material dimension as:		
Manifestation	**Attributes**	**State of Consciousness**
Spirit Form	-Spirit -Non-material manifestation -First Root Race	-God Consciousness
Light Body	-Material; not yet flesh -Luminescent light energy -Able to enter and exit at will -Second Root Race	-Diminishing God Consciousness -Soul-memory still alive
Thought Form or Thought Body	-Physical manifestation -Imaged in the soul mind -Able to enter and exit at will -Gradually hardened as mind dwelt on carnal thoughts -Third Root Race	-Losing awareness of God Consciousness -Soul-memory still alive -Beginnings of individualized conscious mind
Thought Projection	-Projection of an aspect of the soul into physical form -No individual will -Used as servants/ laborers -"Automatons"	-No individual consciousness
Human Body	-Flesh and blood -Birth and death cycle -Density increased with time -Created as the perfect vehicle for the soul to use on earth -Fourth Root Race	-Division of mind into 3 levels: - conscious - subconscious - superconscious

NOTE: This table does not include a reference to the animal forms which the soul experimented with as they are not considered a natural expression of man's development.

As the "first soul group" entered the earth plane in spirit form, the souls looked upon the world and were amazed. They found an abundance of existing life forms, plant and animal, evolving according to an established evolutionary plan. More intriguing, perhaps, were the physical sensations which these life forms were capable of experiencing. The souls soon realized that the denser animal body, or flesh, was capable of experiencing physical sensations which a spirit form could not. Rather than follow the plan for their own soul development, some souls made the choice to project themselves into these life forms so they might experience the physical senses. Once again, the choice of self, in defiance of God's will, was made. The souls that chose this path not only abandoned their own spiritual development, but interfered with the development of earth's life forms, and altered their evolution as well. This selfish projection into matter without regard for natural law was a misapplication of spiritual powers of the highest order.[18] It also marked the souls' first step in the process of devolution, whereby the soul descended from the highest realm of God Consciousness into the limited consciousness of "earthiness."

According to the readings, the first soul group projected into animal, plant, and even mineral forms of life on earth! The creatures which resulted from these projections were not creations of God, but the result of the soul's misapplication of its own creative abilities. At first, the soul was able to project into and withdraw from these forms at will. With each successive projection into matter, however, the soul began to stay in the body for longer and longer periods of time. The denser vibration of the flesh began to interfere with the soul's vibration, and made it more difficult for the soul to enter and exit at will. Eventually, many souls lost this ability completely

and became entrapped in the flesh, unable to return to
their spiritual form.

A Desire to Help

Thousands, if not millions of souls were now trapped
in the earth plane. As they descended into matter and its
subsequent states of lesser consciousness, they had lost
sight of their divine nature and were unable to return to
the celestial sphere. Even the death of the organism was
no guarantee that the soul would be freed from its
earthly bounds, for some were so confused as to their
true identity that they lingered in the earth plane, unable to "return to the light" from which they came. Disoriented and trapped in the earth plane, they often
sought another body into which they could project.

These developments on the earth plane were being
watched with great concern by the millions of souls still
in unity with the God-Force, some of whom had not yet
chosen to manifest in materiality. There were also others who had taken the opportunity to experience materiality in other solar systems, and had not become
entangled in matter as happened on this planet. From
both these groups, many souls unselfishly made the
choice to go and help their brethren, even though they
knew that they too would run the risk of becoming entrapped. " . . . there were then—*from* the other *sources*
(worlds) the continuing entering of those that *would*
make for the keeping of the balance, as of the first purpose of the Creative Forces . . . "[19] The purpose for which
the "second soul group"[20] incarnated, was a noble one,
for they entered the earth plane in an attempt to help
the lost souls regain their identity, an endeavor born out
of unselfish love for their brethren.

Initially, many of these souls remained in spirit form

and did not enter the flesh, knowing that to do so meant loss of spiritual awareness. Others manifested in a "light body," appearing as luminescent beings of tall stature with slightly elongated limbs. Although not a physical body, this light body was of a denser vibration than a spirit form, light being a material manifestation of the energy of spirit.

Unfortunately, many in this second soul group also succumbed to the temptations of the physical sensations of this world, and began to lose sight of their divine nature as they repeated the mistakes of the first soul group. Although some of these souls had experienced materiality in other systems, there was something different about the earth plane. Perhaps it was its intense gravitational pull, or the heavy density of the flesh of earth's life forms. Perhaps it was a combination of these and other conditions unique to the earth that hindered their attempts to help their brethren, and resulted in many of the second soul group becoming trapped in flesh as well.

With the failure of the second soul group, it was clear that the physical sensory sensations of this planet were too much for most souls to resist. It seemed that any soul, no matter how noble its intentions, ran a great risk of becoming entrapped in matter upon entry into the earth. Yet even knowing this, there were still those who were willing to try again. One such soul was Amilius, the First Son and Elder Brother, the first soul created of God.

A Plan for Redemption

Amilius belonged to, and in fact led the group of souls that had never rebelled against the Creator, and still existed in unity and harmony with the Creative Force. Amilius had closely observed the activities of the first two soul groups, and knew the difficulties the soul faced in trying to resist the physical gratifications of the earth. Concerned for his brethren's welfare, Amilius felt that some action must be taken to give these souls the direction needed to bring them out of the chaos into which they had fallen. He realized that somehow, they must be shown a way to overcome the physical influences which were interfering with the spiritual forces of the soul. So great was Amilius' love for his brethren, that he proposed that he take these very conditions upon himself! He proposed that he become as one of them, and experience materiality, for only by experiencing those conditions could he overcome them, and show others the way it could be done.

As a soul in perfect harmony with the Creative Force, Amilius spoke with the Father, and proposed that he enter the earth for the purpose of leading his brethren back to a remembrance of their spiritual selves. God was at first reluctant to permit this, for He knew that once in matter, even Amilius might not be able to resist the physical temptations. Amilius persisted, however, certain that he would not lose sight of his divine nature, certain that he could overcome the entrapment of the flesh. God agreed, however, for He knew Amilius' plan was the only hope for those that had become lost to His Presence.

Yet God did not will that Amilius should undertake this mission alone. He would be accompanied by other souls who also desired to help those that had become lost. Amilius would lead a "third soul group," numbering some 144,000 souls,[21] into the earth plane. This was the time "when the morning stars sang together, and the whispering winds brought the news of the coming of man's indwelling . . . "[22] Together, they would undertake the task of showing their lost brethren the way back to God Consciousness.

The Entry into Materiality

Amilius thus led the third soul group into the earth plane, so that they might experience materiality in order to overcome it. ". . . the first begotten of the Father that came as Amilius in the Atlantean land and allowed himself to be led in ways of selfishness."[23] This did not, however, imply entry into the dense, flesh bodies we inhabit today. For Amilius, endowed with free will and an innate creative desire, had discerned that he could create, from his soul self rather than from existing animal life, a material form of being. These creations were projections from the soul mind, called thought forms, or thought-bodies, which the soul could inhabit and withdrawn from at will. This body was not created through physical means—it was "imaged" in the soul mind and brought into being. "As to their forms in the physical sense, these were much *rather* of the nature of *thought forms,* or able to push out *of themselves* . . . much in the way and manner as the amoeba would in the waters . . . "[24] The soul could enter the thought body for the purpose of learning certain lessons designed to awaken the memory of its spiritual purpose and oneness with God.

Another aspect to this creation was the division of the sexes. To aid Amilius in the accomplishment of his mission, God moved to divide the soul into its two aspects— the active or *yang* aspect, and the receptive or *yin* aspect,[25] so that by working together, their individual strengths would complement one another. ". . . when there was that turning to the within, through the sources of creation, as to make for the helpmeet . . . *then*—from out of self—was brought that as was to be the helpmeet, *not* just the companion . . . "[26]

In their early years on earth, the souls of this group learned to use the attributes of mind as they developed their mental abilities. At first, they used them in pursuit of spiritual matters, expressing the Divine within. These souls, attuned to the Creative Force, and expressing its love in their activities on earth, were known as the "Sons of God."

Gradually, however, some souls began to use more of the carnal mind, and began to live more in the thought of flesh than in the thought of spirit. They began to experience the world through the physical senses, experiencing desire, sex, ingesting first plant food, and later eating animal flesh itself. As they did so, the thought-body began to take on the form of that which they sought, and began to harden, taking on the aspects of flesh as its vibrational rate slowed. "As these took form, by the gratifying of their own desire . . . they became hardened or set—much in the form of the existent human body of the day . . . "[27]

The downward spiral of devolution with its resultant loss of God Consciousness thus continued after the advent of Amilius into the earth. Many in this soul group became versed in the ways of the souls they had come to help. As they did so, these "Sons of Darkness," as they are referred to in the readings, moved deeper into self-consciousness and away from God Consciousness. Self-consciousness became so great that they began to listen to another voice, a voice not of God, and not of evil, but the voice of self. This voice, the self-will as opposed to the God-will, is symbolized in the biblical account of creation as the serpent.

The souls' continued desire for self-gratification led some to project a portion or aspect of themselves into a separate being, a type of "thought projection," which had no will of its own but was subject to the desires and control of the soul which brought it into being. The readings refer to these as automatons " . . . that were retained by individuals or groups to do the labors of a household, or to cultivate the fields or the like."[28] The creation of these beings, and their use as servants or slaves, was to cause great dissension between those who remained true to their original purpose, and those falling ever deeper into the self-gratification of materiality.

As Amilius, the Elder Brother, looked upon the errors that had occurred, he understood that the only way to overcome the physical world was to take on the aspects of flesh and blood itself in order to demonstrate a way of escape from their carnal influences. He accepted that he would have to take on physical form—flesh and blood, and become as one of those lost in the physical world, so that he might experience the flesh in order to overcome it, thus setting an example for all to follow.

> *There is an inmost centre in us all where truth abides in fullness; and around, wall upon wall, the gross flesh hems it in . . . and to KNOW, rather consists in opening out a way whence the imprisoned splendor may escape, than in effecting entry for a light supposed to be without.*
>
> —Robert Browning

2

Our Physical Heritage:
Creation of the Human Body

*So Spider Woman gathered earth, this time of four colors,
yellow, red, white, and black . . . molded them . . .*

*She sang over them the Creation Song, and when she
uncovered them these forms were human beings in the
image of Sotuknang.*

—The Book of the Hopi

THE STORY of the creation of the soul, as depicted in
the previous chapter, illustrates that we were created as
spiritual beings of celestial origin. Yet the entry of the
third soul group into materiality added a new dimension
to our existence and marked the beginning of a long process by which we slowly built the physical side of our
nature. As a result of this process, we reached a point
where we might more appropriately be thought of as a
"soul-body," containing both the physical and spiritual
elements of a whole being. " . . . for in man we find both
the spirit entity and the physical entity . . . "[1]

We cannot ignore the fact that there is a dual aspect to

our existence. To ignore one in favor of the other gives us only a part of the picture, and we need to see the whole if we want to truly understand why we are here, and how our destiny will manifest. In order to completely understand who we are, we must consider not only our spiritual selves, but our physical selves as well. This chapter will first consider the creation of the human body as told in the Cayce readings, and then consider the scientific view of human development, and attempt to see if correlations can be drawn between the two sources of knowledge.

Creation of the Human Body

As stated in the last chapter, Amilius realized that he must experience flesh and blood in order to overcome it. He must take on physical form and yet somehow retain an awareness of his divine nature. He therefore proposed that a new body be created, one capable of existing in the physical world and yet capable of understanding spiritual consciousness. " . . . when one individual [Amilius] first saw those changes that eventually made for that opening for the needs of, or the preparation for, the Universal Consciousness to bring into the experience what is known to man as the first created man."[2] Through this body, the soul would be able to arrest the process of devolution and begin its slow evolutionary climb upward back to God Consciousness. It should be noted that this body, although flesh, was not as dense as the body we know today.

Thus did Amilius lay plans for the creation of the human body. It is this physical creation which is recorded in the second chapter of Genesis. "And the Lord God formed man of the dust of the ground, and breathed into his nostrils the breath of life." (Genesis 2:7) Note the time line here as the spiritual creation of the soul precedes physical creation. While the first creation was spiritual, after the likeness of the God Spirit, the second was earthy or physical, as symbolized by the dust of the earth.

There are indications in the Cayce readings that the creation of the physical body was directed by Amilius, hence making it a creation of the souls, and not a direct creation of God. " . . . the sons of God came together to announce to Matter a way being opened for the souls of men, the souls of God's creation, to come again to the awareness of their error."[3] Physical man, "the last of the creations,"[4] created out of the elements of the earth [the dust of the ground], might best be considered as a result of the soul's development, a necessary consequence of the choices the soul had made. " . . . for when man was brought into being there was a variation in the creation."[5]

Thomas Sugrue, Cayce's well-known biographer and the author of several books based on the readings, echoes this thought " . . . they [the souls] played at creating; they imitated God . . . and what had been set in motion gradually entangled the souls, so that they became trapped in the plan of earth's evolution, inside *the bodies they had themselves created* [author's italics]."[6] Hugh Lynn Cayce, Edgar Cayce's son and an expert on his father's work, concurred with this interpretation, saying that it was man and not the Creator-God who brought our physical bodies into existence and by so doing, limited ourselves to three-dimensional consciousness.[7] The soul, being spirit, was created by God and is therefore eternal. The body, being flesh, was created by God's creation, and has a finite existence.

Amilius, ever the Wayshower, set the pattern the others were to follow. We need to understand that this was not an individual creation but a group creation, which occurred in five places at once, each manifestation representing one of the five "races" of man. "Man, in Adam, (as a group; not as an individual), entered into the world (for he entered in five places at once, we see—called Adam in one . . .)"[8] The "color differences" of these groups were nothing more than adaptations for the environment and climatic conditions they would encounter. The readings also indicate that each group symbolized one of the five physical senses which were to be conquered before spiritual perfection could be attained. The white race in the Caucasus represented sight/vision, the black race of West Africa represented taste/appetite, the yellow race of East Asia represented hearing, the brown race in Lemuria represented smell, and the red race of Atlantis[9] represented touch/feeling/intuition.

Since the actions of the soul had resulted in the path of the flesh over the spirit, it now meant that while in the earth plane, the soul would be subject to physical laws. " . . . when earth became habitable for physical man, man entered in the plane, just as the highest of created forces in the earth plane. Then became man amenable to laws of earth plane, and amenable to physical birth, physical conditions, physical conceptions, physical forces. . ."[10]

It is not clear, however, whether the birth and death cycle, as we know it today, was intended to be a part of the soul experience at this time. One interpretation concludes that the soul was able to project itself into the human body and leave when its experience on earth was complete, much as Enoch and Melchizedek did. This interpretation holds that it was only after humankind, symbolized by Adam and Eve, had done that which was forbidden to them—to partake of the world's physical gratifications—that the soul became subject to the cycle of birth and death. "In the sweat of thy face shalt thou eat bread, till thou return unto the ground; for out of it wast thou taken: for dust thou art, and unto dust shalt thou return." (Genesis 3:19)

For once in the human body, souls chose not to honor the purpose for which it was created, but continued to seek gratification of their own desires over the will of God. Even the Amilius soul, now as Adam, succumbed to this temptation. "Remember Adam."[11] " . . . knowledge without the practical ability to apply same may become sin. For, it is knowledge misapplied that was the fall—or the confusion—in Eve."[12]

Yet no sooner was Amilius' (Adam's) error shown to him, than he repented, and again offered himself, this time as a sacrifice, for the souls he had come to save.[13] He knew that the choice of the physical over the spirit had led to death, and that death itself would have to be overcome as the final barrier to spiritual awareness. "And with error [sin] entered that as called *death*, which is only a transition—or through God's other door . . ."[14]

The Growth of the Physical Forces

Yet whenever it took effect, it was the birth and death cycle which resulted in the emergence of what is sometimes referred to as "ego" or "little self," which is a reflection of what the physical self *thinks* itself to be. As the soul became more concerned with the physical world in which it lived, rather than with the spirit world of its origin, the ego grew in strength, and reinforced the idea that we were physical beings. As the mind sought to learn more and more of the physical world, the vibration of the human body slowed ever further and became more dense, as symbolized in scripture by the putting on of skins upon leaving the Garden of Eden, until it gradually developed into the body we know today. The spiritual realm became little more than a memory, something recalled in myth and legend, something we perhaps caught a glimpse of in our dreams. Knowledge of God Consciousness was pushed down into the deepest recesses of the mind, later to be recognized as the "super-consciousness." As the soul-memory itself (hereafter called the subconscious) was lost from consciousness awareness, many souls completely forgot their divine nature while in the earth, and came to believe that they were nothing more than physical beings. The process of devolution was now complete.

The soul was now firmly entrenched in the physical body. Although spiritual in origin, we had chosen a path which created a physical or genetic heritage. This dual nature we had imposed upon ourselves would hereafter be reflected in the development of the human species. For the faculty of development, which allowed the soul to learn and grow through experience, remained an attribute of the soul-body. As the human species, we were now subject to the physical laws of the universe, and would thereafter develop and evolve according to those laws. "In all ages we find this has been the developing—day by day . . . or the evolution as we see from those forces as may be manifested . . . The theory is, man evolved . . . from first cause in creation . . . "[15]

We are the children of God, yes, but we are also the children of Mother Earth. For that reason alone, we must take a look at what the earth has to say about her children's development.

Evolution: The Scientific View of Human Development

Now that we know what metaphysical sources have to say about the creation of the human body, we turn our attention to the scientific view of human development.

This body of knowledge, based primarily upon evidence in the earth's fossil record, can tell us much about the development of the human species and its relationship to the other life forms on this planet. Before examining the fossil record, however, we first need to understand how science, specifically paleoanthropology, defines humankind.

Phylogenetically speaking, our species is classified as *Homo sapiens sapiens* (wise wise man), and belongs to the Primate Order, which also includes apes, monkeys, and prosimians. This classification is based on anatomical and physiological characteristics, as well as biochemical makeup. Numerous studies have revealed that modern-day humans and apes are very similar in terms of skeletal structure, muscular anatomy, physiological processes, serological reactions, and chromosome patterns.

Over the years, science has defined our species in a variety of ways—an intelligent, tool-making, social, self-aware animal. Today, however, paleoanthropology bases its definition of the human species solely on its physical characteristics. Yet if we look at humankind's physical makeup, there is not one single characteristic that makes us unique. Rather, it is a combination of four specific traits, referred to as a "complex," that distinguishes us as human beings. The human or hominid complex includes: (1) bipedal walking, (2) manipulative hands capable of a precision grip, (3) binocular (three-dimensional) color vision, and (4) a large brain-to-body ratio.

The traits of the hominid complex are interrelated; as one trait developed, it often enhanced the effectiveness of another, thereby creating a positive feedback loop within the trait complex. For example, the development of efficient bipedal walking left the forearms completely free from the task of support and locomotion, thus enabling the hands to be used for other purposes. Our forward-facing eyes, sensitive to color, depth, shape, and hue, allowed us to manipulate objects with our now-freed hands to a fine degree. The ability to precisely manipulate objects led to habitual tool use, which in turn increased our chances of survival. Then, as brain size increased relative to body size, convolution of the brain surface gave rise to increased neural interconnections, thus enabling even further refinement of hand-eye coordination and the development of more efficient tools.

A precise dating of the hominid complex is not yet possible due to gaps in the fossil record. Based on the available fossil evidence, however, most paleoanthropologists agree that the human or hominid lineage split from its closest relatives, the ape or pongid lineage, approximately 10 to 12 million years ago. There is also agreement that the first true hominids, called australopithecines, appeared in the fossil record as early as 5.5 million years ago.

Evolutionary Theory. When paleoanthropologists examine the physical evidence found in the fossil record, they interpret what they find according to the principles of evolutionary theory. Nearly 150 years after the principles of evolutionary theory were first proposed, it remains one of the most controversial and misunderstood areas of scientific study. The reason evolutionary theory remains controversial in some quarters may stem from the fact that many people believe it denies the existence of God, and they therefore reject it on that premise alone. Like all scientific theories, however, evolution neither denies nor confirms God. It simply does not address the issue, as that is not its purpose.

Yet I suspect that there may be more to it than this. I can't help but wonder if the resistance to evolutionary theory stems from the fact that, on the subconscious level, it reminds us of how we, as spiritual beings, separated from God and chose an earthly existence over our celestial home. The theory of evolution may hit a little too close to the heart of the matter, and by calling to mind our "fall" or descent into matter, reminds us of something we would rather forget.

As well as being controversial, evolutionary theory is also one of the most misunderstood areas of science. I've lost count of the number of times I've heard well-meaning lecturers misstate concepts of evolutionary theory, and refer to "descent from monkeys," mention the "missing link," use "survival of the fittest" incorrectly, or state other common misperceptions, none of which are true. For this reason, I want to begin by dispelling some common misbeliefs regarding evolutionary theory.

1. Evolution does not say that man descended from the monkey. What it does state is that the human family, Hominidae, and the ape family, Pongidae, had a common ancestor.

2. Evolution does not search for the "missing link," a supposed half-man/half-ape creature. There is no such thing as a missing link as used in common parlance. The common ancestor of hominids and apes was most likely a generalized "ape-like" primate.

3. Evolution does not say that only the physically fit, or strongest survive. It does say that those individuals possessing characteristics which help them to successfully adapt to their environment tend to live longer than those not possessing those characteristics. They therefore pass these characteristics on to their offspring in greater numbers.

4. Evolution does not say that we came from primitive, brutish "cave men." The groups of hominids, such as the Neandertal tribes who lived in caves during the Ice Age in Europe, had a complex society which included

a family structure, social customs, and even religious beliefs! I wonder how many people would be surprised to learn that Neandertals are classified as the same species as we are! Yes, Neandertals are classified as "*homo sapiens*," specifically *Homo sapiens neandertalensis*.

5. Evolution does not say that individuals evolve. The unit of evolution is the population, a word used to describe a group of interbreeding individuals, or a species. Individuals do not evolve from one form to another. Rather, species change over time as genetic mutations which occur in DNA structure are passed from generation to generation, and exhibit different characteristics shaped by the environment they inhabit.

6. A belief in evolution does not imply a non-belief in God. In fact, you could even argue that God created the process of evolution just as He created other physical laws, and set them up to govern the orderly operation of the universe.

Simply put, evolution is the process by which all living things have developed from simpler organisms to more complex forms. Living organisms develop specific traits or characteristics caused by genetic mutations in their DNA structure. Some traits increase the organism's chance at survival, others may have no effect, while still other traits hinder the organism's ability to survive. Those traits that increase the organism's adaptability, or chance for survival, are passed on to offspring in greater numbers than those traits which hinder survival and result in early death of the organism.

An example of this would be certain color markings on animals, such as the spots on newborn deer, which camouflage the animal and allow it to better hide from predators. This is a positive trait which increases the chance of survival. A negative trait would be albinoism, which makes the animal more visible to predators and would likely result in an early death before the animal reaches the age of bearing offspring. The elimination, often through early death, of those possessing negative traits, and the passing on of favorable traits, is known as natural selection, because it is the result of selective environmental pressures. The process of natural selection therefore addresses the issue of "survival of the fittest" in terms of which organisms are best adapted to their environment.

Charles Darwin is remembered as the father of evolutionary theory, although his proposal was actually presented simultaneously with that of Alfred Russell Wallace, who independently discovered natural selection during the same time. Today, the modern or synthetic theory of evolution has expanded upon their theories and combined them with data drawn from genetic studies. The synthetic theory states that variability among individuals within a population is produced through random mutation, an inheritable change in the chemical composition of DNA which produces new or modified enzymes and alters physical characteristics. The differing characteristics, or genetic variability, is then acted upon by natural selection in the environment. All species of life currently existing on earth are a result of this developmental process. Therefore, in light of evolutionary theory, let's examine the fossil record as it relates to the development of our species.

The Emergence of the Human Species

The earliest fossil evidence of a possible ancestral candidate, which led to modern-day primates, including man, was found in the discovery, in sub-Saharan Africa, of a monkey-like primate called *Propliopithecus*, dated around 35 million years B.P. (before present). It constitutes a link between the earlier lemur-like primates and the true monkeys and apes that first appear about 22 million years B.P.

The most successful of these early apes was the genus *Dryopithecus*, which is believed to include the evolutionary ancestor of both hominids (humans) and later apes such as the chimpanzee and gorilla. As the climate grew drier during the latter part of the Miocene, *Dryopithecus* disappeared from the fossil record, presumably retreating to the tropical forest regions. For many years, it was believed that *Ramapithecus*, dating back 12 million years B.P., was possibly the first direct ancestor of the hominid line. It was adapted to life in the grasslands, rather than the trees of the forest. Further study, however, revealed that there is no evidence that this primate walked upright or used tools, and today most anthropologists feel that it was too early a specimen to be considered a hominid.

A discussion of the true hominid forms found in the fossil record can sometimes be difficult to follow due to the variety of taxonomic classifications within the human lineage. For that reason, the data on hominid forms is summarized in Table 2, *Evolution of the Hominid Lineage*, which outlines the distinguishing characteristics of each species, and suggests the possible relationship of one species to another.

The genus *Australopithecus*, classified as in being in the family Hominidae, contains the first true hominids. Australopithecine remains were first found in Cape Province, South Africa, the Transvall, and later at Lake Turkana in northern Kenya, and are dated from 5.5 million to 1 million years ago. They walked completely upright, had a brain size averaging 410-500 cubic centimeters, ranged in height from three to five feet, and lacked projecting canine teeth (an ape characteristic).

Table 2. EVOLUTION OF THE HOMINID LINEAGE

Genus and Species	Dates B.P.	Habitat	Brain Size Height/Weight	Physical Characteristics	Cultural Associations	Disposition
THE AUSTRALOPITHECUS GENUS						
africanus	3 million- 1 million	East Africa South Africa	450 c.c. 3 to 4 feet 45-90 pounds	-Bipedal -Long arms	-Tool maker -Omnivore -Meat eater	-Possibly died out due to competition with other advanced forms
robustus	2.5 million- 1.5 million	South Africa	500 c.c. 5 ft. 3 in. 110 pounds	-Bipedal -Large cheek teeth -Large skull crest	-No known tool use -Possible vegetarian	-May have given rise to A. boisei
boisei	2.5 million- 1.5 million	East Africa	500 c.c. 5 ft. 3 in.-5 ft. 10 in. 130-175 pounds	-Bipedal -Large skull crest -Small canine teeth -Powerful muscles	-Found with chipped pebbles	-Most likely died out due to competition with Homo genus
afarensis (Lucy)	4 million- 2.5 million	East Africa	410 c.c. 3-4 feet 65 pounds	-Bipedal -Bowlegged	-Family groups -Possible tool use	-Directly or indirectly gave rise to other australopithecines and to Homo genus
anamensis	4 million	East Africa	Small; still under evaluation 110 pounds	-Bipedal -Large canine teeth -Parallel side teeth -Chimp-like ear	-Combines bipedalism with ape-like traits	-Discovered in 1995; still under evaluation

(Table 2, continued)

Genus and Species	Dates B.P.	Habitat	Brain Size Height/Weight	Physical Characteristics	Cultural Associations	Disposition
THE HOMO GENUS						
habilis	2 million-1.5 million	East Africa South Africa	650-850 c.c. 5 feet 110 pounds	-Large brain case -Small face -Broca's Area (speech) -Human-like pelvis	-Stone tools -Use of fire -Hunted game -Simple shelters	-First true "human" -Likely gave rise to Homo erectus
erectus	1.6 million-200,000	East Africa South Africa North Africa Europe China S.E. Asia	880-1100 c.c. 5 ft. 6 in.-6 feet 88-160 pounds	-Thick skull -Broca's Area -Wernicke's Area (understanding speech) -Flat face -No chin	Standard tool kits -Use of fire -Survival in cold climates -Big game hunters -Stone shelters	-Direct ancestor of modern man -Gave rise to Homo sapiens
sapiens neandertalensis Neandertal Man Classic Progressive	250,000-40,000	East Africa South Africa Europe China S.E. Asia	1100-1800 c.c. (1500 c.c. avg.) 5 ft. 7 in. 165 pounds	Classic Forms: -Brow ridges -Small chin -Heavy bones Progressive Forms: -No brow ridges -Modern face -High forehead	-Mousterian tool kit -Careful burials with artifacts indicate religious beliefs -Elderly and handicapped lived to old age -Possible speech -Tents, clothing -Culture	-Likely that Classic Forms died out -Likely that most Progres-sive forms gave rise to Homo sapiens sapiens
sapiens sapiens Cro-Magnon Man Modern Humans	40,000-present	All global areas	1350-1600 c.c. 1400 c.c. avg. 5 ft. 6 in.-5 ft. 8 in. 150-180 pounds	-Frontal brain development - High forehead -Small jaw, teeth -Modern-day man	-Complex Culture -Civilization -Speech, writing	???

They lived in family groups, appeared to be semi-nomadic, and made crude shelters. Some finds have been associated with tool use.

For many years, it was thought that there were only two species of australopithecine. *Australopithecus africanus* was the smallest species and the most accomplished tool maker, while *Australopithecus robustus* was a larger vegetarian form which was thought to have died out. It was generally agreed upon that the *africanus* form was the direct ancestor of man, the first identifiable hominid ancestor. A third species, however, originally identified as *Zinjanthropous boisei*, was later recognized as *Australopithecus boisei*. Even larger than *robustus*, it too is thought to have died out.

Traditional views of human evolution were rocked in the early 1970s as certain East African sites yielded the remains of several relatively large-brained, bipedal hominids who *predated* the earlier australopithecine discoveries. Of these, Skull 1470, uncovered in 1972, is the most difficult to interpret because although it shows a large sized brain, considered an advanced feature, it also possesses a large facial area, a primitive characteristic. Its age also represents a problem, since some rock samples it was associated with date from 2.6 million while others date at 1.8 million years. This puts Skull 1470 right in the midst of the Australopithecine populations! Yet, rather than being classified as an Australopithecine, Skull 1470 was classified as a form of *Homo habilis* by its discoverer Dr. Richard Leakey. This classification, based largely on a brain size of 800 cubic centimeters, indicates that the *Homo* lineage co-existed with the australopithecine populations, and suggests tha the Australopithecines are not in our direct ancestral line.

In 1974, the discovery of "Lucy" at Hadar, Ethiopia, a proportionately large-brained, bipedal hominid, dated at 3.5 million years, created even more controversy. While some anthropologists were quick to classify Lucy as a possible *Homo* form, her discoverer, Dr. Donald Carl Johansen, classified Lucy, along with several other similar specimens, as a form of Australopithecine, naming her *Australopithecus afarensis.* He proposed that this species was a common ancestor of both the *Homo* genus and the Australopithecines! This single-species idea defied the accepted theory that there were two types of hominids—the Australopithecines which became extinct, and the *Homo* genus which evolved into modern humans. The controversy between the Leakey camp and the Johansen camp has continued over the years, and has not yet been resolved.

Into the midst of this controversy in 1995 came news of a discovery which will no doubt create even greater debate. A new fossil specimen dating at 4 million years was uncovered at Lake Turkana in northern Kenya by a Leakey research team. This find may be controversial because it possesses both human and chimp-like characteristics. Although completely upright in posture, as evidenced by a shin bone, it has a small brain, chimp-like traits of parallel rows of side teeth, large canine teeth with wide flaring molars, and a small ear opening. The find has been named *Australopithecus anamensis,* and represents the oldest specimen demonstrating upright posture. It's possible that this specimen may be ancestral to *Australopithecus afarensis,* although an exact determination must await further study.

As of today, however, we no longer have one clearly defined genus in our ancestry; we have a somewhat confusing picture of multiple species, each existing at the same time, adapting to slightly different environmental niches, any one of which might have led to the genus *Homo.*

One of the earliest specimens recognized as belonging to the genus *Homo* was found in 1964 at Olduvai Gorge in Tanzania, by Dr. Louis S. B. Leakey. Leakey named his discovery *Homo habilis* or "handy man," after the many tools associated with it. Other *Homo habilis* fossils have since been found at other African sites, and date from 2 million to 1.8 million years B.P. *Habilis* specimens possess a large brain capacity of 650-850 cubic centimeters, small rear human-like teeth, and skeletal bones similar to those of modern humans. The position of *habilis* in human evolution is still uncertain. Some believe that as the earliest member of the human genus, it represents an evolutionary transition between the australopithecines and the later members of *Homo erectus*, while others think that *habilis* is simply an early form of *Homo erectus* and should be classified as such.

It should be noted that all of the australopithecine specimens, as well as *Homo habilis*, have only been found in Africa. No specimens have been found outside that continent. Evidence of *Homo erectus*, however, has been found in various parts of the world including Java (Java Man), Indonesia, China (Peking Man), southern Africa, eastern Africa, northern Africa (Ternifine Man), and Europe, including Germany (Heidelberg Man), Hungary, Greece, and France. The specimens have been dated from 1.6 million to 200,000 years B.P. Specimens found at Olduvai Gorge and in southern Africa occur in later levels of geologic strata than the australopithecines found there, indicating a clear, progressive time line.

Since the first discovery of Java Man in 1891, *Homo erectus'* position in the human lineage has remained relatively unchanged. *Homo erectus*, "erect man," walked upright, had a large brain capacity of approximately 880-1100 cubic centimeters, developed the acheulean tool culture, made temporary dwellings such as tents, and most importantly, possessed the use of fire. The discovery of fire about 500,000 years ago enabled these populations to expand their territory beyond temperate areas and successfully inhabit cold climates. There is also evidence that *Homo erectus* groups engaged in cooperative hunting of big game animals. The specimens found in the French Pyrenees are noteworthy because they have features similar both to *Homo erectus* and the later appearing *Homo sapiens*. Between 300,000 and 200,000 years ago, traces of *Homo erectus* gradually disappear from the fossil record, replaced by their supposed descendants, the *Homo sapiens* species.

Evidence of the first appearance of our species dates back to 200,000 years B.P., with the appearance of Neandertal Man, so named after the first specimen discovered in a cave in the Neander Valley in Germany. Some people may be surprised to learn that Neandertals, erroneously portrayed for years as dim-witted, brutish, bent-kneed, hairy cave dwellers, are, as previously stated, actually members of the *Homo sapiens* species, specifically *Homo sapiens neandertalensis*. Unfortunately, the earliest studies of Neandertal Man were based on an isolated group of European specimens, later called Classic Neandertals, which possessed more primitive traits such as heavy brow ridges, and which were most likely regional adaptations to their extreme environment. To make matters worse, the most prominent study was based on an individual later identified as having a deformed body due to severe arthritis. The truth is that if you took a Neandertal man, dressed him in a jogging suit, and put him on a bus, no one would give him a second look. He would most likely resemble a short, stocky, muscular athlete.

Neandertals extended the range of human beings even further than that of *Homo erectus*. Specimens have been found in Germany (Steinheim Man), England (Swanscombe Man), Zambia (Broken Hill Man), South Africa, eastern Africa, and the Middle East. Their average brain size of 1500 cubic centimeters *exceeded* that of modern man, which averages around 1400 cubic centimeters, and even ranged as high as 1800 cubic centimeters. As different populations grew and flourished, distinct tool traditions developed. There is also evidence that they practiced ritual, including the elaborate burial of the dead. It's interesting to note that children were often buried with flowers, and aged and handicapped people lived to an old age, indicating that they were supported by the tribe. Given this evidence of complex ritual beliefs, it is likely that they possessed some form of speech, although there is disagreement as to whether or not their vocal cords were capable of true human speech.

About 40,000 years ago, the Neandertal populations disappear from the fossil record, replaced by Cro-Magnon populations, true *Homo sapiens sapiens*. Whether all Neandertal groups evolved directly into Cro-Magnon, or only a few populations of the Progressive or more modern-looking specimens did, with the rest becoming extinct, is still a matter under consideration. What is agreed upon, however, is that modern man first appeared about 40,000 years ago, and was soon on its way to becoming the dominant life form on earth.

The Human Species' Genetic Heritage

While the fossil record tells us a great deal about the physical forms which may have been ancestral to the human body, some of the strongest proof of man's evolutionary origins comes from biochemical studies which compare the body's molecular building blocks with those of other organisms. These studies are both intriguing and controversial, and may yet shed the greatest light on our relationship with other species.

Similarities in chromosome patterns provide fascinating evidence of our close relationship with modern-day great apes. In a comparison of the alpha chain of hemoglobin of humans and the gorilla, 139 of the 141 amino acids in this chain have an identical composition! Comparisons between humans and chimpanzees show no difference at all! This shows an extremely close genetic and evolutionary relationship between these species.

DNA annealing shows similar results. Annealing is the process whereby the double helices of DNA are separated or "unzipped," and mixed with another strand to create a hybrid double helix. In this process, only those molecular units or sites which are identical will unite. When this process was tested using human and chimpanzee DNA, only one unit out of every one hundred was a mismatch. Not surprisingly, serum immunological testing, which matches the immunological response to the albumen in blood, shows similar results.

When the results of such studies were first released in the 1970s, they immediately became a hotbed of controversy, because they placed the divergence of the ape and human lineages at no more than 5 to 6 million years B.P. The fossil record, at that time, placed the divergence at 20 million years, although subsequent fossil finds have pushed that figure down to a date closer to 10 million years B.P. This issue has yet to be resolved within the scientific community.

Physical Evidence Versus Metaphysical Insight: Can We Compare the Two?

Now that we have discussed both the scientific view of the development of the human body, and that given in the Cayce readings, we need to see if we can draw any correlations between the two. While at first glance it might seem as if these two sources of information are contradictory, a closer look at the content of the readings will show that there are indeed similarities.

Refer again to the reading stating that physical man was created out the elements of the earth, of all that had been before: "From among the many physical shapes and sizes that resulted from the mixtures, he [Amilius] selected the form of the present man as the most suitable vehicle for physical manifestation on this planet."[16] This reading indicates that Amilius chose an existing life form as the most suitable vehicle for the human soul!

Thomas Sugrue, the well-known biographer and friend of Edgar Cayce, expounds upon this further and states that this process involved the souls directing or manipulating the evolutionary development of an already existing life form! "A form was chosen to be a proper vehicle of the soul on earth . . . The form already existing which most approached the needs of the souls was what man would call one of the anthropoids."[17] The readings go on to tell how the souls hovered about this species, rather than inhabiting the body, and influenced the species to move toward a different purpose. "They came down out of the trees, built fires, made tools, lived in communities, and began to communicate with each other. Swiftly, even as man measures time, they lost their animal look, shed bodily hair and took on refinements of manner and habit. All this was done by the souls working through the glands,[18] until, at last, there was a new inhabitant of the earth: man."[19]

The developmental process being described here certainly sounds like the hominid complex which led to the evolutionary development of the hominid lineage, and is identical to that reflected in the fossil record. The only difference is that science states that this occurred due to the *natural laws* of evolution while the readings indicate that there was a *"divine" impetus* which sparked this process.

While this may at first sound extraordinary, is the concept of "divine intervention" any more astounding than the scientific probability by which life first appeared on this planet? According to Carl Sagan, the world-renowned astronomer and author, the number which represents the odds of life appearing on this planet haphazardly would start with the numeral one followed by enough zeros to fill the pages of six paperback books! And this number reflects the odds of life itself, and not the even greater odds of intelligent life.

Many people already accept the premise that the laws of nature and physics were created by God to govern the affairs of His creations. Could it be that the evolution of the human lineage which led to the development of the *Homo* genus was not due to the *random* laws of evolution but was rather the product of a well-thought-out *plan* of divine-soul origin which used the evolutionary process to produce a body capable of meeting the needs of the soul in the physical world? Perhaps that's why paleoanthropologists can't explain exactly how and why the hominid complex appeared. Perhaps that's why the consciousness of humankind is unique among all animals. Perhaps we are in a sense a "special" creation which houses the soul, and yet also carries the roots of our genetic heritage.

If we accept the premise that the human lineage was

the result of soul-intervention in the evolutionary development of an existing anthropoid species, the next logical step would be to see if there is a way to cross-reference the fossil record with the various groups of "man," as given in the readings, to determine when the culmination of this process—the human body capable of housing the soul—appeared. Regretfully, attempts to cross-reference material in the readings with evidence in the fossil record are sketchy at best, due to differences inherent in the framework of the two thought systems themselves.

One of these differences stems from the fact that in the readings, the word "man" is not always used to refer to our physical aspects. It is used to refer to any of our developmental stages, sometimes referred to as "root races," including spirit form, the light body, and thought form, in addition to the human body. (Refer to Table 1 on page 16.) The fossil record, of course, deals only with the physical remains of a species. Since our earliest manifestations on this planet were not in physical form, much of the material in the readings cannot be verified by the fossil record.

A related problem is that the word "flesh," as used in the readings, has more than one meaning " . . . all spirit being one spirit. All flesh not one flesh. Flesh being that as has merited by its development in its plane of existence."[20] This seems to indicate that when Cayce speaks of a flesh body, we cannot assume that he is necessarily speaking of the one we possess today.

Another difficulty stems from the fact that the readings often give a date in a relative sense, rather than an absolute sense. "In the period, then—some hundred, some ninety-eight thousand years before the entry of Ram into India—there lived in this land . . ."[21] Using this passage as an example, we must first identify who Ram was, and what year, as we count it, he entered into India. Such relative references make it difficult to pinpoint events in the readings to a specific time. Combine this with the fact that we must also determine in which form the soul manifested, and you can see the variety of interpretations that can result.

There are however, several readings, which when considered together, can be used as the basis for making inferences as to the appearance of physical man in the earth. To begin, the earliest date given in the readings for the entry of a soul into the earth plane, in spirit form, is 10.5 million years ago. This indicates that the soul's intervention or direction in the evolutionary process had to occur after that time. No doubt this was a lengthy process which required generations of manipulation and refinement in accordance with the laws of evolution which do not work quickly. This scenario does agree with the scientific record which indicates that the human and ape lineages split sometime between 6 million and 10 million years B.P., each thereafter following its own separate evolutionary paths.

From the readings, we also know that the Atlantean civilization lasted approximately 200,000 years, until its final destruction in 10,500 B.C. At first glance it might seem that, since Amilius was present in Atlantis, his activities in directing the evolution of a new body would have had to occur within that time frame. Keep in mind, however, that the 200,000-year period refers to the Atlantean "civilization," and not necessarily its earliest inhabitation. Amilius' plans for the creation of a human body could, therefore, stretch back further, even to the millions of years as noted above.

Further, we need to remember that the readings refer to the existence of thought forms during the earliest years of Atlantis, implying that the human body had not yet been perfected. The readings indicate that "Adam," the Amilius soul who directed this process and who is associated with the appearance of a human body much like our present one, appeared during the course of the Atlantean civilization. " . . . in the Atlantean land . . . in those periods *before* [author's italics] Adam was in the earth . . . among those who were then 'thought projections' . . . "[22] Another noteworthy reading includes a reference to *present*-day man " . . . much in the form of the present-day man (were one chosen of those that were, or are, the nearest representative of the race of peoples that existed in this first period as the first destructions came about) . . . The ones that became the most *useful* were those as would be classified . . . as the *ideal* stature, that was of both male and female . . . and the most ideal (as would be called) was Adam . . . "[23] This reading is most significant because it is given in terms of a definable date, namely the first destructions in Atlantis. Interpretations of other readings indicate that these upheavals may have occurred at approximately 52,700 B.P.

These readings therefore indicate that a physical form, much like our present-day *homo sapiens* body, had appeared sometime between 200,000 and 50,000 years ago. This corresponds to the fossil record, for Neandertal Man, a member of our own species, was flourishing in many areas of the world at this very time, with *Homo sapiens sapiens* spreading across the globe by 40,000 B.P. The worldwide appearance of *Homo sapiens* also finds a correlation to the appearance of five racial groups as cited in the readings.

Yet other than these broad generalizations, no other correspondences between the fossil record and the readings are evident. However, assigning a specific group of archaic humans to a particular time as described in the readings, or determining exactly when the soul, as represented by Adam, entered the physical body, may not be as important as recognizing the overall common message found in both the fossil record and the readings. That message is clear in both sources, namely, that the physical development of the human species has been ongoing for a very long time, and that we share a genetic heritage with all other life forms existing on this planet. Though our origin is divine, we adopted the earth as our mother eons ago, and while in the earth plane, we live as her children.

The Human Species: No Stranger in the Earth

It should be clear by now that the soul, whether as a spirit entity, thought form, or in the physical body, has been involved in the affairs of this planet for a very long time. We know that the earliest date given in the readings for the entry of a soul into the earth plane, in spirit, not physical form, is 10.5 million years ago! We also know that "present-day man" has been in existence for over 50,000 years, a fact supported by the fossil record as well. The readings further state that our present-day body is the result of a lengthy process whereby a pre-existing species was influenced or directed by the soul force, so that it might evolve into a physical form capable of housing the soul while in the earth plane so that the soul would not lose sight of its spiritual nature. Based on this information, we can therefore conclude that physical man, in the human body, has been developing for hundreds of thousands, if not millions of years. Consider this extract from the readings:

> Man *did not* descend from the monkey, but man has evolved ... from time to time, time to time, here a little, there a little, line upon line ... the prepara-

tion for the needs of man has gone down many, many thousands and millions of years, as is known in this plane, for the needs of man in the hundreds and thousands of years to come.[24]

This certainly sounds like a restatement of the evolutionary process. Remember, evolution doesn't teach that we descended from the monkey. In fact, if you look up the definition of evolution in a dictionary, you will find such words as "develop, emerge, mature, result, and unfold." Evolution simply teaches that species change from simple to complex form, a process reflected in the fossil record. One-celled organisms became complex organisms with multi-cellular structures. Rudimentary neural systems evolved into elaborate neurological networks with millions of synapses and interconnections. Simple vocal systems developed into the intricate symbology of human language. Science contends that these developments are the result of the natural and random laws of evolution. The Cayce readings contend that they are the culmination of a divine-soul plan, which manifested in the earth according to natural evolutionary law.

Either way, the human species has been a long time in the making. We did not magically appear out of the ethers, nor were we transported here by an alien civilization. Our biochemical makeup, nearly identical to that of several other species, clearly shows that we were created out of the "dust" of the ground, the elements of this planet. A recent successful bone marrow transplant, wherein an AIDS patient received the healthy bone marrow of a baboon, serves as testimony of the close relationship of humans to others in the primate family. According to the readings, we can expect our development in the earth to continue for hundreds and thousands of years to come.

Remembering the Divine Within

By the time the human body came into existence, souls in the earth plane had begun to think of themselves as physical rather than spiritual beings, seeing only the physical aspect of their nature. Although the First Cause was an inherent part of the soul, memory of our divine nature became as a whisper, a quiet voice within, an echo within our consciousness minds, prompting us to remember our divine origin. At times the memory of the First Cause broke through to consciousness, as evidenced by the works of the poets, the dreamers, and the great thinkers of history, who dared to believe that we are more than we appear to be. Throughout history, it has remained a primary driving force of the soul.

Yet it was through the human body that the soul would be able to express the constructive force of the mind and use its mental faculties to manifest its spiritual attributes rather than physical desires. Our journey in the earth plane thus became one of progress, not decline, here a little, there a little, the enlightenment overcoming the darkness. " . . . and man's evolving, or evolution, has only been that of the gradual growth upward to the mind of the Maker."[25] For through the constructive force of the mind, the soul reversed the downward spiral of devolution and began instead an evolutionary journey back to the state of God Consciousness which was ours at the beginning of our creation.

What a piece of work is man. How noble in reason. How infinite in faculty . . .
In action how like an angel. In apprehension how like a god.
The beauty of the world. The paragon of animals!
—William Shakespeare, *Hamlet*

3

Our Mental Legacy: The Evolution of Human Consciousness

In the Word was the Beginning . . . the beginning of Man and of Culture.
                    —Leslie A. White, *The Science of Culture*

As WE consider what we know of man's dual nature, it might seem that such an existence would be one of continual turmoil and chaos, as the individual is pulled in two directions, one emphasizing spiritual attributes and the other emphasizing physical desires. Fortunately, there is a third aspect or component of ourselves, which helps us bridge the gap between the two. This aspect is the mind, or our mental abilities, which mediates between the promptings of the soul and the desires of the body. In this chapter we will first consider what the readings say about the constructive power of the mind, and then examine the scientific evidence regarding the evolution of human consciousness.

According to the Cayce readings, mind was a creation of God, given to the soul as a gift, a part of its birthright. "There was, there is, as we find, only three of the creations as is given, matter, force, and mind."[1] It was through the mind, or the mental abilities, that the soul was to express the attributes of free will and development. Although mind was spiritual in origin, it found expression in physical matter when man entered the material plane. In fact, mind is identified as the constructive force through which all things, physical and spiritual, are brought into manifestation. Hence the Cayce readings' adage that "mind is the builder."

Mind therefore operates within both the spiritual and material worlds. It can build from the spiritual ideals which a soul holds, or it can build from the material desires of the individual, depending upon how the soul chooses to express its will. "What, then, is *will?* That which makes for the dividing line between the . . . divine and the wholly human, the carnal and the spiritual. For the *will* may be made one *with Him,* or for self alone."[2] Mind then, can be used as a positive force to bring into material expression spiritual attributes in harmony with universal law, or it can also be used as a negative force to create chaos and conflict.

The Three Levels of Mind

According to the readings, the devolution of the soul into matter caused the mind to divide into three levels: (1) the conscious, (2) the subconscious, and (3) the superconscious. The conscious mind might best be thought of as the portion of the mind concerned with "earthiness" and the physical body; it creates in the physical plane through one of the five physical senses.

The conscious mind controls those physical functions governed by the central nervous system, as well as heredity, environment, and cultural influences. This is where the concept of self or the ego exists. The subconscious mind corresponds to the soul-memory; it can create in both the physical and spiritual worlds. It controls those physical functions regulated by the autonomic nervous system, the endocrine glands, dreams, and memories of our existence beyond the physical world. The superconscious is that part of the mind which corresponds to the spirit, the life-force of the soul. It has no connection with the physical world. The superconscious mind normally manifests only in terms of spiritual insight or revelation. It is the area of our mind which connects us to the Universal Mind or God Consciousness. This is where the "higher self" resides.

These categories of mind as given in the readings have a similar, though not direct, correspondence to those delineated by Sigmund Freud, and used by psychoanalysts today. Freud also recognized three parts of the mind, which he identified as the ego, the id, and the superego. The ego was identified as the conscious portion of the mind, dedicated to ordinary thoughts and functions needed to guide a person in daily behavior. The id was an unconscious level of mind, responsible for instinctive behavior as well as repressed memories. The superego was recognized as the part of the mind that holds cultural values, ideals, and prohibitions, and through these beliefs, sets the guidelines for behavior. When the ego doesn't behave in accordance with these guidelines, the superego imposes feelings of guilt on the individual. The conflict between the ego and the superego was identified as the root cause of emotional problems and mental disorders.

These two schemes of the mind are similar in that

both recognize that a portion of the mind is conscious, or aware of and expressing through the physical senses while another portion of the mind is unconscious, or hidden from our conscious recognition. We can control the conscious mind, because we are aware of our thoughts on this level. It is the unconscious portion of the mind which causes us the most difficulty, however, for with it we can create things and conditions without even being aware that we are doing so.

The Body-Mind Connection.   In recent years, medical science has reaffirmed the fact that the mind can create and influence physical conditions within the body. It has been documented that people who are despondent or dissatisfied with their life situation tend to contract illness at a greater rate than people who express contentment or happiness with their lives. This phenomenon is called the psychoimmunological connection.

A person's mental attitude has also been linked to the ability to recover from injury and disease. Doctors are even going so far as to acknowledge that creative visualization techniques can help fight infection and aid the recovery process. Cancer and AIDS patients are taught creative visualization techniques designed to help fight the spread of tumors within the body. Patients recovering from serious illness or injury are being taught to visualize such things as normal blood flow within organs and the knitting together of broken bones.

Today, I think most people would agree that the mind does have a definite impact upon the body, and can create conditions of health or disease within the physical system. What we need to do, however, is to take this line of thought one step further and recognize that the mind force creates all the circumstances and conditions which we encounter in life, even though we are not consciously aware of many of the things we bring into manifestation.

Mind as the Builder

As the constructive force of creation, mind is responsible for the evolution of everything we know in the material realm. ". . . there is the evolution of the soul, evolution of the mind, but not evolution of matter—save through mind, and that which builds same."[3] All creation first begins with a mental thought held by the mind. As an individual thinks on the mental image held in the mind, the thought becomes an idea, capable of being expressed in words. As the individual continues to dwell on the idea, he or she puts into place plans and preparations so that the idea may manifest in the physical.

The phases an architect goes through in designing a building provide an excellent analogy of the creative process. An architect first imagines or "images" a building in his mind. This is the mental thought of the building. He then draws a blueprint which expresses the idea of what the building will be. He can manipulate this blueprint or idea, making changes as he deems necessary. After the blueprint is completed, the physical steps are taken to bring the building into manifestation—the foundation is laid, the framework is set, and carpentry and masonry begun. The end result will be a tangible, three-dimensional structure which exists in the material dimension. This is what Cayce means when he says that thoughts are things, for the thoughts you dwell upon will manifest in the physical world. The thought is the cause; the physical result of that thought is the effect.

Since the creative force of mind can bring any thought into manifestation, it can be used to create works of great beauty and harmony, as well as those things which bring great destruction. It all depends upon the ideal held by the person, and whether that ideal is to work in harmony with universal law, or to work only for self-gratification. In the same way, if we continually dwell on undesirable circumstances or negative thoughts such as fear and hate, we will create those conditions in our lives. If we concentrate on constructive ideas, however, we can create those conditions which will help us live a happy and productive life. The idea that "thoughts held in mind produce after their kind,"[4] has long been recognized by many spiritual disciplines and philosophical schools of thought. This concept of the cause-and-effect power of the mind first made its way into the popular domain with the publication in 1952 of the bestselling book *The Power of Positive Thinking*, by Dr. Norman Vincent Peale. Oddly enough, the sports world was one of the first disciplines to recognize the potential of actively applying the power of this cause-and-effect relationship. World class athletes in many countries were taught to repeatedly visualize the perfect execution of a physical movement or set of movements as part of their training. Soon coaches were giving testimony that this process greatly improved an athlete's actual performance. By the 1980s the ability of the mind to create conditions and circumstances in one's life was the subject of numerous books on the "creative visualization" process.[5] In recent years, self-help books dealing with the application of this phenomenon in daily life have created one of the fastest growing book markets.

From Devolution to Evolution

According to the readings, the creative power of the mind force was to be the means by which the soul could reverse its descent into the limited consciousness of the earth, and expand its awareness back to its original state of God Consciousness. Once in the earth as a soul-body, humankind would be able to look at the world of which it was now a part and begin to rediscover those hidden truths which were carried within, but could no longer be consciously remembered. By using the faculty of reason, we would be able to fight our way back from the limited consciousness of the material world and rediscover our spiritual self.

Following Adam and Eve's choice of the physical over the spiritual, humanity reached the bottom of its devolutionary spiral away from God Consciousness. There was no connection, no memory of the spiritual state from which we had come. Anyone familiar with the tenets of Alcoholics Anonymous knows that every alcoholic must first "hit bottom" before he or she is ready to begin the journey back to sobriety. Just as an alcoholic must first "bottom-out" before beginning to "climb out of the bottle," so the soul had to plummet to the depths of materiality before it could begin the long climb back from whence it came.

Through the faculty of reason, and the application of patience and faith, humankind began to raise itself upward. The forgotten, inner, heavenly knowledge of the soul expressed itself as mystic dreams, religious revelations, philosophy, and theology. Music, the arts, mathematics, and geometry appeared and flourished. As humankind continued to apply reason and logic to the world in which it dwelt, science resulted and expanded its knowledge even further. Civilizations rose and fell. With each generation, humankind expanded its awareness not only of the world, but of itself as well. As it did so, it began to question its reason for being and its relationship with the universe. Thus human consciousness began its upward spiral.

The Development of Human Consciousness

While the creative power of mind can create those things which are visible in the physical world, it also creates those things which are manifest in the material world but are intangible in nature. This includes such things as behavior patterns, belief systems, paradigms, and spiritual and cultural ideals. The mind is therefore responsible for the development or evolution of human consciousness.

As you may recall, human consciousness refers to the way the human species perceives the world, and can be defined as those universal beliefs, values, and attitudes, which the human species, as a whole, holds to be true. Imbedded in human consciousness are the universal paradigms through which humans filter incoming information. A paradigm[6] is the framework or standard of reference from which we analyze all sensory input regarding our world. Paradigms establish the limits for our beliefs, define rules for successful behavior, and since they filter information we receive, they influence our perception.

As the human species evolves, human consciousness evolves with it. As the human species learns more about the world in which it lives, human consciousness "shifts" or "expands" to accommodate that new perception. Major shifts in human consciousness can be identified by the paradigm shifts which accompany them. As paradigms change, they create a variety of repercussions which can affect all areas of human existence, much like the ripples in a pond created by the throw of a stone.

For example, in the fifteenth century, we see the beginnings of what might be called the paradigm of "individual worth." This was the recognition, in Western culture, that each individual has an inherent self-worth, independent of his or her social or economic status. The appearance of this paradigm coincided with the changing concepts of God, man, and man's relationship to the universe brought about by the Reformation and the Renaissance. Prior to this, individual life was held in little esteem. The wealthy and powerful thought nothing of exploiting, abusing, or even killing a person relegated to the status of serfdom. The rise of the Humanistic Movement, an educational and philosophical outlook which emphasized the personal worth of the individual and the importance of human values as opposed to religious belief, can be seen as a direct reflection of this paradigm shift. As the concept of individual worth gained acceptance, the feudal system of serfdom began to disintegrate, and soon afterward we see the rise of a growing middle class. In later centuries, the paradigm of individual worth would lead to the abolition of slavery and the establishment of human rights in countries throughout the world.

While there have been many shifts in consciousness throughout human history, there are three major or primary shifts which were particularly significant, having the effect of altering the course of human history thereafter. These three primary shifts in consciousness preceded and were related to three of the most monumental developments in cognitive evolution, these being the discovery of fire, the development of language, and the emergence of culture.

Harnessing the Power of Fire

The ability to systematically use and control fire was a major evolutionary development in the history of the human species. It was the first step in learning to take control of our environment by using what it offered, rather than being at the mercy of the elements. It is still the one characteristic that is uniquely human; no other animal possesses this ability.

The ability to control fire no doubt involved a shift in human consciousness. The human species had to change its perception from one which regarded fire as something to be feared, to one which regarded fire as a beneficial "tool," an instrument which could be used to improve not only our comfort but also our chances of survival. Prior to this shift in consciousness, we no doubt ran from fire as other animals still do, fearing its destructive power. Somehow, humans had to overcome their fear of fire and set it aside rather than acting upon it. The shift in consciousness occurred as humans moved from a paradigm of "behavior by emotion" to a paradigm of "behavior by reason." The reasoning ability of the human mind enabled man to control the emotional urgings of fear so that it no longer was a determining factor of behavior.

While we will never know the circumstances by which the first human learned to control the flames of fire, we can speculate. It's likely that man first learned of the beneficial aspects of fire by drawing near to already existing fires, such as those caused by lightning. Perhaps he or she drew near due to curiosity, and found the warmth of the fire inviting on a cold night, or welcomed protection against nearby predators. Most likely it was a child, spurred by curiosity and undaunted by the fear experience brings, who first ventured near the flames. As cold hands and feet warmed in the glow of the flames, the idea that fire had beneficial aspects was conceived in the minds of those individuals. A new perception of fire as friend rather than foe was born.

Once we understood that fire could be a friend as well as a foe, early hominids most likely tried to keep alight fires that were started by natural means. Perhaps one night, as a family huddled around the flames eating their evening meal, a piece of meat accidently fell into the fire. Since food was precious, it was quickly retrieved with a nearby digging stick, and since no one could afford to waste food, the charred meat was eaten. Imagine that person's surprise when he or she realized that the flames had made the meat more tender and easier to chew. Eventually, we learned to preserve the smoldering embers of a fire and control them, so that they might be fanned at a later time when a large fire was again needed.

While we do not know how humans first harnessed fire, we do know that the systematic use of fire had occurred one-half million years ago, in *Homo erectus* populations. These groups were the first to consistently use fire for warmth, cooking, and as protection from predatory animals. Remains at Terra Amata, in the French city of Nice, reveal living floors in oval huts made of branches braced by stone. Inside each hut was a hearth sheltered by a windshield of stones. Caves in the French Pyrenees also revealed evidence of habitation and consistent fire use. Excavations at Choukoutien, China, gave evidence of fire pits associated with prolonged habitation.

The shift in consciousness which made possible the systematic use of fire started the human species on the road which led to our becoming the dominant species on earth. As the human brain developed and cognitive thinking abilities expanded, reason replaced emotion as the basis for behavior. Although we possessed emotion, we recognized that we could control it, and no longer had to act on its promptings. Equally as important is the fact that this shift in consciousness planted the seed that said we, the human species, could learn to control the forces around us, rather than allowing them to control us. It was our first step in learning to use the ideas of the mind to bring about change in the physical environment.

Language: The Expression of Symbolic Thought

Language has become such an integrated part of our existence that we take this ability for granted. It is even inconceivable to most people that at one time, the human species did not possess this capability. Yet language was not always a part of the hominid lineage, and the ability to communicate through language involved another significant shift in consciousness, this time from a paradigm of "concrete reality," meaning that which is tangible, to a paradigm of "abstract thinking," specifically the ability to symbolize. A symbol is anything which stands for or represents something else. The two do not have to be intrinsically related. A symbol can be a company logo, a nation's flag, the sign of the cross, or in language, a sound which has been given a specific meaning. Different sounds are then combined and arranged into a word, which represents a specific object or concept.

The use of language is such a natural part of our lives that we seldom give it any thought. No one really remembers the exact instant when he or she first became aware that sounds or words signified something else. Yet that instant was a most significant milestone in human evolution. For without symbolic thought, the sharing of information with another person is limited to rudimentary expressions based in the physical world. Communication of abstract ideas and thoughts is virtually impossible as is the transmission of cultural traditions. In order to understand the full significance of that instant when language first became meaningful, we must turn to the story of someone to whom symbolic thought came as a revelation in later life.

Helen Keller, who was left deaf and blind due to an illness in infancy, remembered the exact moment at which she established contact with another human being. She gives a moving account of the afternoon that she, with the help of her teacher Anne Sullivan, experienced a dramatic revelation.

> Someone was drawing water and my teacher placed my hand under the spout. As the cool stream gushed over one hand she spelled into the other the word "water," first slowly, then rapidly. Suddenly I felt a misty consciousness as of something forgotten—a thrill of returning thought; and somehow the mystery of language was revealed to me. I knew then that w-a-t-e-r meant the wonderful cool something that was flowing over my hand. That living word awakened my soul, gave it light, hope, joy, set it free![7]

Helen Keller's revelation was a shift in consciousness as her perception of symbolic thought awakened after lying dormant for many years. For the first time in her life, she was able to communicate ideas and concepts with another human being. Her experience gives us some indication of how this shift in consciousness must have affected those early humans who first developed the cognitive ability to understand symbolism and communicate through language.

While it is doubtful that we will ever be able to determine the exact conditions under which language became a part of human behavior, there are certain areas of the brain which have been identified as controlling aspects of speech production, and they may provide a clue as to when language occurred. Specifically, an area in the left hemisphere (in right-handed people) of the frontal lobe, known as Broca's area, has been identified as controlling the ability to produce meaningful, spoken speech. Wernicke's area, located posterior to Broca's area, has been identified as controlling the ability to understand spoken speech. Trauma to Broca's area results in the inability to string sounds into words while injury to Wernicke's area results in the inability to understand words or word sequences. These linked speech centers produce a swelling in the skull, a characteristic identifiable in skeletal remains. Since these areas are identifiable in fossil skulls, they provide the best clue available as to when language may have appeared in the human species.

Evidence of these areas in the brain exist as early as 2 million years B.P. A clearly defined bulge inside the skull of *Homo habilis* reveals the existence of the speech-producing Broca's area. However, it is doubtful that the laryngeal structure of *habilis* was capable of producing the same types of sounds as modern humans do. Broca's area becomes even more prominent in *Homo erectus* populations, and increases again in size amongst Neandertal groups. The complex ritual beliefs of Neandertals certainly indicate that they had to possess some type of language capability. What is clear, is that by the appearance of Cro-Magnon populations, dated at 40,000 B.P., the ability to communicate through language had become a defining characteristic of the human species.

Although the more than 6,000 identifiable languages known today at first seem to be diverse, the differences are only superficial. Most linguists agree that all languages are essentially similar in structure, function, and expressive ability. Even the seemingly disparate sound systems are similar in structural and organizational components. All of this indicates that language develops throughout the human species in a similar pattern. This amazing uniformity across all languages suggests an essential physiological and cognitive parity among the many populations of the human species.

While language appears to be a learned behavior, meaning that a person will learn to speak the same language as those he is raised with, it's interesting that a learned behavior so quickly became a universal characteristic of the human species. Psycholinguists have long been aware that the usual methods of learning, such as imitation, practice and reinforcement, failed to adequately explain the child's early acquisition and creative use of grammar. The apparent innateness of language acquisition led to speculation that language had a biological component as well, which controlled a person's "language competence," the knowledge of a language that enables a speaker to encode (construct) and to decode (understand) grammatical structures. Noam Chomsky, a renowned pioneer in theoretical grammar, went so far as to postulate the existence of a "language acquisition device" in the brain. As the forebrain evolved, this "language acquisition device" became a part of man's biological makeup, something that was passed on genetically from generation to generation.

Today, it is generally recognized that language is a uniquely human mental faculty consisting of two components—performance and competence. Performance refers to actual speaking and comprehension, which are determined by learned, cultural factors. Competence refers to the innate knowledge of language structure and grammar, a faculty controlled by biologically determined structure and principles.

Since language is based upon the ability to symbolize, it is likely that language development followed the shift in consciousness from concrete reality to symbolic thought. Whether this shift in consciousness was a result of physical changes in the evolving human brain, or whether the emergence of symbolic thought initiated changes in the brain structure and function, is something we cannot determine. Perhaps the two developments went hand-in-hand, each reinforcing the selective advantage of the other.

We do know, however, that the shift in consciousness which accompanied abstract, symbolic thinking, had far-reaching effects upon the future evolution of the species. Through language, humans were able to expand their awareness beyond the physical world of the five senses, and ponder nonphysical concepts such as religion, philosophy, aesthetics, and even scientific theory. Eventually, humans would come to question all aspects of life, including their creation, their creator, their relationship to the universe, and the meaning of their existence.

The Emergence of Human Culture[8]

It was the development of language which made possible the remarkable complexity of human culture. Anthropologists define culture as "the set of learned beliefs, values, and behavior, shared by members of a society,"[9] as well as the material objects particular to that society. Culture is a uniquely human characteristic, its primary attribute being its transmissibility through social mechanisms rather than biological means. The experiences of a culture are transmitted from generation to generation through the medium of language, and it is through language that children acquire knowledge of the culture in which they are raised. Although certain species among the primates demonstrate a variety of customs or behavior patterns acquired through social learning, no other species demonstrates learned, cultural behavior to the extent that humans do.

While there is a great deal of cultural diversity expressed throughout human societies, all cultures share the common characteristic wherein biological urges are controlled, regulated, and modified by the behavioral mores of the culture. This is because the emergence of culture no doubt followed, or perhaps coincided with, yet another shift in human consciousness. This time, our paradigms of behavior shifted from those governed by "biological instinct" to those governed by "learned behavior."

For example, strong biological instincts such as sex and hunger became modified by the rules of a culture. The sexual behavior of humans is regulated in all societies by certain taboos, which define those relationships within which sexual relations are permitted and prohibited. The dietary taboos of a culture are held in such reverence that even people suffering from hunger will refuse food that violates their dietary laws or religious prohibitions.

The emergence of culture is intimately connected with the development of the human lineage, and may even date as far back as the australopithecines. Stone tools used to cut meat may indicate some type of cultural tradition, although there is no way to discern the existence of any other australopithecine cultural beliefs. By the time the *Homo* lineage appears, however, cultural traditions were showing increasing complexity. Toolmaking had diversified into a complex array of implements. Campsites reveal living areas where families shared meat and other food. Perhaps the most remarkable evidence of culture was the discovery of man-made structures built by *Homo habilis*. A site at Olduvai Gorge has revealed the existence of a stone circle about thirteen feet in diameter, which supported a circular hut made of branches. Very similar to modern shelters still built in parts of Africa today, this first known human structure dates to 1.8 million years. Elaborate tool cultures, semi-permanent hearths and shelters, and cooperative big-game hunting by *Homo erectus* show that cultural traditions were becoming more complex as the human lineage evolved. The systematic use of fire, cooking of indigestible plant foods, and perhaps the wearing of fur, all of which enabled *Homo* populations to expand into intemperate climates, demonstrate that cultural evolution began to play a larger role in man's development than biological change.

By the time Neandertal appeared, there is no doubt that humans possessed complex, cultural traditions. We have evidence which indicates that Neandertal culture had progressed to the point of including art, ritual and even religious beliefs. Artistic endeavors included the creation of bone amulets worn for decoration, scratched pebbles, and lumps of red iron oxide and rubbed manganese, used to decorate the body.

There is also clear evidence that Neandertals deliberately buried their dead. Bodies were normally placed in a sleeping posture, and surrounded with grave goods such as tools and food. Many were placed on a bed of woody horsetail, with the head resting on a stone pillow, and flowers scattered about the body. Remains of elderly persons, crippled by arthritis and other deformities, show that they must have developed the faculty of compassion, for these people could only have been kept alive with the help of others. All of this suggests that Neandertals attached significance to both an individual's life and death. Today, many cultures bury their dead with food and other implements because they believe they will be needed by the deceased after death. The inclusion of food and tools with Neandertal burials certainly indicates a belief in an afterlife.

With the appearance of Cro-Magnon populations around 40,000 B.P., we have the rapid expansion of cultural traditions across the globe. This time in human history has been called "the Great Leap Forward," marked by a proliferation in art and ritual practices. Interestingly, this time period also corresponds to that given in the Cayce readings for the emergence of the fifth or "Adamic" root race of humankind. Innovations in art included elaborate cave paintings and sculpture in bone, ivory, antler, and stone. Some illustrations depict part-human, part-animal figures, supposed to represent shaman. Could they, perhaps, be memories of that long-ago time when the soul wrongly projected itself into animal bodies, interfering in the natural evolution of earth's animals? Still other paintings show geometric patterns which may represent notational systems, and there is speculation that one illustration depicts the phases of the moon.

Cro-Magnon burial demonstrates increasing complex symbolic ritual beliefs, involving differentiations in wealth and status. It appears that mourners sprinkled the dead with red ocher, possibly symbolizing the life-blood, again demonstrating a belief in an afterlife. Some corpses were more richly ornamented than others, indicating there were now social status differences based on wealth or authority. A most interesting find, dating to 23,000 B.P., was discovered east of Moscow. The burial consisted of one elderly man, elaborately dressed in beaded fur clothes. Beside him lay two boys wearing beaded furs, ivory rings, and bracelets. Nearby lay long mammoth-tusk spears, and two strange, scepter-like carved rods called *batons de commandement*, taken to be symbols of power and authority. Such burials foreshadowed the elaborate burials of royal personages at a much later time in history.

The emergence of culture is considered by many to be the crowning achievement of the human species. Yet it is the shift in consciousness which made culture possible that holds the most importance, for it was the point at which the human species first learned to overcome the physical side of its nature, and control the biological urges which up to that time had governed all behavior. It marked the dominance of the mental abilities, or mind, over the physical, or biological instinct. No longer were we subject to the promptings of unconscious, innate urges. We could decide not only how we would think, but how we would behave, how we would act upon our thoughts, and the manner in which we would live. The human species had taken the final step which would raise it above the level of the animal consciousness, as humans became "cultural animals," dependent upon culture, rather than biology, for their existence.

The Ascendance of the Human Mind

As evidenced by the above discussion, when we speak of the evolution of the human species, we must consider not only changes in the physical body, but changes within the mind as well. Shifts in human consciousness should therefore be seen as a natural part of our species' cognitive evolution. As humans become capable of viewing their existence in a new way, they discover unforeseen horizons of opportunity which alter the course of human development just as surely as the changes physical evolution brings.

A close examination of the three primary shifts in human consciousness will show that a common thread runs among all three. Each was characterized by a paradigm change wherein a paradigm based on the sensations of the physical world was replaced by a paradigm rooted in the mental world of thought. Emotional response was replaced by action based on reason, the concrete reality of the physical senses was replaced by the abstract quality of symbolic thinking, and biological instinct was replaced by learned codes of behavioral rules. (Refer to Table 3, *The Evolution of Human Consciousness.*)

Table 3. THE EVOLUTION OF HUMAN CONSCIOUSNESS

Primary Paradigm Shifts		Associated
Old Paradigm	New Paradigm	Development
Behavior by Emotion	Behavior by Reason	Systematic Use of Fire -500,000 B.P. -*Homo erectus* -Control of the elements
Concrete Reality	Symbolic Thought	Language -Linked speech centers in brain (Broca's area & Wernicke's area) -*Homo habilis/ erectus ??* -Neandertal -Communication of abstract ideas and thought
Biological Instinct	Learned Behavior	Emergence of Culture -Coincident with human lineage -100,000 B.P. Neandertal cultural evidence -40,000 B.P. Cro-Magnon culture spreads -The Great Leap Forward -Transmission of learned behavior and knowledge across the generations

When considered together, the primary shifts in human consciousness form a pattern whereby the human species gradually moved away from behavior governed by physical sensation and toward behavior governed by the mental faculties of the mind. Slowly, through the development of the mental faculties, humankind began to access information long-buried in its soul-memory and learned to control, modify, and even create the physical environment in which it lived. By learning to use and apply the creative power of the mind in the physical world, humankind began to find its way beyond the limitations of its physical existence. The devolution of the soul into matter thus became evolution of the soul-body into higher states of mental consciousness. By exercising our creative abilities within the earth plane, we were taking the first steps in reclaiming our true relationship as co-creators with God.

Every animal leaves traces of what it was;
man alone leaves traces of what he created.
       —Jacob Bronowski, *The Ascent of Man*

Part II

Embracing Our Present

4

Three in One: Body, Mind, and Soul

As far as we can discern, the sole purpose of human existence is to kindle a light in the darkness of mere being.
—Carl Jung, *Memories, Dreams, Reflections*

WHILE PART I discussed humankind in terms of its origin, this section will focus on the present state of humanity, both on the microcosmic or species level, as discussed in this chapter, and in macrocosmic or global terms, as will be discussed in the following chapter.

As we have already learned, human beings are indeed unique and complex creatures comprised of three distinct yet interrelated components: our physical body, the intangible quality of the mind, and the ethereal soul. While the last section sought to examine the body, mind, and soul in terms of their origin, this chapter seeks to address them in terms of who we are today.

The physical body easily lends itself to analysis. The human mind, however, is not corporeal in nature, and therefore cannot be directly observed or measured. As for the soul, we may never find any concrete means to measure or assess this spiritual aspect of ourselves. Yet it is possible to examine all three, whether directly or indirectly, so that we might come to a better understanding of who we are.

The Abilities of the Five-Sensory Body

Humankind has come a long way since the day its ancestors first stepped out of the forests and learned to manipulate and control their physical environment. It wasn't long before humans were expressing a power and presence across the world that had never before been seen in the history of the planet. Yet, if you carefully consider the characteristics of the human species, one comes to understand how truly remarkable this development was.

There is nothing particularly outstanding about the human body when compared with other species. Our eyesight, the most highly developed of our five physical senses, may be capable of binocular, color vision, and yet our vision pales in comparison to the vision of most bird species who can spot a tiny rodent from a distance of hundreds of feet. Our night vision is feeble and cannot begin to measure up to that of nocturnal animals, including the common house cat! Our tactile abilities are well-developed in that we have an extensive network of tactile sensors on our fingertips, and yet this is very comparable to that of other primate species. You need only think of the family dog to realize that our hearing ability and sense of smell are quite unremarkable when compared with those of many other species. There is nothing exceptional about our sense of taste either.

If you look at our other physical attributes, it becomes even more incredible that our species became the dominant one on earth. Our size is moderate and our physical strength minimal when compared with the large cats, the canine family, bears, and even our fellow primates. Pound for pound, a chimpanzee can exert three times more physical strength than a human. There is no doubt that the gentle gorilla, if so motivated, could rip an arm from its socket as easily as it gently strips a leaf from a tree. In terms of speed, we are no match for other animals our size. We also possess little means of natural defense, lacking sharp teeth, horns, or claws. In fact, physically speaking, the human being is a puny, almost pathetic creature.

Yet there is one physical characteristic which humans alone can claim, and it is this characteristic which has given us an advantage over all other species. This outstanding feature is the complex brain which humans possess. As noted earlier, the human brain is a part of, as well as a result of, the hominid complex, and partially made possible by the development of bipedal, erect posture. Humans possess a larger brain-to-body ratio than any other land animal, and yet it is not brain size in itself which is most important. It is the way the human brain evolved, particularly the development of the forebrain and the "index of cephalization" which has made the human brain so unique. The index of cephalization refers to the amount of brain tissue in excess of the required amount necessary for transmitting impulses to and from the brain. Studies show that there has been a progressive evolutionary encephalization in vertebrates which culminates in the human species.

Related to this was the evolutionary development of the forebrain, a characteristic found only in the human lineage. This greatly expanded and convoluted brain mantle contains the neuronal centers necessary for understanding and producing language as well as the capacity for conceptualization, abstractions, judgment, and contemplation. The convolution or folding of brain tissue allows for an increased number of neurons than could exist on a smooth brain surface. It is estimated that the human brain contains approximately 10 billion neurons, a nerve cell specialized for the transmission of information into, within, and out of the body. Each brain neuron in turn may have several thousand direct connections to other nerve cells in the body. Scientists speculate that we use only ten percent of our neuron capacity at any given time. It was this unique physical development of the human brain which was responsible for the quality of the human mind. It was not, therefore, our physical attributes which made our species great, but the mind force of the soul which resided in the body, which gave the human species an advantage over all others. It was the mind force of the soul, termed "intelligence" by some, that differentiated us from the rest of the earth's species and made us the dominant life form on this planet.

The Human Mind: The Source of Man's Uniqueness

There is no doubt that the reason the human species rose to dominance on this planet is because of the incredible faculty of the human mind which resides in the physical brain. For years, scientists sought to explain the mind in terms of brain function alone. The father of modern neurosurgery, Wilder Penfield, initially believed that brain studies could ultimately explain everything about the mind and body. Fifty years later, however, after extensive research, Penfield came to the conclusion that something indefinable distinguished the physical brain from the mind. "After a professional lifetime spent in trying to discover how the brain accounts for the mind . . . during the final examination of the evidence . . . the dualist hypothesis (the mind is separate from the brain) seems the more reasonable of explanations."[1]

Since direct observation and measurement of the mind is impossible, its functioning is often determined through the study of intelligence, which can be inferred from observable behavior in various situations. There is no consensus today on the definition of intelligence, or the number of factors of intelligence that can be tested. Initially, intelligence was conceived of as a singular power or faculty of the mind, an innate brain power that distinguished the more highly evolved animals from simpler organisms. Today, however, scientists understand that the development of intelligence is partially determined by heredity but also depends on the character of the environment in which an individual is reared.

While individual variations in intelligence are numerous, the intelligence of the human species as a whole far outstrips that of all others. Because of intelligence, humans did not need sharp teeth and claws as a means of defense against predators. Intelligence enabled us to make tools which more efficiently served the purpose of teeth and claws. Because of intelligence, humans did not require enormous strength or speed to bring down large game. Intelligence enabled humans to become cooperative hunters, whose combined efforts could defeat any animal on earth. Because of intelligence, humans did not need the protection fur provides against the elements. Intelligence enabled humans to make clothing and shelter so that they could survive in all climates. Finally, through intelligence, humans were able to pass down learned knowledge from generation to generation, so that culture became possible.

The human mind is an awesome wonder. It allowed a relatively physically insignificant creature to gain true dominion over all other life forms. Unfortunately, we have not always used this faculty wisely, causing the extinction of other species, the wanton despoliation of our environment, and even threatened the very existence of all life on this planet as we developed the capability of nuclear destruction. Why, for all our supposed intelligence and knowledge, has the human species moved from being the caretaker of this planet to being known as the source of vast devastation and even the potential destroyer of the very planet itself?

The answer to this, I think, lies in the fact that all too often, the human mind lost touch with its spiritual foundation, the soul, the true source of its reason for being. We have too long ignored our spiritual aspect, the true nature of ourselves. As we dwelt more and more in the earth plane and lost sight of our soul self, we came to see ourselves as physical beings, the "thinking animal." We fooled ourselves into believing that this gave us the inherent right to use other species as well as the earth itself for our own gratification and desires. The same erroneous thinking which entrapped the soul in the earth plane in the beginning was repeated once again by the human species.

Evidence of the Soul: The Auric Energy Field

The human body is certainly visible through physical means, and although not directly observable, the human mind can be indirectly assessed by the behavior it induces and controls. The soul, however, is much less tangible, incapable of being observed by physical means. For centuries, however, humankind has sought to define the soul and prove its existence.

Democritus, a fifth-century Greek philosopher believed that the "bonds of the soul" were controlled by the brain. The Catholic Church proposed that the soul could be divided into different functions, and went so far as to offer opinions as to where these functions were located in the brain. The theory of dualism, still widely accepted today, was first proposed by the French philosopher René Decartes, who maintained that the soul was separate from the body/brain, and was indivisible, immaterial, immortal. Many people simply believed that the seat of the soul resided in the heart, although the modern miracle of heart transplants has caused this belief to go out of favor.

Today, most people realize that proving the existence of the soul may be something which is outside the boundaries of science. You either have to accept the existence of the soul on faith, or reject the concept entirely.

Mystics and clairvoyants as far back as ancient Egypt, India, Greece, and Rome, however, have claimed to possess an ability which allowed them to see the "aura," an energy field which emanates from all things which exist in nature, including animals, plants, and minerals. Reports of this purported emanation were long believed to be evidence of the soul force. Auras were described as sometimes swirling patterns of different colored light which surrounded and penetrated the body. Psychics agreed that auras reflected the state of a person's mental, emotional, and even physical health. Prior to death, the aura was reported to become faint, departing the body when life ceased. Edgar Cayce possessed the ability to see auras and called them the "weathervane of the soul."[2]

There is an interesting story concerning Edgar Cayce and his ability to see auras.[3] One day as he was about to enter an elevator, he stopped and took a step back, feeling a sense of repulsion. Yet he couldn't identify what caused that feeling. He took the stairs instead. Seconds later, the cable to that elevator snapped, and the elevator dropped six floors to the basement, killing all its occupants. Cayce would later realize what it was that had disturbed him. None of the occupants in the elevator had an aura.

Until recently, there was no scientific way to observe the auric phenomenon described by psychics. A recent technological development, however, may have come the closest yet to helping prove the existence of the soul. While it is not capable of observing the soul per se, it may indirectly measure the energy the soul emits, much as the mind is evaluated by the behavior it controls. This development is Kirlian photography, which has proved the existence of the human energy field known as the aura.

Kirlian photography was developed in 1939 by the Russian scientist Semyon Davidovich Kirlian. The technique involves photographing objects in the presence of a high-frequency, high-voltage, low-amperage electrical field, which shows glowing, multicolored emanations coming from the subject. Kirlian photography remains controversial within scientific circles, although independent researchers have conducted a number of experiments which have verified that the auric field is affected by changes in emotional states. One experiment conducted at the University of California's Center for the Health Sciences at Los Angeles, by Thelma Moss and Kendall Johnson, showed that even the auras of plants reacted when the plant was injured, or when a leaf was removed.

The controversy surrounding Kirlian photography is not so much that it works, as it is what the auric field represents. Many people believe that the aura as photo-graphed by Kirlian photography represents a physical manifestation of the soul force, particularly since it disappears upon the death of the organism. This, of course, corresponds with traditional metaphysical teachings which have long described the aura as a reflection of the soul. This is not to say that the aura is the soul, but only a *reflection* of the soul force. "The aura, then, is the emanation that arises from the very vibratory influences of an individual entity, mentally, spiritually—especially of the spiritual forces."[4]

Integrating Our Separate Selves:
Union of Body, Mind, and Soul

It may seem that humans are fragmented, splintered beings, possessing three separate selves which are constantly at odds with one another. Yet we know from the Cayce readings that the human body was designed as a perfect vehicle capable of allowing the spiritual attributes of the soul to manifest through the action of the mind. We infer that the souls altered the evolutionary pattern of an existing primate species by "working through the glands," so that our present body might be developed. What, then, was this alteration? To what glands are the readings referring? Might they hold the key to the way in which the mind, body, and soul can be brought into attunement with one another? How is the body capable of connecting to the soul so that we might express its spiritual attributes? What role does the mind play in this process?

The answer to these questions can be found in ancient Sanskrit concepts, as confirmed by the information given in the readings. According to both systems of thought, the connection between the physical body and

the soul resides in the endocrine system, and this connection can be activated through the direct application
of the mind force. Let's therefore consider the endocrine
system, examining it first in terms of its physical structure and function, and then in terms of its metaphysical
significance.

The Endocrine System: Bodily Connection to the Soul

The endocrine system is comprised of specialized
glands located in various parts of the body. These glands
are "ductless," meaning that they have nothing connecting them to their target organs or tissues. They secrete a
variety of hormones and chemical agents which are responsible for the regulation of bodily processes including growth and metabolism. Only mammals possess
true endocrine glands. These glands include the pituitary, the pineal, the thyroid, the thymus, the adrenals,
and the gonads.

The endocrine system shares control of all bodily activities with the nervous system. The nervous system
acts quickly and produces instantaneous response while
the endocrine system produces slow and long-lasting
effects. Both systems are similar in that they secrete
chemicals that convey regulatory messages to different
areas of the body.

Of the endocrine glands, the pituitary is considered
the "master" or "control" gland. It is responsible for production of the growth hormones as well as the production of "tropic" hormones, which stimulate all the other
endocrine glands, particularly the thyroid, adrenals, and
gonads. Not surprisingly, the pituitary is located in the
center of the brain, between the center of the eyes.

Connected to the posterior wall of the third ventricle

of the brain, in a position slightly behind and above the pituitary, is the pineal gland. It lies above the cerebellum and is richly supplied with nerve fibers and blood vessels. The pineal gland produces melatonin, a hormone associated with the regulation of a number of biorhythms, including the onset of puberty and seasonal behavior displays in certain animals. In various species of fish, frogs, and lizards, the gland is associated with a light-sensitive organ which is actually called the "third eye" by biologists (not to be confused with the metaphysical Third Eye, associated with the pituitary). Although encased deep within the brain, in all species the pineal is responsive to and affected by light. René Decartes, the father of the philosophy of dualism, proposed that the pineal gland, although not the soul itself, might be the likely "seat of the soul," since he felt it was here that the mind and body came together.

The thyroid gland, located in the throat area, secretes thyroxine and triodothyronine, hormones which play a major role in the regulation of the body's metabolism, particularly the growth rate and maturation of the individual. Through the secretion of calcitonin and the parathyroid hormone, it acts upon blood calcium levels, thus influencing bone development.

The adrenals are composed of two endocrine tissues, a medullary region and a surrounding cortex. They are located on the upper anterior end of each kidney. The hormones they secrete, epinephrine and norepinephrine are released in response to emergency or emotional situations and increase the heart rate, thus stimulating the vascular system. This is responsible for the "fight or flight" response in mammals. They also secrete several steroid hormones which play a role in stress adjustment through the regulation of the blood sugar level, anti-inflammatory action, and reduction of sodium and water excretion by the kidneys.

In addition to being an endocrine gland, the thymus serves a dual function as a vascular organ of the lymphatic system. Located just behind the breastbone and heart, the thymus is the principal organ that controls the production of lymphocytes and antibodies, which are responsible for the proper functioning of the immune system.

Although not a gland of the endocrine system, the spleen, which is the largest organ of the lymphatic system, must also be considered here. It is a richly vascular organ which filters cellular waste products and old red blood cells from the system. It also manufactures antibodies and certain blood cells.

The gonads are responsible for production of the steroid sex hormones that stimulate the reproductive process and the development of secondary sexual characteristics, as well as influencing growth and behavior. The gonads consist of the ovaries in the female and the testes in the male.

The endocrine system, therefore, is intricately connected to the development of the individual. In terms of evolutionary theory, alterations in this system would definitely lead to evolutionary changes within a species. This is borne out by the fact that mammalian evolution may have been predicated upon the development of the endocrine system itself. It is no stretch of the imagination, therefore, to understand that if an "outside force," such as that noted in the readings, wanted to influence the development of a species, it could do so by adjustments to the endocrine glands. It should not be surprising that endocrinology is one of the component disciplines which contributes to the field of genetic engineering being carried on by scientists today.

Yet how do these glands, which are very much in the

physical body, connect to the soul? According to both Hindu and Buddhist teachings, as well as the readings, each gland and its surrounding area is connected to a specific "chakra," a Sanskrit word meaning wheel. A chakra is a vortex or energy center where various energies, including the universal life force, are received, transformed, and distributed.[5] While there is no scientific proof to verify the existence of chakras, they have long been recognized by Eastern religions as well as various Western metaphysical traditions.

Body and soul "meet" within the endocrine/chakra system when the constructive power of the mind force is focused on spiritual expression, rather than physical wants and desires. Body, mind, and soul, thus act as one. The "spiritualization of the body" occurs when the mind draws the universal life force through the glands and applies it in accordance with universal laws. "In the psychic forces, or spiritual forces, there has even then been a vehicle, or portion of the anatomical forces of the body, through which the expressions (meaning spiritual expressions) come to individual activity."[6] Thus, through the direction of the mind force, an individual can bring the spiritual attributes of the soul into expression in the physical world. To better understand this process, we turn now to an examination of the human chakra system.

The Human Chakra Energies: Gateway to the Soul

The chakra system can be considered as representing the human energy field. Each chakra is said to resemble a multi-petaled flower or spoked wheel which rotates at various speeds as it processes energy. There are seven major chakras along with dozens of minor ones. The chakras are connected to the body and one another through a *nadi,* or channel of energy. The acupuncture meridians often parallel the *nadis* of the chakra system. The central *nadi,* called the *sushumna,* rises from the base of the spine and culminates in the *medulla oblongata* at the base of the brain. The *medulla oblongata* is a nerve fiber-rich organ which processes all incoming and outgoing neural information between the brain and the body.

In various religious traditions as well as certain alternative treatment therapies, it's acknowledged that chakras play a role in physical, emotional, and mental health, as well as spiritual development. Each of the seven major chakras is associated with a specific endocrine gland or nerve plexus, a specific color, a physiological function, and a psychic function. (See Figure 1: The Chakra System.) Problems in any area can develop when a chakra is out of balance, either due to a blockage or an excess of energy. It is likely that most people have some chakras which are out-of-balance at any given time.

There are slight differences in the way the chakra system is described in various traditions. The information presented here represents the most widely accepted synthesis of the existing body of information.[7]

The Root Chakra.   The first chakra, also called the root or base chakra, is located at the base of the spine and is associated with the gonads. Its color is red. It represents our connection to the earth and material reality and is the source of our physical energy and vitality. Deficient energy in this chakra can lead to a lack of energy, self-destructive tendencies, or inability to focus, while excessive energy can lead to egotism, a domineering personality or inappropriate expression of sexual energy. Physical problems might include poor circulation, low blood pressure, and infections of the genitourinary tract. A healthy root chakra results in a well-grounded, self-

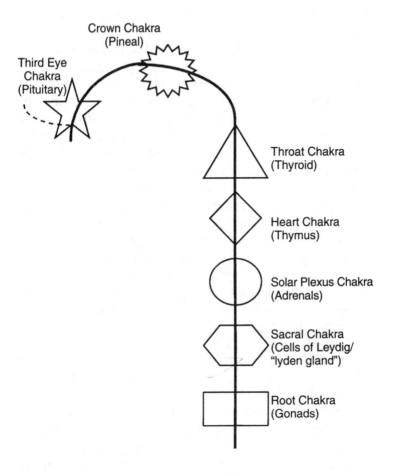

Figure 1. The Chakra System

sufficient personality characterized by sufficient physical energy.

The Sacral Chakra.   The second or sacral chakra lies near the genitals. The Cayce readings associate it with the cells of Leydig (lyden gland) which reside on the gonads, while most other traditions associate it with the spleen. It is normally associated with the color orange. It is the seat of self-creativity, and governs sexuality and the reproductive urge. Lack of energy at this center might result in feelings of fear and an intense separation from life. An abundance of energy might result in emotional instability, aggressive tendencies, and the need for frequent sexual gratification. Physical ailments could include kidney weakness, chronic allergies, and a consistent lack of energy. The readings associate schizophrenia with an imbalance here. A well-balanced sacral chakra is characterized by a well-adjusted personality, creative imagination, good sense of humor, and attunement to one's own feelings.

The Solar Plexus.   The solar plexus resides just above the navel and is a nerve network where vast numbers of blood vessels and neural fibers interconnect. This third chakra is connected with both the solar plexus and the adrenal glands. Yellow in color, it affects the pancreas, liver, stomach, and other digestive organs. According to the readings, it is the seat of our emotional karma. The third chakra is also the center of personal power. Various martial arts traditions consider it the center of "chi," the life force energy.

According to Paramahansa Yogananda, the third chakra is ruled by the conscious mind and is only active when one is awake. With training, however, it can be used for creative thinking which will provide access to, and influence, the subconscious mind. It therefore controls the power of negative or positive thinking.[8]

Lack of energy through the third chakra can lead to worry, depression, lack of confidence and the feeling that you have no control over life. Excess energy may be indicated by a judgmental attitude, extreme prejudice, perfectionism, and a superiority complex. Physical ailments may include high blood pressure, digestive problems, liver disease, and gallstones. An equilibrium of energy within this chakra will result in a healthy self-respect, a strong sense of personal power, concern for others, and a general positive outlook on life.

The first three chakras are called the "lower" chakras, and are considered to be connected to the physical earth and conscious mind. The fourth chakra, the heart chakra, is the gate through which the energy moves into the three "upper" chakras where higher levels of consciousness are attainable.

The Heart Chakra. In many traditions the fourth chakra is associated with the heart, although the Cayce readings connect it with the thymus gland which lies directly behind the heart. It is the door leading to higher levels of consciousness through the ability to manifest unconditional love. Green, the color of healing and nature, is the color of the heart chakra. As the color at the middle of the light spectrum, it is the most balanced of all colors. Pink, the color of love, is also associated with this chakra. It is the chakra of compassion, humanitarianism, and healing on all levels—emotional, mental, and physical. Too little energy processed through the heart chakra may result in paranoia, abnormal fears, a sense of unworthiness, and abandonment. Too much energy processed through this chakra may result in manic-depression, a martyr complex, or an overly demanding, critical attitude. Physical disorders can manifest as heart problems, high blood pressure, insomnia, and a tendency toward cancer, particularly leukemia. A healthy heart chakra manifests as a friendly, outgoing person in touch with his/her feelings, and characterized by empathy, compassion, and a desire to be of service.

The Throat Chakra.   The first of the upper chakras is the throat chakra, associated with the thyroid gland and the color turquoise. It is the center of communication, and the beginning of spiritual enlightenment where the individual will can be brought into alignment with universal law. A deficit of energy in the fifth chakra can result in an inconsistent, timid personality, afraid of expressing his/her own thoughts. An excess of energy here can result in an arrogant, self-righteous personality, as well as addictive tendencies. Physical problems may be ulcers, chronic back pain, hypo/hyperthyroidism, high blood pressure, frequent skin irritations, and mental exhaustion. Balance within this chakra leads to contentment, a feeling of centeredness, musical or artistic expression, and an interest in meditation.

While Eastern religious traditions identify the sixth chakra as the "third eye chakra," and the seventh chakra as the "crown" chakra, largely because the pituitary is located slightly below the pineal, the Cayce readings emphatically state that the position of these two chakras have been reversed, and maintain that the crown chakra is actually the sixth chakra while the third eye should be considered the seventh spiritual center. Other than their relative positions, there is little difference between the information in the readings and that of other traditions regarding the two chakras' functions. We will follow the Cayce scheme for purposes of this book.

The Crown Chakra.   This chakra is linked to the pineal gland located slightly above the pituitary, at the top of the brain. The crown chakra's color is purple, and it cannot be completely activated until all other chakras have been cleared and balanced. When complete attunement is achieved, the color of this chakra manifests as white. It is thought that this chakra is the source of the halo of saints and mystics, as portrayed in art throughout the centuries. The readings identify it as the seat of the Christ Consciousness. Deficient energy through the crown chakra may result in a joyless, nearly catatonic personality. Excessive energy in this chakra may result in a psychosis, destructive tendencies, or manic-depressive behavior. Associated physical illnesses include depression, migraine headaches, and nervous disorders. A balanced flow of energy in this chakra may result in the ability to access both the subconscious and superconscious minds, a sincere interest in spiritual, rather than material, concerns, and the manifestation of psychic abilities.

The Third Eye. This chakra is linked to the pituitary gland and is associated with the conscious awareness of spiritual enlightenment, as well as intuition and psychic abilities. The color of the third eye chakra is a blue-purple or indigo. An inadequate amount of energy within this chakra can lead to an undisciplined or withdrawn personality as well as a schizophrenic personality, unable to distinguish between the ego and the Higher Self. An extreme amount of energy might result in egomania and a manipulative, authoritarian personality, as well as religious dogmatism. Physical problems associated with this chakra include chronic pain, agitation in the intestines, and mental exhaustion. Balance in this chakra will lead to an interest in spiritual matters rather than material concerns, a love of life yet no fear of death, as well as the manifestation of such things as telepathy, astral travel, past life recall, and experience with the cosmic consciousness.

The reason for the difference in the order of the sixth and seventh chakras between that given in the readings and most other traditions, is that the readings use the analogy of the "shepherd's crook" to describe the alignment of the chakras. The staff or shepherd's crook (refer to Figure 1, *The Chakra System*) is used as a symbol in many of the religions of the Middle East, including the ancient Egyptian, Judaism, and Christianity. In Egypt, the power of the Pharaoh was symbolized by the crossed "crook" and flail. Moses asserted the power of his God, Jehovah, over Pharaoh by use of the same shepherd's crook. Jesus, known also as the Good Shepherd, carried on this symbology. In terms of the human body, the rod of the crook represents the spine, while the curved portion represents the outline of the brain case. According to this analogy, the tip of the shepherd's crook is the pituitary gland, and hence its position as the seventh, rather than sixth chakra.

Symbolism of the Chakras. It's interesting to note that the first three or lower chakras are all associated with organs which consist of two separate glands. In the heart chakra, however, we have the merging of the two into one organ, with two sides. This represents the fact that it is only through the unconditional love of the heart chakra that we may enter into the higher realms of consciousness, where the physical and spiritual meet. As we move into the upper chakras, the organs associated with them consist of a single gland. The separation between the spiritual and physical, between God and man, has been eliminated. Further, as we move from the heart chakra to the throat chakra, we must pass through the very narrowly defined area of the neck before we can pass into the chakras through which we achieve Christ Consciousness. The narrowness of the throat passage is said to represent the difficulty of the footpath and the "narrow gate"[9] which the soul must traverse on its way back to unity with the Creative Force.

Spiritualization of the Body Through the Chakras

A healthy chakra/endocrine system is therefore important not only for the maintenance of good health, but for those seeking unity with the God-Force. The endocrine glands, along with their associated chakras, are referred to in the readings as the "spiritual centers of the body" through which our spirit force finds means of expression. "In the body we find that which connects the pineal, the pituitary, the lyden, may be truly called the silver cord [that which connects the soul to the body], or the golden cup that may be filled with a closer walk with that which is the creative essence in physical, mental and spiritual life . . . "[10] Development of the chakra system can therefore be thought of as the key to reconnecting with our spiritual side, which has long laid dormant.

A main principle in understanding the chakra system is the belief that the universal life force enters the body through the chakra at the top of the head and then filters down through the other chakras, which transform it into usable energy. We have forgotten, however, that a spark of the Creative Force itself resides *within* us as well. The key to spiritual development lies in the ability to raise that spark of the divine within, called *kundalini,* and activate its creative properties in accordance with universal law.

The readings as well as Hindu and Buddhist traditions teach that spiritual cleansing and balance of the chakras can be accomplished through the application of the mind force working in accord with universal law. An individual may, through patience, practice, and application of the mind, awaken the *kundalini* within, and balance all chakras so that the *kundalini* can be *raised up through* them and activated. The body is then "spiritualized," as body, mind, and soul are brought into attunement with divine will, and the spiritual attributes of the soul find expression in the physical world through that individual's actions.

The Meditative Process. The primary means by which the mind force can be applied to balancing the chakras is through the practice of meditation. Meditation is capable of "spiritualizing" the body by raising the very vibrational rates of the glands themselves, which then affect all other portions of the body. While an explanation of meditative techniques is outside the scope of this book, a brief description of the energy flow process which occurs during meditation is given below.

Interestingly, the meditative process as described in the Cayce readings parallels the process of the development of the human fetus in the womb. At conception, the sperm and ovum unite to create the body-to-be. As cellular division begins, the first gland formed is the pituitary. Following this, the creative process forms the adrenals, followed by the other five endocrine glands.

During meditation, the *kundalini* energy is raised within the gonads of the root chakra and released through the lyden gland which opens the door for this energy to move through the system. At this point, the mind of the soul, the subconscious mind, rises to the pineal, the Christ Consciousness. As the *kundalini* energy rises to the pineal, it joins with the universal energy entering through the crown chakra. This energy is then directed to the pituitary, and from there it passes to the adrenals. Following that, it is distributed to the remaining spiritual centers. As it passes through the chakras, it cleanses and illuminates them, bringing them into attunement with the Creative Force. Just as the process of fetal development creates a new human being, the consistent practice of the meditative process creates a new "spiritual man/woman within."

The gonads of the root chakra are no longer used simply as a means for raising the life force through physical reproduction. Their purpose is redirected as they become the means whereby the *kundalini* life force is first raised. The lyden gland, which the readings call the control-center of the soul's activity, are the "door which must be lifted up"[11] before the soul can begin the spiritualization process. The lyden gland brings a balance of male/female characteristics to the individual which represents the sublimation of purely physical desires so that we may become channels for spiritual purposes. The adrenal glands, which stimulate the body in times of stress or danger, turn their purpose from one of individual survival to one which brings courage, perseverance, and patience. Negative emotions are removed and all emotional energy is used constructively. Cleansing of the adrenals enables the individual to seek out the good in all things.

Perhaps the thymus gland, active in the body's defense against infection, is located near the heart because all healing comes from love, a heart quality. When spiritualized, the heart chakra will manifest unconditional love, the type of love the Christ exhibited toward His fellow humans, even those who crucified His body. It is only through unconditional love that we can pass on into the higher chakras which lead to the higher levels of consciousness.

Once spiritualized, the energies of the thyroid which were concerned with maintaining metabolic balance, turn toward the balancing of psychic energies. This is the beginning of the expression of psychic abilities such as clairvoyance, telepathy, and intuition. The pineal gland regulates puberty and our biorhythms, and is therefore responsible for a child maturing into an adult. Through daily meditation, the pineal redirects its purpose to the process whereby the individual matures into a spiritualized being, capable of communion with the Christ through the Holy Spirit. It becomes the center at which the arising *kundalini* meets with the descending force of the Holy Spirit. Stimulation of this center may bring about the ability to prophesy.

The master gland of the entire chakra system is the pituitary, which biochemically controls all of the endocrine glands, and it is through this gland that the ultimate spiritual awakenings occur. As the pituitary becomes purified, healing through laying on of hands becomes a possibility, much in the manner that Jesus did. When attuned through meditation, the pituitary becomes the center of contact with the Father through the awakening of the superconscious. Here we return to the original state of our being—unity with the Creative Force. We come to understand that we are spiritual beings, at one with our Creator. We have at last overcome the physical body, even to the point of overcoming death itself, as exemplified by the Christ soul, the first to reclaim His birthright as a co-creator with the Father-God.

Thus the endocrine system, a part of the physical body, contains within it the capability which enables us to rise above the physical and regain our spiritual identity. As the mind force works in harmony with universal law, and attunes itself with divine will, our physical self is reconnected to the soul, and then becomes subject to it. As the physical body becomes spiritualized, the veil imposed by the material world is lifted and we begin to see with the eyes of spirit and become more receptive to spiritual phenomena. " . . . but development in the spiritual sense—by meditation, prayer—[is] dependent upon the external forces, or the creative energies, for its food, rather than upon that which is wholly of the material, develops that as may be termed the psychic [spiritual] development of individuals."[12]

We must keep in mind, however, that spiritualization

through meditation is not meant to make us feel "special" or superior to others. Rather, if practiced in the right spirit, it will make us as humble as the carpenter from Nazareth who chose to walk among the lowliest of sinners rather than dwell in the palaces of kings. ". . . as the progress is made, as the understanding comes more and more, *never, never* does it make the manifested individual entity other than the more humble, the more meek, the more long-suffering, the more patient."[13] For it helps us understand that each soul, as created by God, is equally loved and "special," in that each is an individualized expression of the divine love of the Creator.

Spiritualization as an Agent of Change

It is important to understand that the process of spiritualization as described above is more than a tool for attaining personal spiritual enlightenment. It is also a mechanism by which evolutionary change—physical, mental, and spiritual—occurs. It is a mechanism which works subtly, however, and it was seldom recognized for the evolutionary agent it truly was. After all, if meditation was the practice of the few, how could spiritualization be a driving force for evolutionary change? The answer is that, although meditation is the most formalized means by which this process can be advanced, it is not the only one. Each time an individual chooses the spiritual over the physical, spiritualization occurs. Every time a person chooses to think a loving rather than a hateful thought, or chooses to put someone else's needs above their own, or decides to serve as a channel of service to others, the process of spiritualization is fostered. Thousands if not millions of people practice and employ spiritualization without even being consciously aware of doing so.

Since spiritualization has been an ongoing process since the beginnings of humanity itself, one might even say that it is an innate trait of the human species. It has served as the primary force responsible for the true progress humankind has made throughout the centuries, because it is the process through which memory of the First Cause is being brought to conscious awareness. Through this process, the human species has manifested the so-called virtues of humanity—including compassion, mercy, forgiveness, empathy, faith, hope, charity, service, altruism, and unconditional love, the attributes of the soul.

What makes this particular time in history significant, however, is that people throughout the world are consciously awakening to the existence of this process and actively employing it not only for personal spiritual growth, but as a means by which we can awaken memory of the First Cause within the human species and bring it to consciousness awareness. Formalized methods to accomplish this include not only meditation but such practices as positive thinking, creative visualization, the use of affirmations, and even effective prayer. The annual World Wide Day of Prayer for Peace, sponsored by Unity, which occurs every September, is an excellent example of this initiative.

Those who are aware of the species-wide ramifications of spiritualization must continue to pursue this path and encourage others to join in the effort as well. Each time one person moves toward the integration of body, mind, and soul, whether it be through meditation, positive thinking, or simply a kind word to another, we all, as a species, move that much closer to overcoming our physical nature and reclaiming the birthright of our soul.

Every time that we mediate we are lessening the self-ish and evil influences in the world.

The degree to which evil seems to be lessened may be of minute proportions,

but once Spirit is loosed, there are no limits to its far-reaching effects.

—Joel Goldsmith

5

World Culture Today

Although the world is full of suffering, it is full also of the overcoming of it.

—Helen Keller

IN THE last chapter we examined the human condition in microcosmic terms, meaning that we examined human nature in terms of body, mind, and soul. In this chapter, we will examine the human condition in macrocosmic or global terms, as we examine human culture as whole. As you may recall from Chapter Three, culture is defined as the set of learned beliefs, values, behavior, and material objects which are shared by members of a society. While anthropologists tradition-ally apply this definition to a particular culture, it can be applied to the human species as a whole, as we consider the dominant beliefs, values, behaviors, and technology which characterize human culture today.

In looking at human culture as a whole, it is best to consider it as a cultural system, consisting of three levels or strata: the philosophical strata (beliefs and values), the sociological strata (behaviors), and the technological strata (material objects). All are interrelated to the extent that a change in one area affects the other two. As the means by which the life process of the human species is carried on throughout the generations, culture has, in a sense, taken on a life of its own. Cultural systems change, grow, adapt, and evolve, much like a biological organism.

The Paradox of Culture

Human culture today is sometimes described as a paradox, or world of great extremes. The reason for this is that technological progress has occurred so rapidly in the last century that philosophical ideals and social systems have not had time to adapt to the ramifications that these changes have caused.

It's quite evident that humanity has made great scientific and technological advances over previous generations. Diseases which once were the scourge of childhood have all but disappeared. We possess the medical knowledge necessary to revive a heart after it has stopped beating, literally giving us the ability to return the dead to life. Telecommunications links millions of people in dozens of countries in a worldwide network that stretches to the farthest recesses of the globe. Computers are indispensable teaching aids and children now begin using them at the preschool age. The greatest achievement of this technological progress is still considered by many to be the landing of man on the moon. In this generation, after centuries of dreaming, the impossible became a reality, and humankind took its first step toward the stars.

Yet for all of our technological wonders, the question remains as to whether humankind has truly made any significant progress in other areas. We have grown technologically, but have our value systems and behavior towards one another experienced an equal growth? Have we learned to show mercy rather than judgment? Have we learned to practice forgiveness rather than the taking of revenge? Have we learned to love our brethren rather than hate them for ancient grievances either real or perceived? Have we made the world a better place in which to live through manifestation of the spiritual attributes of the soul?

A cursory look at recent headlines might lead one to believe that the answers to these questions is a resounding "no," and that human culture today is characterized primarily by turmoil, violence, and destruction. Poverty is still commonplace in many areas of the world, and unfortunately, is no stranger in this country either. Although many thought it would never again be possible, wars of genocide have occurred once more in such diverse lands as Iran, Cambodia, Bosnia, and Rwanda. It has become apparent that in some areas ancient ethnic hatreds still run deep, as a war of ethnic cleansing such as the world has not seen in fifty years still rages in southern Europe. Further, how many have lost their lives in the centuries-old struggle of Northern Ireland?

In our own land, violence appears to be on the rise. Crimes once restricted to "poverty-stricken" areas have spread into all neighborhoods, making people feel as if there is nowhere they can be safe. Hate groups appear to be on the rise and no longer hide their activities but boldly proclaim them on television talk shows. No sooner did science eradicate many fatal diseases than a

new and more deadly disease—AIDS—appeared to take
their place.

Yet despite all of these tragic events, there is also evidence of great good in the world culture. Social systems are changing to the betterment of humankind. The fall of the Berlin Wall in 1989, in what was a relatively bloodless overthrow of the communist Soviet government, is something few people ever thought they would see in their lifetime. Who could have imagined that Yasir Arafat, once considered the world's foremost terrorist leader, would one day take up a role as an advocate for bringing peace to the Middle East. Many people were astounded when the apartheid government of South Africa released Nelson Mandela after a twenty-five-year imprisonment. Even more astounding was the political change of fortune in that country which resulted in the election of Mandela to the presidency in 1994. Who would have thought that possible even a mere ten years ago? And yet it became a reality. While many South Africans have lost their lives during the struggle for racial equality, the actual change of government proceeded in a relatively orderly manner.

There have also been tremendous changes in the human value system, particularly in this country in recent years. Concern for the environment and a sincere desire to halt the damage humankind has done has received nationwide attention from many corners. Other "movements" such as the drive for civil rights for all races, equal rights for women, and the recent advocacy of the rights of children are all signs of a coming shift in consciousness. The massive concern for the humane and ethical treatment of our fellow species literally forced many major corporations to cease the needless use of animal testing for various products. In the 1950s, it would have been a safe bet that the majority of American women desired to own that most visible status symbol—a fur coat. That is certainly not true today, however, and there is a strong coalition of well-known celebrities who publicly campaign against the archaic practice of harvesting animal pelts for their fur.

It's also recognized that newspapers, and the television/radio media, purposefully concentrate on "negative news," because these stories attract attention. A newspaper which carried only "positive" news would not have much of a circulation and would soon be out of business. When we do hear something of the good in humanity, it is often in connection with a disaster of some sort, a violent accident perhaps, or a natural disaster, where people joined together to help one another. We seldom hear of the little kindnesses many people do for others on a daily basis as a way of life.

What we do see today, then, is a paradoxical world of extremes. There is much good in the world, and there is also much evil, both on a national and individual level. Why, one may ask, do we see such extremes being manifested within human culture? How can humans who are capable of such good, also be capable of such evil? The answer to these questions can be found in the metaphysical principle of the karmic Law of Balance. The concept of karma is useful in helping one understand the state of human culture today, as well as speculate about the future of humanity.

A Time of Balance

The Karmic Law of Balance. According to the Cayce readings, the law of karma falls under the universal Law of Cause and Effect. Universal laws[1] are fundamental laws of mind and spirit and are the basic principles by which life, or the universe, operates. They were brought into being by the Creative Force to help and guide us on our way back to God Consciousness. They are immutable and affect you even if you are unaware of their existence. Once you are aware of them, however, you can learn to operate within their framework and use them to resolve problems, create peace and joy in your life, and help manifest the spiritual attributes of the soul.

The Law of Cause and Effect simply says that every effect which manifests has a cause; nothing that happens in the world happens randomly. Corollaries of this law are "like begets like," and "as you sow, so you reap," both of which mean that a cause will result in a like effect. Whatever seed you sow in the world will result in the growth of that seed. If you sow hate, you reap hate. If you sow love, you reap love. A subsequent corollary is that "nothing happens by chance." There are no accidents in that all results are consequences of the causes that preceded them.

Karma is a reflection of the Law of Cause and Effect. A Sanskrit word meaning "deed," it means that every action you have done, every thought you have had (the cause), will return to you in some form (the effect). Your thoughts, purpose, aims, and desires result in the situations and circumstances which manifest in your life. The readings discuss karma in terms of reincarnation,[2] a philosophy that the readings support, and state that in each lifetime the soul chooses to work on certain lessons which, if learned, will bring that soul to a closer union with God. If the lesson is not learned, however, the lesson is repeated until it is mastered. This explains why we often have difficulty accepting circumstances, and wonder what we have done to deserve them. The answer could be that we are meeting karma from another lifetime, and have chosen to work to resolve a particular issue that we may have handled incorrectly in another life.

Not all situations are karmic, however. Another possibility is that we have simply chosen a particular experience because it gives us an opportunity to manifest the attributes of the spirit and therefore to glorify God.

You do not have to believe in reincarnation, however, to accept the idea of karma, because you can think of karma as a process which occurs in one lifetime only. In a sense, the traditional Christian concepts of heaven and hell reflect the concept of karma. If a person lives a good life in accord with the church's teachings, he or she reaps the rewards of that goodly behavior in heaven. The person who lives a life of selfish gratification at the expense of others, however, reaps the consequences of that behavior in hell.

A Time of Testing

The world situation we are experiencing today is the result of karmic conditions set in motion by humanity ages ago. According to the readings, the reason for the manifestation of such extremes of good and evil may lie in the fact that we have entered a pivotal point in history, a period of "trial by fire," in which each soul is being afforded the opportunity to make the ultimate choice between good and evil. This is a time when all of humankind is being afforded the opportunity to make the choice as to whether they will continue with old behavior patterns which lead only to destruction—the physical path—or if they will take a step forward and choose not to act on ancient hatreds and biases, manifesting instead the fruits of the spirit—the spiritual path.

Several readings given by Edgar Cayce indicate that this generation, taken to mean the era 1938-1998, was to enter a testing period prior to the establishment of a "new world order." The readings, given prior to the outbreak of World War II, go on to say that this would be a time of trial and tribulation wherein all of humanity would be tested or "tried so as by fire," so that our destructive behaviors could be finally eradicated and the way paved for a return to the state of God Consciousness.

Yet why is such a "trial so as by fire" necessary? Perhaps because history has shown that the human species is slow to learn from mistakes it has made. How many times has humankind sworn to never again allow a certain offense to happen, only to have a similar atrocity recur again and again? For example, a lesson learned from the Holocaust was that humankind vowed never to permit such a tragedy to occur again. Yet it has. During the 1970s and '80s in Cambodia, over one million people lost their lives at the hands of the Khymer Rouge. In 1995 in Rwanda, it's estimated that the ruling tribe of Hutus killed over one million Tutsis and exiled another 700,000. Even now, the so-called ethnic cleansing by the Serbians in Bosnia has resulted in the as yet uncounted deaths of Muslim and Croat citizens in actions very similar to those of the Nazis. To paraphrase the words of a popular song of the 1960s, "how many times must the horrors of man's inhumanity to man be made manifest before we ultimately reject them?" Indeed, how long? Perhaps trial by fire is the only way we truly learn our lessons.

The Choice to Return. If universal law states that nothing happens by chance, it cannot be by chance that souls have come to the earth plane at this critical time. In fact, the gift of free-will guarantees each soul the opportunity to choose the time and circumstances of its birth into the earth. Each soul chooses the family and circumstances into which it is born, and does so with the intent of choosing those factors which will aid it in mastering the lessons it has come to learn.

The readings also make it clear that the soul chooses which lessons it wishes to work on in any given lifetime; the lessons we encounter are not arbitrarily imposed upon us by God. We decide when we are ready to meet a particular karmic lesson and attempt to balance the scales. This does not imply that such lessons are necessarily easy. In fact, the lessons of karma are often extremely difficult because it is easier to resort to old, familiar behavior patterns than to assert the will and choose the way of the spirit.

Meeting Ourselves—The Atlantean Parallel. The Cayce readings also mention that this time period is attracting many souls who were present in Atlantis, and who are incarnating for the specific purpose of saving the world from the destructive influences similar to those that brought about the demise of the Atlantean civilization.

According to the readings, this is the first time in the history of humankind that human culture has reached a cultural level similar to that developed in Atlantis. Cayce's story of Atlantis could fill volumes in itself, and is far beyond the scope of this book. Suffice it to say that the readings describe a glorious civilization, characterized by spiritual awareness as well as scientific endeavors which paralleled and even exceeded our own, such as telepathy and the overcoming of gravitational forces themselves. Unfortunately, however, one group of Atlanteans misused the powers they had mastered, turning their knowledge to exploitation of others for selfish purposes. Although a second group which honored the spiritual truths stood opposed to them, they realized too late what was happening, and were unable to stop the chain of events set in motion by the selfish motives of the others. The end result was that the Atlantean civilization destroyed itself through a series of three cataclysmic events, the last of which occurred in 10,500 B.C.

This event saw the final immersion of the three re-maining islands of the once great continent into the At-lantic Ocean. With that destruction, all evidence of Atlantis disappeared as well, although survivors made their way to other lands including Egypt, the Pyrenees, the Yucatan peninsula, and Peru. Today, there is no agreed upon scientific evidence which supports the existence of such a civilization, although the readings in-dicate that a record of Atlantis will eventually be discov-ered in Egypt.

Nevertheless, the readings are clear that Atlantis did exist, and that this group of souls has reentered the earth plane at this time so that we might avoid a similar de-struction, possibly through a nuclear holocaust that would destroy not only one continent, but perhaps the entire world.

The Karma of the Nations

In addition to individual and group karma, the read-ings also speak of the karma of the nations, and indicate that each nation is also meeting itself according to the laws of karma. Each nation, when it was first established, was brought into existence according to certain ideals and tenets. How well a country honors those ideals in subsequent generations creates the karma its popula-tion must one day face. In fact, the readings emphasize that the spirituality of a people will shape its destiny. "Each nation, each people have builded—by the very spirit of the peoples themselves—a purposeful position in the skein, the affairs not only of the earth but of the universe!"[3] It was, after all, the loss of spiritual ideals, which brought about the downfall of Atlantis, Rome, and many other civilizations throughout history. As a country has acted, according to the seed it has sown, so will be the harvest it reaps.

A series of readings given in 1944 provided an account of the karma which the major nations of that day would soon have to face. England was cited as the land from which the idea, not ideal, came of being a little bit better than others. She would have to grow to the level at which she felt she deserved to be known. England was also described as having the capability of becoming the "balancing power" in the world, which, through consideration of her relationships with other countries, would be able to help control the world for peace. France would meet a pattern of gratifying the desires of the body. The fulfillment of self-gratification at the expense of others would have to be overcome there. The nation "first which was first Rome"—Italy—would have to answer for the activities which caused its fall—the enforcement of slavery—so that a few might enjoy a better life and "declare their oneness with the Higher Forces." Although this way seemed right at the time, it was morally wrong, and led the Romans down a road ending in spiritual decay and destruction.

India was cited as being the cradle of knowledge, and yet she applied this knowledge only within herself, rather than sharing it with others. China erred in that it was content to be satisfied with that of itself alone, and has not awakened to the idea of a brotherhood of nations. Even so, the readings state that one day, although it is a day far in the future as time is counted, China will become the cradle of Christianity! The readings puzzled many when they stated that out of Russia would come the hope of the world. " . . . that each man will live for his fellow man! The principle has been born. It will take years for it to be crystallized, but out of Russia comes again the hope of the world. Guided by what? That

friendship with the nation that hath even set on its
present monetary unit 'In God We Trust.' "[4] In 1944, the
strength of communism in the Soviet Union made this
prediction seem dubious at best. Recent events, however, have come to make it much more believable.

What of the United States? What do the readings have
to say about one of the youngest and yet most powerful
countries on earth? The readings indicate that the
American nation was unique in that it was not only
founded upon spiritual ideals of brotherhood and freedom, but that it put these ideals in writing, forming as it
were a pact with God to honor those ideals and guarantee that they would be brought into existence for all generations to come. The karma America will have to meet,
however, is that she has at times forgotten to apply the
very ideals upon which she was founded within herself.
The readings admonished that if America did not actively apply the ideals of brotherhood and equality in all
areas, she would face riots, social dissension, and possibly even a revolution within her borders. However, the
readings do go on to say that the peace of the world
would be shaped upon the ideals as set by America.

Hopefully, some of the karmic conditions contained
in these readings have already been met and successfully
resolved. Following World War II, England can certainly
be seen as emerging as a stabilizing influence in the
world. The self-sacrifices of the French, and the experiences of the Italian people during World War II, may very
well have been the meeting of those countries' karmic
conditions.

As for India, she has, in a sense, shared her knowledge
with others, as her ancient Hindu and Buddhist spiritual
teachings have made their way to other countries. The
teachings of Mahatma Ghandi, who led India to independence, are known worldwide and have certainly in-

fluenced more than one reformer, including Dr. Martin Luther King, Jr. The Russian people, as well as many other countries, did successfully break the yoke of communism. Although some may argue that the collapse of the Soviet Union has resulted in even worse economic and political situations, we must still maintain hope that, through the guidance of America and other nations, these problems will be resolved, and the example set by the Russian people will eventually serve as an example of hope to the world.

The situation in China is more difficult to comprehend. The swift and violent quelling of student protests made it seem as if there is little hope that the communist regime is weakening. Yet the very fact that college-age students launched such a protest in the first place, and were willing to risk their lives to make their voices heard, is proof that the communist program of educational indoctrination from the earliest age has not worked! If it had, the students raised by that system would not have launched a protest in the first place. The truth that freedom sings is one that cannot be silenced by any government, and eventually that truth will again awaken among the Chinese people.

As for the United States, one can only hope that the riots and social dissension mentioned in the readings refer to the turmoil this country passed through during the 1960s. Americans, however, must never let up on actively applying the ideals upon which this country was founded, to all people, within her borders and abroad. Many religious doctrines teach that the greatest sin is that of a person who knows the truth, and yet does not apply it. Those who know they are doing wrong will be judged more harshly than those who do wrong but do not realize their error. America knows the truth of the spiritual ideals upon which she was founded, and if we ever abandon them, her demise will not be far behind. If we honor those ideals, however, not only in word but in action as well, this country can set the pattern for all to follow as we enter the next millennium.

There has been a great deal of speculation as to whether the nations of this generation have successfully passed through the threat of a nuclear holocaust. Although many believe that the demise of the Soviet Union marked a successful passage through this test, there are those who believe that the nuclear threat is still very real. It is quite possible, however, that this generation successfully passed through this test many years ago, in fact, as the United States and the Soviet Union passed through the tense drama of the Cuban Missile Crisis in 1962. Although it was not known at the time, taped recordings of presidential briefing sessions released years later revealed just how close this planet came to mutual destruction by both parties. In fact, when one listens to the tapes, one wonders how we escaped having pushed that button.

The answer as to how we escaped destruction may actually be related to something which occurred two years earlier, in connection with the 1960 presidential election. The idea I present here came to me during a moment of "intuitive insight," and although it cannot be proven, I share it with you nevertheless. I am not referring to the politics of the candidates themselves so much as that one candidate, John Kennedy, represented for many a choice for change and the acceptance of a new system of thought that has been likened to the ideals of legendary Camelot, while the choice of the other candidate, Richard Nixon, represented the maintenance of the status quo which had already led us to two world wars. Perhaps it was the metaphysical ramifications of that choice by the American people themselves which spread out across space and time and gave the necessary impetus which helped our planet pass through that test of nuclear destruction.

While the detonation of a nuclear bomb by a lone, "rogue" country is still a possibility, it is unlikely that any country could or would be allowed to wage a full-scale nuclear war. Sister nations would no doubt respond swiftly and without hesitation so that detonation of a second device would not be likely. In fact, in 1991, Pentagon officials deleted the scenario of a global war from the United States' Defense Planning Guidance. Hopefully, the world's nations have reached a level of consciousness where they realize that nuclear destruction means the destruction of the entire planet, and they intend on doing everything within their power to prevent that from happening.

A New World Order

If individuals and nations successfully meet the lessons of karma and manifest attributes of the soul such as love, forgiveness, mercy, and understanding, we can take the first steps toward establishing a new world order based on spiritual principles, as described in the readings. As we begin to manifest the attributes of the spirit "No longer is the entity then under the law of cause and effect—or karma, but rather in grace it may go on to the higher calling as set in Him."[5] It was the Christ soul who set the law of grace into motion, by setting the pattern and serving as the example by which we might enter the spiritual state of grace.

The readings offer this advice as to how we can help bring about this cultural change: "As ye show the wisdom, as ye show the love of thy fellow man, so may the love be shown, so may the wisdom, so may the guiding

steps day by day be shown thee. Be ye joyous in the Lord
. . . He is not in heaven, but makes heaven in thine own
heart, if ye accept Him."[6] " . . . know that right, justice,
mercy, patience . . . is the basis upon which the new
world order MUST eventually be established, before
there IS peace. Then, innately, mentally, and mani-
festedly in self, prepare self for cooperative measures in
all phases of human relations . . . "[7]

As for the new world order referred to in the readings,
the emergence of a new way of interaction should not be
so surprising if we realize that social, political, and economic changes often accompany a shift in human consciousness. A reading given in 1938 states that the
transition to this new order will occur between 1958-
1998. "It is . . . understood, comprehended by some, that
a new order of conditions is to arise; that there must be
many a purging in high places as well as low; that there
must be the greater consideration of each individual,
each soul being his brother's keeper . . . Though there
may come those periods when there will be great stress,
as brother rises against brother, as group or sect or race
rises against race—yet the leveling must come."[8] The
"leveling" spoken of refers to a redistribution of the
world's wealth, power, and resources, so that the needs
of all, rather than the few, would be met in the future.
This "leveling" is no doubt a by-product of the shift in
consciousness that the human species will experience
in the next millennium, much as the emergence of capi-
talism followed the acceptance of the paradigm of individual worth.

The reading also provides hope that this transition can
be accomplished without turmoil and disruption. It goes
on to say that if men of principle and vision would rise
to the task, the social, economic, and political reforms
necessary to bring about this leveling could be brought

about through peaceful means. If not, however, humanity will resort to the only tools available—crime, riots,
and revolution. Perhaps Mikhail Gorbachev will be remembered in history as one of those "men of principle
and vision" for his role in the relatively nonviolent overthrow of the Soviet government.

The Power of Choice

The world in which today's generation lives is indeed
a culture of paradox. In some ways, the evils we see are
akin to the "dark night of the soul,"[9] the lowest point to
which the human soul descends, the point at which the
soul believes it has been forsaken by God and all others,
left alone to die in the dark. Perhaps we must come to
this place of darkness and desolation because it is here
that the light can shine the brightest; it is only here that
we truly become conscious of the light within and can
make the choice to embrace the light of our spiritual self
so that we can move out of the darkness of the physical
world and into God consciousness.

According to the readings, each soul present on the
earth plane today is here by choice, and has the opportunity to make manifest the love of God on earth. Thousands of years ago, the Atlantean people had just such
an opportunity. They knew their true identity as spiritual beings, yet they chose to take the path of physical
self-gratification which led to their destruction. Because
of that choice, the spiritual knowledge they possessed
lay buried with them, forgotten for generations. It has
been a long road back to the reawakening of that knowledge. Many of those same souls are here again, under
similar conditions, hoping that this time, they can make
the right choices to help bring about the establishment
of a new order based on spiritual principles.

Back in 1968, the *Star Trek* television series aired an episode in which a man of the late twentieth century—a genetically engineered superhuman called Khan—was revived nearly four hundred years into the future. After observing the world around him, he remarked that humankind had not really made that much progress in the four hundred years he had been in stasis. Oh, there had been technological improvements, he remarked, but humanity was still pretty much the same killer species it had always been. The series hero, Captain Kirk, disagreed with him, pointing out that humans had overcome their violent era, put aside their differences, and united as one species, spreading out to the stars in the spirit of peace, harmony, and a desire to learn about the universe around them. Khan, however, was not impressed. Humanity still had the killer instinct, he responded. Perhaps, Kirk countered, but every day we can make the choice not to act on that instinct. *We can make the choice.*

Those living on this planet today have chosen to come to earth at perhaps the most pivotal time in human history. After thousands of years in the shadows, the human species is beginning to see the light once again. It is coming to understand that it does have a choice. By making a conscious choice of love, justice, mercy, and understanding, we can hasten the shift in human consciousness which will change the world. We can ensure that the next millennium is remembered as the time humankind finally overcame the divisive paradigms of the physical world and began to see itself not as a collection of separate beings, but as one united species. This is more than a chance to make a better world. It is the next step that humankind must take before we can proceed any further on our evolutionary journey back to unity with God.

This is the whole law (love), this is the whole answer to the world, to each and every soul. That is the answer to world conditions as they exist today.
                                                              —Edgar Cayce

Part
III

Accepting Our Future: Coming to Terms with the New Millennium

6

Biological Evolution: Emergence of the Multisensory Human

All of our great teachers have been, or are, multisensory humans. They have spoken to us and acted in accordance with perceptions and values that reflect the larger perspective of their multisensory being, and therefore, their words and actions awaken within us the recognition of truth.
—Gary Zukav, *The Seat of the Soul*

IN PART II, we explored the question of human nature as it exists today on both the microcosmic (species) and macrocosmic (global culture) levels. In considering questions on the future evolution of humankind, it is necessary to take the same approach. To that end, this chapter and the next will focus on biological and cognitive change occurring within the human species itself, while evolutionary changes on the global level are addressed in the final two chapters.

The Threshold of Evolutionary Change

In terms of microcosmic change, there is growing evidence that the human species is developing from a five-sensory species to a multisensory species, as more and more people demonstrate the capability to discern information not perceptible to the five physical senses. Not surprisingly, the physical ability to perceive phenomena beyond that of the three-dimensional world is also having a direct effect upon human cognition.

The concept of evolutionary change is neither new nor surprising. Through science we have come to understand that evolution has been an ongoing process since life first appeared on this planet. The fossil record reveals a gradual progression of species development wherein all species develop from simpler ancestral forms. Evolution is the mechanism by which species continue their existence across the generations of time. It is understood that if a species does not adapt to changing environmental conditions, it dies out and is lost forever.

What makes this particular juncture in our development so exciting, however, is that for the first time in history, the human species is becoming cognizant of its own evolutionary process. With this realization has come much speculation as to what form this evolutionary change will take. One idea proposes that there will be a spontaneous change in the human brain-wave pattern which will result in a significant expansion of mental capabilities. Others have suggested that humanity will experience a type of "spiritual awakening," whereby we have immediate access to all spiritual knowledge and will transcend the body and move on to other realms of development. Still others have proposed that a radical physical change will take place, such as the instantaneous mutation of the human genetic code or DNA structure, which will endow us with extraordinary psychic and mental capabilities.

What these proposals fail to consider, however, is the fact that the unit of microcosmic evolution is the population or species, and not the individual. Quadrupedal primates did not suddenly leave their niche in the trees, venture to the savannah, and suddenly stand erect anymore than the terrier-sized, three-toed ancestor of the horse suddenly tripled in size and magically merged its toes to become the single-hoof horses we know today. These changes did occur, but it took hundreds of generations for them to manifest. The simple fact is that in terms of physical evolution, species evolve; individuals do not.

All that we know of our physical and spiritual development teaches that the process of evolution is natural, slow, and orderly. The souls' devolution into matter took millions of years. The development of the human body as a perfect vehicle to house the soul took millions of years as well. The development of human consciousness, or cognitive evolution, has been a continual process since the first hominid became self-aware. Millions of years of evolution—physical, cognitive, and spiritual—have led to this point in time, and the changes we are experiencing are the product of that evolutionary process.

Why then, do so many people seem to be suddenly expressing new perceptual abilities and levels of cognitive comprehension? The answer is that the human species as a whole has evolved to the point where it is experiencing the effects of changes which first appeared in its genetic code generations ago, changes which likely govern internal brain structure and function. Although little is known as to how genes regulate the development of the nervous system, sociobiologists do acknowledge that genetic coding has an effect upon brain structure and function which ultimately affects behavioral traits. A good example of this is the growth in size and the internal reorganization of the human brain which is believed to have made language possible. The evolutionary process has reached the point where this genetic coding has been passed on to a significant number of individuals, and the resultant traits and behaviors are now manifesting on a large scale.

The transformation that the human species is about to face may seem "instantaneous" because we are seeing only the end result, and not the entire process. That is why some people have leapt to the conclusion that these changes are spontaneous developments, miraculous acts of God, or the result of alien intervention. Rather than fearing this development and the consequences it may bring, we need to understand that it is the natural result of biological changes occurring within the internal structure and function of the human brain, the next step on the upward evolutionary spiral our species has been pursuing for millions of years.

If this premise is true, it would follow that there should have been signs or signals in our past—evidence that would indicate these changes have been in progress for a long time. Indeed, there is evidence of humans who have already demonstrated the ability to perceive non-physical stimuli and who spoke of experiencing a new state of consciousness based on spiritual rather than physical reality. Documentation of this phenomena is scattered throughout human history, for the changes now being manifested by the many, were first manifested by the few. Records of those individuals who first manifested new physical and cognitive abilities have been preserved in the mystic branches of various religions and in the shamanic traditions of many cultures.

Message of the Mystics

The Mystic Experience. A mystic has been described as a person who has experienced a transcendent state of consciousness at which he or she is able to perceive phenomena not discernible by the five physical senses, including the perception of light or colors, the hearing of voices, and the ability to see entities existing in spirit rather than physical form. Mystics have appeared throughout the course of human history, and often are remembered as the great thinkers, teachers, poets, artists, and religious innovators.

The great philosopher Plato held dialogues with the inner voice he called "Daemon." Lao-Tzu, Jesus, Buddha, Mohammed, and the Old Testament prophets all had experiences with expanded states of consciousness. The fact that many Christian saints such as Joan of Arc, St. Francis of Assisi, St. Teresa of Avila, St. Catherine of Siena, and St. Ignatius Loyola, described having mystic experiences should not be surprising when we remember that St. Paul's conversion to Christianity began with a mystical vision on the road to Damascus. Henry David Thoreau, Dante, William Blake, William Wordsworth, and Johannes Brahms, are but a few of the well-known creative talents who spoke of the mystical experience as the source of their creativity. The list of historically known mystics could go on and on, yet for each recognizable name, there are countless unknowns who left records of their experiences in their personal notes and diaries.

Describing the mystic experience is difficult at best. Words are inadequate to express the impact such an event has upon the individual. The following excerpts of firsthand accounts, however, can at least provide a glimpse into the depth of the mystic experience.[1]

"I felt the most incredible flow of energy and power coursing through me and had, what I believe to be, an experience of Timeless Reality . . . of consciousness that took in everything without limit . . . but reacted to nothing except in the sense of 'knowing' and 'loving.' " (Moyra Caldecott, twentieth century, South Africa, upon the occasion of her confirmation.)[2]

"Then I was floating on my back in a river of peace, under bridges of silence. It came from nowhere and flowed nowhere. Then there was no river and no I. The I had ceased to exist." (Arthur Koestler, British Journalist, upon his imprisonment in Spain during the Spanish Civil War.)[3]

"The treasure I found cannot be described in words, the mind cannot conceive of it. My mind fell like a hailstorm into that vast expanse of Consciousness. Touching one drop of it, I melted away and became one with the Absolute. And now, though I return to human consciousness, I see nothing, I hear nothing. I know that nothing is different from me." (Shankaracharya, seventh-century Hindu philosopher.)[4]

"I was conscious of a lovely, unexplainable pattern in the whole texture of things . . . and weaving the pattern was a Power; and that Power was what we faintly call Love. I realized that we are not lonely atoms in a cold, unfriendly, indifferent universe, but that each of us is linked up in a rhythm, of which we may be unconscious." (F. C. Happold, 1936, upon the birth of his stillborn son.)[5]

"I immediately feel vibrations that thrill my whole being... These are the Spirit illuminating the soul-power within... I realize at such moments the tremendous significance of Jesus' supreme revelation, 'I and my Father are one.' Those vibrations assume the forms of distinct mental images . . . Straightaway the ideas flow in upon me, directly from God." (Johannes Brahms, nineteenth-century composer describing the "inspired moods" during which he composed.)[6]

"The boundary between my physical self and my surroundings seemed to dissolve and my feeling of separation vanished . . . I had suddenly come alive for the first time . . . I remember feeling that a veil had been lifted from my eyes and everything came into focus... I was surrounded by an incredible loving energy, and that everything, both living and nonliving, is bound inextricably with a kind of consciousness which I cannot describe in words." (Wendy Rose-Neill, twentieth-century psychotherapist and medical journalist, upon tending her garden.)[7]

"I saw that in its depths there are enclosed, bound up with love in one eternal book, the scattered leaves of all the universe—substance, and accidents, and their relations, as though fused together in such a way that what I speak of is a single light." (Dante, fourteenth-century author.)[8]

"A kind of glory descended upon the gathered company . . . I looked at the faces of those around me and they seemed to be suffused with an inner radiance . . . I experienced in that moment a sense of profoundest kinship with each and every person there. I loved them all—but with a kind of love I had never felt before . . . which bound us together indissolubly in a deep unity of being." (Unidentified twentieth-century man, in the waiting room of a railroad station filled with strangers.)[9]

"From separation I passed into Unity; all the illusions of life disappeared like a phantom show. Now whenever I cast my glance, I see Him alone, and none other. The Muslim, the Hindu, and the Jew have all become the same to me—they have all merged in the glory of my one Beloved." (Nazir, eighteenth-century Sufi poet.)[10]

"I cannot now recall whether the revelation came suddenly or gradually . . . I cannot say exactly what the mysterious change was . . .I saw no new thing, but I saw all the usual things in a miraculous new light . . . it was not that for a few keyed-up moments I imagined all existence as beautiful, but that my inner vision was clear to the truth so that I saw the actual loveliness which is always there, but which we so rarely perceive." (Margaret Prescott Montague, twentieth-century novelist and poet, suffering from progressive blindness and deafness, during recovery from painful surgery.)[11]

"I saw that a light, beautiful and blissful beyond measure . . . surrounded me and shone through me and illuminated me entirely . . . and in the light and in the joy, I saw and sensed that . . . there it was given me to see my soul clearly and particularly with spiritual vision, as I have never seen anything with physical eyes . . . and what marvels I saw and recognized in it, all humans together could not put into words." (Sofia von Klingnau, Toos Convent, Germany, thirteenth century.)[12]

"Once released from the narrow confines of the 'self,' with its mundane suffering and petty emotions, a man will have stepped into a new, undiscovered world . . . Now that I had discovered and actually begun to live in that 'new world'. . . my narrow self ceased to exist and the only recognizable entity was the totality of existence . . . It was in Cell 54 that I discovered that love is truly the key to everything . . . When my individual entity merged into the vaster entity of all existence, my point of departure became love of home (Egypt), love of all being, love of God." (Anwar Sadat, Egyptian patriot, during his imprisonment in Egyptian Cell 54.)[13]

A close examination of these and other reported mystic experiences show that they are more than accounts of bright lights, dreams, and visions; the common elements run much deeper than that. The mystic experience is an instant where the individual comes into direct and personal contact with the divine. During a mystic experience, time and space seem to be suspended, and the individual experiences intense feelings of peace, joy, love, a sense of seeing things in a new way as if awakening from a dream, and a feeling of unity with all of creation where the individual self merges into the universal whole. Afterward, the individual contends that words are inadequate to convey but a slim shadow of the real experience. Further, the mystic does not just believe in the reality of the experience, but *knows with an absolute certainty* the truth of the revelations encountered while in the mystic state.

The mystic experience appears to happen to individuals on a singular basis. It is not formalized in any way, and can happen to anyone at any time. It describes a state of being whereby the individual is able to transcend the physical world of matter and through the faculty of the mind, enter and experience the nonmaterial, etheric world of energy or spirit. There is, however, a ritualized tradition which teaches the achievement of such a state. Those who are chosen for, and survive, the rigors this training demands, master the ability to shift among altered states of perception. They are known in anthropological literature as shaman.

The Shamanic Tradition. An oversimplified although accurate definition of a shaman is a person who is able to walk with one foot in the physical world and one foot in the spirit world. Shaman live in the physical world but can enter the spirit world at will. Like the mystic experience, shamanic traditions are cross-cultural customs found globally throughout history. While the mystic experience is individual in nature, and seldom understood by the society in which it occurs, shamanic traditions are ritualized institutions, which fulfill a specified role within a culture.

The word shaman was chosen for use by anthropologists because of its very specific meaning. The word comes from the language of the Tungus tribe in Siberia and denotes a person who travels in an altered state of consciousness to a "nonordinary" reality. In most cultural traditions, a shaman could inherit his position through family lines, be chosen by the spirits, or voluntarily seek to become one.[14] As a youth, the election of a shaman-to-be is preceded by a change in behavior. He becomes moody, withdrawn, and may experience visions. The youth normally contracts a life-threatening illness which leaves him unconscious for a time. It is believed that his soul is carried away to the spirit realm where the youth speaks with gods, spirits, and ancestors, and receives information on life's secrets. Sometimes, the youth is beset by unfriendly spirits who seek to kill him (the symbolic death of the ego). If the youth proves himself worthy, he is returned to the body and resumes perfect health. After this initiation experience, he continues rigorous training with elder shaman before assuming a position as shaman in his own right.

The altered state of consciousness which the shaman achieves is normally induced by certain techniques, the most common of which is the repetition of a sound, such as the beating of a drum. The use of psychedelic drugs to attain this level of awareness is much less prevalent than commonly believed. A shaman undertakes a journey into the spirit world—nonordinary reality—for any number of reasons. He may undergo a journey to obtain information for the diagnosis and treatment of illness, for divination or prophecy, to obtain guidance from teachers, guardians, and spirit animals, to contact the spirits of the dead, and to help others make the transition to the spirit realm. A shaman is a well-balanced, well-grounded, and centered person. He or she must have a firm foundation in ordinary reality in order to be able to step into and out of it so easily.

Shamanic traditions were once found worldwide, appearing in Siberia, Native American cultures in Canada, North and South America, Scandinavia, India, and various African cultures as well. The development of state religions, and the establishment of organized churches, however, discouraged the practice of shamanism, and in many cases caused its near extinction. Shamanism was seen as a threat to the control and authority exerted by state religions because it taught that any person could have direct access to the divine. State religions much preferred that people turn to its priests and clerics as intermediaries in their quest for spiritual enlightenment.

Mystics and Shaman: Forerunners of Change. The state of consciousness described by mystics and shaman certainly seems to be one in which the physical sensory boundaries of the material plane are broken. The only difference is that the shaman has been taught the means by which to initiate and control this process while the mystic experience comes upon a person without forewarning. In this state the individual is no longer limited to the capabilities of the five physical senses, but through the faculty of the mind-force is able to perceive phenomena which exist beyond the three-dimensional world. The individual can now perceive mental and even spiritual stimuli which exist outside the three-dimensional world of physical matter.

The idea of the mystic as a harbinger of evolutionary change is not new. Various Sufi texts and teachings speak of an evolutionary potential for soul development given in "the message of the mystics."[15] It was proposed at least as early as the nineteenth century by the Canadian physician Maurice Bucke, who believed that mystics had reached an advanced state of consciousness, which, through the evolutionary process, would one day be common to all humankind.[16] Bucke began his historical study of mystics after having such an experience himself. F.C. Happold, a British schoolmaster made a similar study following a mystic experience during World War I. He concluded that the elevated consciousness of the mystic was the next step in human evolution.

"May it not be the growth of an ever higher state of consciousness . . . which will result in the ability to understand aspects of the universe as yet only faintly glimpsed . . . may we not see in the mystics the forerunners . . . which will become more and more common as mankind ascends higher and higher up the ladder of evolution?"[17]

The mystic experience and the shamanic journey become all the more important when we see that they are universal phenomena that transcend time and cultural boundaries. Similar reports of mystic experiences as described above can be found in diverse cultures throughout the centuries. A handful of such reports might be dismissed or easily explained away. The cross-cultural and historic milieu from which such accounts emerge, however, preclude any explanation other than that the experiences as reported, are authentic. The patterned ritualization of the mystic experience in shamanic traditions may vary by culture, but the altered state of consciousness attained remains the same. This universality across time lends even more credence to the hypothesis that mystics and shaman represent a new development in human evolution.

The mystic experience and the shamanic journey, once the vision of the few, are finally becoming the reality of the many. A new type of human, a multisensory human, is about to make its entrance upon the evolutionary stage of life.

The Development of Multisensory Perception

If we consider that the human species is composed of three components—body, mind, and soul, it should not be surprising that humans would eventually develop "mental" and even "spiritual" sensory abilities capable of perceiving phenomena unobservable through the physical senses. While it has been suggested that we are witnessing the development of a sixth sense, frequently referred to as "intuition," I propose that the sixth sense, a "mental" sense, has already manifested within the human species. In fact, the sixth sense has been a part of our makeup for millions of years; it simply has not been recognized as such. I suggest that the sixth sense is what we have come to call "imagination."

Imagination—The Real Sixth Sense. According to psychologists, imagination is a cognitive process, a mental "faculty" which understands and forms the idea of external objects. It is the creative faculty which makes art, music, literature, fantasy, and dreams possible. It is also the faculty upon which scientific thought is built because it allows for speculation and hypothesis building. Through imagination, the mind is released from the strictures of objective reality and allowed to roam freely so that it might "image" or imagine ideas which do not have their basis in the physical world. It is therefore the faculty through which symbolism is possible, where the mind can impose a relationship upon two inherently separate objects.

Imagination enabled the early hominids to look at a rock and see the possibility that it could be modified to create a tool. It is the faculty that enabled those early humans to look at fire and see it as something other than a destructive force to be feared. It is the faculty that enabled the development of language, the creative arts, and the composition of music and literature. It is imagination, therefore, that has been responsible for all the significant cognitive advances throughout human history.

But more than that, imagination has been the means by which humans were able to transcend the limitations of the physical world. It is the means by which they could see beyond three-dimensional, objective reality, and conceive of possibilities not inherent in the physical world. For this reason, I propose that imagination is more than a "faculty" or mental process—it is actually the sixth sense, a "mental" rather than physical sense, through which we are able to perceive phenomena within the mental realm of thought and ideas. Just as the five physical senses enable us to perceive and interpret the physical world, the sixth sense of imagination enables us to perceive mental reality and translate the phenomenon of creative thought into physical form. As imagination developed, humans were able to integrate two components of themselves—the body and the mind—into a conscious, functional element of their being, with the mind now directing the activities of the body.

Intuition—The Emerging Seventh Sense. If imagination, as the sixth sense, facilitated the integration of body and mind, it might follow that the seventh sense, termed "intuition," would facilitate the integration of our third component—the soul—into our conscious awareness. The word intuition comes from the Latin *intueri*, meaning "to know," and has come to take on the meaning of "knowing without reasoning," or "an immediate or instinctive perception of a truth." Intuition transcends the reasoning process of the mind and depends upon an internal "knowing" which is only possible through the soul and its connection to the Universal Consciousness.

This intuitive sense of knowing is exactly what has been described during the mystic and shamanic experience. It enables the body-mind to incorporate the soul within its conscious awareness. Once the intuitive sense is activated, memory of the First Cause is awakened, and the individual understands his or her true spiritual nature. We now have the integration of all three of our components, body, mind, and soul, into what might be termed the "fully integrated human."

By bringing memory of the First Cause into consciousness awareness, the fully integrated human is able to transcend the physical world of matter and perceive phenomena which exist in the etheric world of pure energy, commonly called "psychic" phenomena. The perception of auras, the ability to access the Universal Consciousness, the comprehension of spiritual principles, and the perception of spiritual entities, such as angelic beings, are all a part of the expanded realities that the fully integrated human is starting to perceive through its multisensory perception.

The Human Species in Transition

The fact that human sensory perception has shown a steady progression of increasing complexity is consistent with the general premise of evolution whereby simpler forms develop into more complex forms. These developments did not happen overnight, however. They are the result of a gradual process whereby the biological changes in brain structure and function which governed these developments, were first expressed by a few individuals within the species.

As a five-sensory species, humans could only perceive material objects in three-dimensional Euclidean space, and were therefore restricted to three-dimensional objective reality. As the mental sense of imagination evolved, humans were able to experience the world of thought and ideas, as well as symbolic relationships. Through integration and application of the mind force, humans not only unlocked the secrets of the physical world, but expressed the power and beauty of the creative thoughts of the mind in the form of art, music, literature, and other creative endeavors. With the emergence of the seventh sense of intuition, the fully integrated human is beginning to tap into the etheric world of pure energy.

The recent rise of interest in so-called psychic phenomena and spiritual issues may very well indicate that multisensory perception is becoming the norm rather than the exception. Although the "mystic movement" can trace its beginnings back to New Thought spiritualism[18] of the late nineteenth century, it was long regarded as nothing more than a passing fad of the fringe element of society. Today, however, that is no longer the case. People from all walks of life, educational backgrounds, social and economic status, including trained scientists, are embracing the reality of psychic phenomena. Angels made the cover of *Time* magazine, physicians proclaim the success of holistic medical therapies, and scientific studies validate of the power of prayer in healing. It was even recently revealed that the Pentagon employed psychics in its espionage activities! Thousands of people are not only accepting the possibility of mystic occurrences, but admitting that they themselves have had some sort of psychic experience in their own lives. More and more individuals are awakening to the fact that sensory perception is not be limited to the five physical senses, and that the perception of other levels of reality is possible.

Imagine what experiences await us as a multisensory species which understands that "reality" consists of much more than that which is visible through our physical senses. Imagine what possibilities open up to us as we begin to see ourselves less as individual beings and more as an integrated part of the whole of creation. The manifestation of an additional sensory ability may well be the most significant step forward since the development of language! Yet a development such as this should really come as no surprise. It is just one more step on a journey we started a very long time ago.

Inorganic matter, animal and plant species, and human nature . . . comprise an evolutionary triad in which the first two have transcended themselves, inorganic elements producing living species, animals giving rise to humanity . . . In each of them there arose a new order of existence.
—Michael Murphy, *The Future of the Body*

7

Cognitive Evolution: Perception and Human Consciousness

This is an age which will be remembered not just for the progress it has made in science and technology . . . but also for the advances that have been made in the growth of human consciousness.
—James Stallone and Sy Migdal, *Consciousness and the Search for Self-Realization*

THE DEVELOPMENT of a new sensory ability, as described in the last chapter, is going to have significant impact upon the way we perceive the world, and hence be the motivating factor underlying new developments in human cognitive evolution. As fully integrated humans capable of receiving nonphysical stimuli, our perception of the world will, of necessity, change. As our perception and analysis of the world itself changes, the paradigms which govern human consciousness will change as well.

The Process of Perception

Science has long known that a species' perception of the world depends upon biological factors, the foremost being the physiological means by which it receives physical stimuli from the environment. Species differ in their sensory abilities and therefore do perceive the world in the same way. For example, not all species see the world as humans do because not all species possess the eye-brain structure which makes three-dimensional, binocular, color vision possible. Some species see only in black, white, and shades of grey, or perceive only certain primary colors. Still other species do not possess three-dimensional vision, but perceive the world as a two-dimensional reality.

Yet perception is dependent upon more than the reception of physical sensory input. It is also affected by the way in which that stimuli is analyzed. The way an organism views and interacts with the world depends upon the receipt *and* analysis of the stimuli it receives from its environment.

Perceptual Schemata. Cognitive or constructivist psychology was one of the first disciplines to define perception as more than the simple recording of information contained in visual, tactile, or auditory stimuli. According to this school of thought, perception is "formulating and testing a perceptual process . . . The eye collects visual information . . . The retina and brain analyze this information in various ways . . . The brain uses the products of visual analysis to test and modify 'hypotheses' about the 'meaning' of the visual information."[1] Perception is thus an active, cyclic process regulated or defined by internal structures called "schemata." A schemata is defined as the portion of the perceptual cycle which is *internal* [author's italics] to the perceiver, *modified* [author's italics] by experience, and specific to what is being perceived.

This idea can perhaps be more clearly demonstrated by a few well-known examples of how this process works. A birdwatcher in a forest, a biologist staring through a microscope, a tracker following a trail, or a doctor reading an x-ray, are all specialists who see details invisible to the untrained eye. They perceive a different "reality" because their schemata have been altered by experience (training), and they expect to see more than you or I would see.

The same can be said for the ability to perceive size, distance, and even color. Anthropologists have long known that the Pygmy tribes of Central Africa had a unique perception of size and distance due to the density of the tropical forests in which they live, where objects more than a few feet distant were rarely visible. Upon leaving the forests, and seeing elephants in the distance, they commented on how tiny the creatures were, believing they were actually the size of small insects. They did not possess a perceptual schemata capable of analyzing the visual input in any other way. The perception of color constancy works in a similar manner. Ethnographic studies have shown that there are cultural differences in the way color is perceived. Some cultures distinguish between a vast array of colors while others have a single word to represent a variety of shades of the same hue.

The faculty of hearing perhaps even more clearly demonstrates the link between expectation and perception. Most people have difficulty understanding an unfamiliar name the first time they hear it because the sounds don't "register." The same is true upon hearing a foreign language for the first time—the sounds tumble together and seem like little more than a disorganized assembly of noise. With time, however, the person comes to recognize phonemes as distinct units, and can distinguish words and sentence groupings.

Cognitive Schemata.   Just as perceptual schemata determine physical perception, mental perception, termed "cognition" by psychologists, is mediated by "cognitive" schemata, which operate in a similar fashion. Rather than serving to order and analyze incoming stimuli received through the physical senses, cognitive schemata accept, analyze, and are modified by stimuli received through the mental senses or thinking process.

For example, when children are first shown water being poured from a wide beaker into a narrow beaker, they inevitably state that the second beaker contains more water, primarily because the water level is higher. As the experiment is repeated, and they observe that the process is interchangeable, they come to understand that the amount of water remains the same. Their cognitive schemata has been modified by experience in that they have learned to differentiate between quantity of water and height of the water. They now expect the water quantity to remain constant and therefore perceive it as doing so. Therefore, just as physical perception is not an absolute, neither is mental perception. Both are dependent upon the observer's expectation, beliefs, and experience.

Modern science therefore recognizes that perception is not an absolute. We can only see what we know to look for. We perceive the external world as being made up of objects in three-dimensional Euclidean space because we expect to. Perception thus depends upon more than biologically determined sense reception. It is also dependent upon the expectations, experience, and theoretical framework (paradigms) through which the observer analyzes the stimuli it perceives. Change any one of these, and you change the observer's perception of reality.

A Model of Multisensory Perception

If our perception of the world is not an absolute, but depends upon perceptual and cognitive schemata, which are internal to the observer and subject to change, what, then, is reality? Can reality be defined? Is there a "real world" or does reality exist only in the individual mind? Fortunately, there is a model which may be useful in addressing these concerns. It is a model based upon teachings found within the Hawaiian Kahuna system of shamanism.

Within the Polynesian worldview or *huna* philosophy, "the world is what you think it is,"[2] meaning that each person creates their world according to their way of thinking. This system further acknowledges that there are four basic levels of experience—the ordinary world, the psychic world, the dream world, and the world of being. Each is based on a specific set of beliefs which define that given reality. Most people are unaware of these different levels of reality or perception, and move among them unconsciously. The shaman, however, is aware of their existence and can consciously travel between them by consciously choosing which set of beliefs to operate within.

The basic premise of this system is very similar to that presented in the Cayce readings which teach that "mind is the builder" and that "thoughts are things," and incorporates the concept of perception similar to the way it is defined by constructive psychology. The sets of beliefs referred to in this system correspond to perceptual schemata and are in fact paradigms. Since this system also permits consideration of how different sensory abilities affect perception, it can be adapted to provide a model of multisensory perception which enables the fully integrated human to perceive the world in a new way.

According to this model, the first perception is that of ordinary or objective reality. It is based on the paradigm that "all is separate." It is the world of physical matter and objects, and is perceived through the five physical senses. The second perception is subjective reality, and is based on the paradigm that "all is connected." It is the world of thought, ideas, and mental communication. It is perceived through the sense of imagination. The third perception is symbolic reality, which is based on the paradigm that "everything is representative of something else." This is the world of associations, patterns, and dreams. Like subjective reality, it is perceived through the sense of imagination and possibly through intuition. The fourth perception is holistic reality, based on the paradigm that "all is one." It is the world of unity and cosmic consciousness, where the individual self merges with the God-Mind. It is perceived through intuition and possibly through spiritual senses yet unknown.

Figure 2, *A Model of Multisensory Perception*, is a graphic representation of this model. In this figure, the circle represents the world, or reality. As people develop new sensory abilities, their perception of the world expands as they become capable of perceiving stimuli that were not visible before. Consider the analogy of a garden. As a five-sensory human, you perceive that portion of the world denoted by the letter "A," which is objective reality. You notice the color and fragrance of the flowers, see the sun overhead, feel the grass beneath your feet, and notice the butterflies flying by. You perceive the physical aspects of the objects around you.

As an individual who has integrated the body and mind, your perception expands so that you can also per-

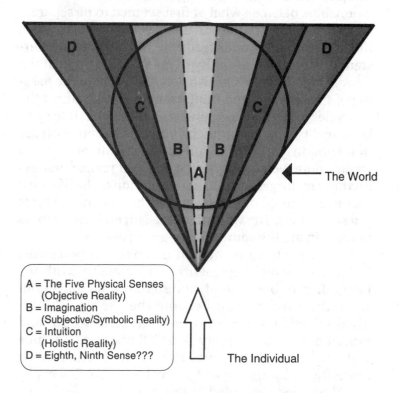

A = The Five Physical Senses
(Objective Reality)
B = Imagination
(Subjective/Symbolic Reality)
C = Intuition
(Holistic Reality)
D = Eighth, Ninth Sense???

The World

The Individual

Figure 2. A Model of Multisensory Perception

ceive the world as "B," which encompasses subjective and symbolic reality. You are now conscious of yourself as a physical and mental being and become aware of relationships between what at first seemed to be separate objects. The light of the sun enables the plants to grow; the rain from the clouds feeds them as well. You understand the role the butterfly plays in the life cycle of the flowers it pollinates. You also become aware of the passing of the seasons, and understand how they affect the life cycles of the plants around you. With a shift into symbolic reality, you integrate the body and mind, with the mind now in control of the physical self. You see patterns where there were none before and you realize that everything in the garden is a representation of the life force that runs throughout all creation. The song of the birds is a song of joy. The warmth of the sun and the wetness of the rain are the source of life-giving energy.

The fully integrated human is capable of perceiving "C" as well, which represents holistic reality. With the integration of body, mind, and soul, you no longer observe the garden—you become the garden. The individual self merges into the universal whole and experiences a state of unity with all that exists. You shine with the light of the sun, you fly with the freedom of the butterfly, and you glow with the colors of the flowers.

"D" has been included in this model to allow for the future emergence of yet unidentified eighth and ninth sensory abilities as alluded to in the Cayce readings. What worlds these senses may open to us, can only be imagined.

Reality and the "New" Physics

From Figure 2, it is clear that the world itself never changes; the observer simply becomes aware of segments of the world which were not discernible prior to the development of certain sensory abilities. Reality thus does not change; only our perception of it does.

Interestingly, the idea of different perceptions of reality is supported by recent discoveries of quantum and particle physics. This should not be surprising since it was physicists who first demonstrated the unitive nature of existence when they discovered that matter was really a denser form of energy, being composed of billions of atoms packed so tightly and vibrating so slowly that it gives the perception of a solid object.

Dr. Erwin Schroedinger, who won the Nobel Peace Prize in physics in 1933 for his studies in wave mechanics, has speculated "that all consciousness is essentially one."[3] This continues to be a common idea held by physicists today, as evidenced by Fritjof Capra, author of *The Tao of Physics*, and popularized by author Gary Zukav, both of whom agree that one of the most important revelations to come out of modern physics is the insight it has given into the basic oneness of the universe. Gary Zukav even goes as far as to argue that scientists such as William James, Carl Jung, Benjamin Lee Whorf, Niels Bohr, and Albert Einstein were mystics, in that "in the depths of their own thought they each saw much too much to be limited by the five senses, and they were not. Their works contribute not only to the evolution of psychology, linguistics and physics, but also to the evolution of those who read them."[4]

Research in the new branches of physics continues to reveal an even more uncertain and unpredictable universe. Physicists now know that all matter is composed of several types of fundamental particles. One of these particles—the boson—is a building block of matter, and yet it has no mass! Experiments conducted in particle accelerator chambers have shown that subatomic particles disappear without explanation only to reappear where they should not be, while others can even appear simultaneously in two places at once! Quantum physics has demonstrated that certain subatomic particles, such as electrons, possess not only the properties of matter but of energy as well, as they exhibit "wave properties" and can be diffracted in the same manner as light. Discoveries such as these have demonstrated that our former concepts of reality may be not adequate to explain the true nature of the universe. They prove that world of physical matter is fluid and changeable, and that energy is just as "real" as physical phenomena. They thus open the door to the scientific possibility of expanded perceptions of reality.

The Upcoming Change in Human Consciousness

As stated earlier, changes or shifts in human consciousness can be attributed to changing perceptions of reality. As you may recall from Chapter Three, the primary shifts in human consciousness, as outlined in Table 3, followed a pattern whereby behavior governed by physical sensation was replaced by behavior governed by the mental faculties of the mind. The shift in consciousness we are experiencing will continue that pattern although it will take it one step further. The perception of "divergence," which has long governed our interactions and relationships with others, will be replaced by a perception of "unity," which has its origin, not in mental thought, but in spiritual truth. This particular shift in human consciousness will be more than a step in our cognitive evolution—it will mark a significant advancement in our spiritual evolution as humans come to accept a paradigm based on spiritual values rather than physical perception.

Paradigms for the New Millennium

Moving from "I Believe" to "I Know." Facilitating the shift from a paradigm of divergence to a paradigm of unity will be the ability of the fully integrated human to move from a state of "believing" to a state of "knowing." At first glance, there may not seem to be much difference between the two. Yet, if you take a moment to examine them, the depth of the difference will become apparent.

Consider the difference in the following statements. "I believe there is a God" and "I know there is a God." Which carries more force? Belief implies the capacity for change so that what you believe to be true today, you may believe to be true tomorrow. Knowing, however, implies a permanence that is inherent in the understanding itself. Who is more dangerous, the revolutionary fighting for a cause he believes is just, or the fanatic who *knows* he is on a holy mission from God? One is willing to fight and sacrifice for his beliefs, the other is willing to die for what he knows to be true.

"Belief" is based upon a supposition that is assumed to be true. It is often predicated upon an analysis of sensory input which we intellectually evaluate and analyze. We believe an object to be solid because our senses tell us it is. We believe a person is good because of what we have heard about their character and reputation from others. Our mental faculties conclude that something is so because our physical and mental senses tell us it is. Belief thus depends upon something external to our perception, whether it is sensory input, faith based on religious tenets, or personal experience.

"Knowing," however, is based upon an inner cognizance or awareness of what is inherently true. The soul understands the limitations of physical and mental sen-

sory input and therefore does not rely on them as a yard-
stick of evaluation. By bringing the soul to conscious
awareness, the fully integrated human will learn to rely
upon its inherent knowledge of "what is," rather than
what "appears to be."

*From Divergence to Unity: Keynote of the New Millen-
nium.* The Model of Multisensory Perception in Figure
2, described above, can be useful in understanding the
approaching shift in consciousness. In each of the realities described within the model, the sense of separation
grows less and less as perception moves from physical
(objective) reality to mental (subjective/symbolic)
reality and finally to spiritual (holistic) reality. This is because all paradigms based on the concept of "divergence" have their basis in the material world. The rigid
lines which separate physical objects become more fluid
in the realm of mental thought and finally disappear
completely in spiritual reality as the individual self of the
fully integrated human merges with the cosmic whole
and a state of unity is achieved.

The legendary tales of Camelot also help illustrate this
concept. Contained within those tales are the chronicles
of the boyhood training King Arthur received from the
mystic wizard Merlin. Anyone familiar with these tales
knows that Merlin employed the shamanic technique of
"shape-shifting" to teach Arthur about the world. One
time, Merlin transformed Arthur into a hawk. As he
spread his wings and took to the sky, Arthur questioned
Merlin about the boundaries which separated the many
fiefdoms into which England was divided.

"Where are they?" Arthur asked. "I can't see them.
They must surely be large enough to see from up here."

Merlin explained that Arthur couldn't see the boundaries because they didn't really exist. They were imaginary divisions imposed upon the people by men who

sought to gain power through the land they "owned."

"But if they're not real," cried Arthur, "why do men fight and die for them? It doesn't make sense."

"Exactly the point," replied the wise magician. "I see you have learned your lesson."

Through this lesson, Merlin was trying to teach Arthur that such divisions have no basis in the real world of spiritual truth. They are arbitrarily imposed standards based on perceived physical criteria and have no inherent meaning. They emphasize perceived physical differences over the true unity which exists in the spiritual state. It was a lesson to which Arthur would return again and again, as he valiantly tried to unite England into a state governed by spiritual rather than physical principles.

This lesson will also serve as the foundation principle for the paradigm shift of the next millennium. The development of new sensory perceptions will allow the fully integrated human to see the illusion of divisions based on physical and cultural differences and acknowledge the unity of all creation as experienced by the mystics. Distinctions based on physical attributes such as skin color, nationality, and religion will cease to hold any importance. Through the sense of intuition, memory of the First Cause will be consciously awakened as the soul self is brought to conscious awareness and integrated with the body-mind. For the first time in history, we will *know*, not believe, but *know* that we are spiritual beings, and that the superficial, surface differences which have so long divided our species are not real. We will come to understand that we are not separate individuals, but one united species.

The seeds of this paradigm shift are already apparent within our popular culture, as evidenced by bestselling books such as *The Celestine Prophecy*, which emphasize the interconnectedness of all life, the immense popularity of movies such as *The Lion King*, which stresses the unity of "the circle of life," and the success of the bestselling song, *Not That Different*, made popular by country singer Collin Raye. As these seeds grow, we will embrace the paradigm of "at-one-ment" realizing not only our interconnectedness with one another, but with all aspects of creation. We will finally understand our role as caretakers of this planet, rather than its exploiters. We will come to accept a truth long known in "native" cultures, namely that the spirit of the Creative Force exists in all its creations.

The Paradigm of Co-Creation. The next step in the expansion of human consciousness does not end with the understanding of the interconnectedness of all life, however. For this realization is but the first step toward attainment of true Christ Consciousness, whereby we acknowledge not only our spiritual nature and bonds with all creation, but *claim* our birthright as co-creators with God Himself. The acceptance of paradigms based upon the spiritual truth of unity is the first step toward achieving that goal because we cannot see ourselves in union with God unless we first see ourselves united with others.

As we begin to reconnect with our true spiritual nature and bring to awareness our spiritual origin and purpose, we will rediscover a power we have always possessed—the power of conscious evolution. No longer will we see ourselves as the pawns of impersonal laws which operate around and amongst us. Instead, we will understand that through the conscious application of our mental faculties, applied in accordance with divine law, we can exercise the co-creative abilities which are our birthright.

The Principle of Critical Mass
(The Hundredth Monkey Theory)

With so much strife and division in the world today, the concept of a major paradigm shift as described above may seem like little more than a "pipe dream," which didn't work for long in Camelot and certainly won't work now. Some might question if it will ever be possible to reach the point where all human beings accept a paradigm of unity instead of the long-held values of divergence. Yet it is not necessary that every human being fully integrate body, mind, and soul, because there is another factor which will play a role in the evolution of human consciousness. This factor will have the effect of hastening cognitive change and extending it throughout the entire species. This factor is the principle of critical mass, or the hundredth monkey theory.

In physics, critical mass refers to the amount of mass within a celestial body required for the internal forces of heat and compression to initiate a thermonuclear reaction which transforms the celestial body into a star. A more practical application of this principle is the fact that it does not take a force equal to one hundred percent of the mass of a fulcrum to tip it—a fulcrum balanced on a pivot point will tip when a force equal to fifty-one percent is applied.

The principle of critical mass was first applied to behavior in 1952, to explain a phenomenon observed by anthropologists studying troops of Japanese macaques. During the study, the anthropologists supplemented the monkeys' normal diet with a supply of sweet potatoes which they placed in the sand. While the monkeys enjoyed the potatoes, they did not like the sand, spitting it out in disgust. One day, in the troop on Koshima Island, an eighteen-month-old female, named Imo, picked a potato from the sand, took it to a nearby stream, and washed it. She taught this to her mother, and shortly thereafter, all her playmates and their mothers were copying this behavior. Soon all the young monkeys in the troop had learned to wash the potatoes. The only adults who learned this behavior, however, were those who had children and had imitated their behavior. Other adults continued to eat the sandy potatoes, and for six years, showed no interest in performing this simple behavioral task.

Then, in autumn of 1958, something unexplainable happened. The anthropologists awoke to find all the monkeys in the troop washing their sweet potatoes! It was as if "overnight," all the remaining monkeys suddenly adopted a behavior that for six years they had ignored. More surprising, however, was the discovery that shortly thereafter, colonies of monkeys on neighboring islands, as well as on the mainland, had begun to wash their potatoes as well! It was not possible that a monkey from Koshima had traveled to the other islands and transmitted this behavior. It was as if by some unknown means, the spontaneous knowledge of this behavior had spread throughout the entire Japanese macaque species overnight. A behavior which had been practiced by a few, suddenly became the norm for the many.

The means by which this behavior was transferred to other macaque species has continued to puzzle scientists. One explanation which has been offered applies the principle of critical mass to the transmission of learned behavior. According to this model, any new level of perception, comprehension, or behavioral trait always begins with one individual. If the trait has an adaptive advantage, other individuals become aware of this new knowledge/behavior and adopt it as well. As more and more individuals come to adopt this change, it spreads out exponentially on an unconscious level and becomes incorporated within the collective unconsciousness of the species itself. At some point, as a certain "critical" number within the species adopts this behavior, critical mass is reached, and this knowledge enters the consciousness of all members of the species, regardless of geographic location. It was suggested, somewhat jokingly, that it took one hundred monkeys to achieve this effect. Hence the name "the hundredth monkey theory."

Although the story of Imo was the first time this phenomenon came to prominent attention, a similar phenomenon was actually documented in the 1920s by Harvard psychologist William McDougall, who observed a similar occurrence in rats who had been trained to swim mazes. After several generations of testing, it was observed that the descendant rats were able to swim the mazes ten times faster than the first generation. Even more interesting was the discovery that rats involved in similar experiments just beginning in other countries, began at the same level as the advanced rats in the McDougall study.

Morphogenetic Fields. In 1981, English biologist Rupert Sheldrake proposed a highly controversial theory[5] to explain how this transmission of learned behavior might occur. Sheldrake theorized that there is an invisible, organizing field which is unbounded by space and time that permeates all levels of existence. A change in one system or species is reflected within this "morphogenetic field," and expands outward to affect like systems and species in all parts of the world. A new behavior thus results in a morphic resonance within the field which will eventually affect all members of the species, creating what appears to be a spontaneous instant such as observed in the Japanese macaques.

Although the existence of such a morphogenetic field remains debatable, the "spontaneous" transmission of learned behavior within the macaque troops and McDougall's rats did occur. Today, the concept of the hundredth monkey theory is accepted by scientists in various fields, although the mechanism by which it operates is not yet agreed upon. It has also attracted considerable attention by those who are following current advances in cognitive evolution, particularly, the pending shift in human consciousness. It holds particular interest for this area because it provides an explanation as to how such a cognitive change may occur throughout an entire species.

The Advent of a Spiritual Consciousness

If the human species is successful in achieving the critical mass necessary to ignite a species-wide acceptance of a spiritual paradigm, it will mark the beginning of a new era. While there is no way to predict the consequences of such a paradigm shift, it's likely that the changes which follow will be as great as those which followed the discovery of fire, the development of language, and the emergence of culture.

Observers of the human condition have already noted the beginnings of this change, which many have described as a spiritual awakening. James Redfield, author of the bestselling *The Celestine Prophecy*, refers to it as "the process of clearing and opening ourselves psychologically and the exploitation of a variety of spiritual paths."[6] Award-winning author Gary Zukav refers to it as evolution from "a species that pursues external power (power based upon the perceptions of the five senses) into a species that pursues authentic power (power based upon the perceptions and values of the spirit)."[7]

Psychiatrist, psychologist, and author, Carlos Warter, refers to this phenomenon as "recovery of the sacred" or the "spiritualization of culture."[8] Warter goes on to say that "A new *spiritual consciousness* [author's emphasis] is entering the planet, one that connects all of us . . . Business people are reevaluating what they want in life, and are finding that their families are more important than their careers. There is a movement in progress in this country that involves people acting with kindness towards others for no other reason than the connection that exists among all people . . . We are realizing that all mankind came from the same traditions . . . Physicists . . . view the world and the universe as an organic whole, not a fragmented reality. It is the realization of these numerous connections that is bringing mankind forward into a time of spiritual awakening."[9]

Yet before a new order can begin, the vestiges of the old must first be eliminated. Although most people will embrace the spiritual paradigms that such a shift in consciousness will bring, there are still areas of the globe where malice and darkness prevail, where people cling to ancient hatreds, living only to exact violence upon those they perceive as enemies. These old ways serve only one purpose—self-destruction, and must be abandoned before the shift in human consciousness can be fully implemented.

Unfortunately, there will be those who seek to maintain the status quo, unwillingly to give up the power they possess within the old world order. They will cling to old paradigms and reject the truth that is being revealed to them through new sensory perception, refusing to see beyond the physical differences that have always separated them from others. Something must get the attention of those who persist in preserving the old ways and cause them to reevaluate their destructive thinking. That "something" may very well be cataclysmic events which have the effect of so devastating our way of life that we must turn to our spiritual source and rely upon one another in order to endure the hardships these cataclysms may bring. For just as the human species is standing at the crossroads of evolutionary change, so the planet Earth itself is about to experience an evolutionary transformation of her own, as the microcosmic evolution occurring within the human species is echoed on the greater macrocosmic scale without.

> *"A new spiritual awakening is occurring in human culture, an awakening brought about by a critical mass of individuals who experience their lives as a spiritual unfolding..."*
> —James Redfield, *The Celestine Prophecy: The First Insight*

8

Ancient Prophecies, Modern Visions: Predictions for a Changing World

Thirteen Heavens of decreasing choice, Nine Hells of increasing doom, and the tree of life shall blossom with a fruit never before known in creation. And that fruit shall be the New Spirit of Man.

—The Mayan Prophecies

As Above, So Below; As Within, So Without

THE BIOLOGICAL and cognitive developments described in the last two chapters are not the only changes the human species will be facing in the next decade. Even more dramatic than the microcosmic changes occurring within the species will be the macrocosmic changes occurring in the world without. This is due to the effect of a universal law or principle, originally attributed to Hermes Trismegistus, the supposed architect of the Great Pyramid and originator of mystic knowledge. This principle is expressed as "as above, so below; as within, so without."

This concept was known by the great masters. It refers

to the fact that everything which exists in the world of spirit—the above, can be brought into manifestation in the physical world—the below. It is based on the belief that physical laws are secondary to spiritual laws, and can be superseded by the spiritual when spiritual principles are applied in the earth plane. This accounts for such things as miraculous healings, whereby the physical laws of disease are suspended by the application of spiritual energy in the form of prayer, faith, and hands-on-healing.

A secondary corollary to this law is the principle "as within, so without," meaning that the external or physical world is a reflection of the internal or spiritual world. Scientists have long known that the inner or atomic world of matter reflects the larger world of the universe. In the atom, electrons revolve around a nucleus of protons and neutrons, much in the same way planets revolve around a star, and solar systems revolve around a galaxy. This concept has also been recognized in medical science as the mind-body connection, in that a person's physical health (external) is dependent upon his or her mental health and emotional well-being (internal). This principle applies to all areas of life, including evolution. Since the human species is experiencing extensive biological and cognitive changes within itself, it should not be surprising that these changes are even now, and will continue to be, reflected in the greater world at large in the form of political, economic, and geophysical change.

Prophetic Convergence

In the 1960s, a popular song entitled "The Age of Aquarius" spoke of the dawn of a new age, an age marked by "harmony and understanding," and "the mind's true liberation." While the song was new, the idea was not. There are many prophecies, both ancient and modern, which speak of global change, including social, political, economic, and geophysical changes which are expected to occur within the next few years.

Yet interest in the "Age of Aquarius" alone cannot explain the rising interest in the new millennium and the sense of expectation it is generating in so many corners of the world. What is it about this particular time in history that is causing so many well-educated, scientifically oriented people to be drawn to the idea that this new millennium will indeed be a time of significant change? Perhaps one reason lies in the fact that as individuals experience biological and cognitive changes within themselves, they become more attuned to the changes which are occurring in the outer world.

Equally important is the fact that the time lines of numerous prophecies are converging upon this decade as the time for the fulfillment of like predictions. Ancient calendrical systems pinpoint with precision accuracy the ending of the current epoch and the beginning of a new era in human history. Accounts of cyclic, cataclysmic change involving worldwide destruction by flood, ice, or fire, can be found in the mythology and legends of diverse cultures throughout the world. These destruction myths are often creation myths as well, because they actually tell of the creation and destruction of a series of worlds, of which this is the most recent. Such myths do not stop with the creation of this world, however. While many speak of the inevitable destruction of the current world order, they also predict the subsequent appearance of yet another, "new world." Apparitions of divine beings appear to people from all walks of life in countries around the world. Signs which are to precede the coming changes, as given in these prophecies, have, for the first time in history, been fulfilled. Modern prophets recount visions of the future which echo these ancient themes, and describe in great detail the unfoldment of earthshaking events, giving dates which coincide with those of the ancient predictions. Many of these prophecies specifically cite the years, such as 1998-2012, as the time of drastic change.

If one or two such prophecies were to pinpoint the same date, it could be dismissed as an isolated coincidence. But the fact that numerous prophecies, drawn from unrelated culture areas across the globe, spreading across thousands of years, all converge upon this particular time, must be considered as a significant indication that *something* will happen at the close of this millennium.

People *are* more highly educated than at any other time in history. They are aware of the progression of astrological cycles, have read Nostradamus' quatrains, and are familiar with the Hopi prophecies. They know that the more "new physics" finds out about the universe, the more questions are raised. People understand that one soothsayer can be overlooked as an anomaly. They also understand, however, that a gathering of soothsayers may indeed portend the future.

Cycles, Myths, and Visions

The prophecies discussed below fall into four basic categories—cyclic prophecy, divine revelation, prophetic visions, and apparitional phenomena. The cyclic prophecies include systems of counting time which are tied to a defined calendar system. This may be based on the cosmic clock of planetary movement, or a specific calendar. Those discussed here include astrological cycles, the Buddhist Wheel of Dharma, and the Mayan

Prophecies. Divine revelation, meaning the imparting of knowledge from a divine being to a group of people, is represented by the biblical apocalyptical literature and the Hopi prophecies. The futuristic visions of Nostradamus and Edgar Cayce, both modern seers, are discussed in detail. The significance of apparitional phenomena, where supernatural beings appear to individuals in isolated incidents, is illustrated through a discussion of the Marian apparitions.

The examples discussed here were chosen because they represent a comprehensive sampling of the world's prophetic literature of the last four thousand years, as drawn from diverse cultures, religious systems, and ethnic groups.

Cyclic Prophecies

Astrological Cycles. In astrology, the zodiac is divided into a series of twelve signs or constellations, equally spaced in a celestial sphere in the sky above. As the earth rotates on its axis, it wobbles, causing the first point of Aries (the vernal equinox) to appear to rotate backward through the different astrological signs. This is known as the "precession of the equinoxes."[1] The time spent in each constellation is a cosmic month, approximately 2,152 years in length. Rotation of the vernal equinox through all twelve constellations comprises a cosmic year consisting of approximately 25,826 solar years.

The earth's apparent reverse transit through a constellation during the cosmic month is considered to be an age or epoch in itself, when humankind is guided by the positive and negative potential of the sign in which it is transiting. The ending of one age and the beginning of the next cannot be pinpointed precisely, but are considered to occur within a 200-year range. The first point of

Aries entered the constellation of Pisces over 2,000 years ago and is now moving towards the constellation of Aquarius. Although there is some variation in astrological calculations, there is agreement that the first point of Aries will move into the constellation of Aquarius by 2,011 A.D., with its full effect manifesting sometime after the year 2,200 A.D. This particular transit becomes even more significant when we realize that Pisces is the last sign of the zodiac and marks the end of the cosmic year.

The Wheel Dharma.   The teachings of Gautama the Buddha (560-483 B.C.), included a belief in the Wheel Dharma or truth teachings. The teaching of truth was equated metaphorically to a great wheel that turned once every 2,500 years. Buddha predicted that the next great turn of the wheel would begin around 2,000 A.D. when a great teacher named "Maitreya" would appear. The appearance of Maitreya would be known worldwide, as the new teacher would revitalize the momentum of the wheel, and move the world into a new era of truth seeking.

The Mayan Prophecies.   The most complex of the cyclic prophecies comes from the Mayan culture of southern Mexico. The Maya can trace their history back to 7,000 B.P., when egalitarian fishing communities appeared along the Caribbean and Pacific coasts. By 4,000 B.P., the Maya had moved inland and adopted agriculture as a way of life. Contact with the Olmec civilization in 3,200 B.P. led to the development of a stratified society, which, at its zenith, consisted of more than two million people, living in communities concentrated around ceremonial centers. A vast network of trade routes extended the Mayan influence throughout Mesoamerica. They developed a sophisticated water management system to support their intensive agricultural efforts. For reasons still unknown, these centers were suddenly abandoned in 830 A.D., and the population dispersed throughout the countryside.

Builders of pyramids and complex temples, they possessed written language and were keen mathematicians and astronomers, whose interest in the study of numbers led to the development of a complex calendar, by which they were able to predict solar and lunar eclipses, as well as the equinoxes and solstices.

The Mayan calendar consisted of three separate systems of counting time—a cycle of solar years, a cycle of sacred years, and a cycle of Thirteen Heavens and Nine Hells. The solar year, or *Haab*, was used for agricultural purposes. It consisted of 365.29 days, and was divided into eighteen months (*vinal*) consisting of twenty days each, with five additional days (*vayeb*) at the end of each year. The sacred year or *Tzolkin*[2] was used for ceremonial and religious purposes. It was calculated using two interlocking wheels, a digit wheel of thirteen numbers and a symbol wheel of twenty glyphs. (Refer to Figure 3, *The Mayan Calendar System.*) As the wheels intermeshed, each of the numbers would be associated with one of the twenty glyphs, making a 260-day year known as "the count of days."

The sacred year or "long-count" calendar was also used to track the passing of the Cosmic Cycle, or the time (actually 25,920 years) it takes for the vernal equinox to pass through each of the twelve zodiac constellations. It is this Cosmic Cycle which holds the most interest in terms of the prophetic aspects of the Mayan calendar. The Cosmic Cycle was divided by the Maya into five periods of 5,125 years, each of which was considered a Great Cycle or world era, and represented in the Mayan calendar by a sun glyph. Glyphs of the first four Great Cycles were arranged in a circular pattern around the

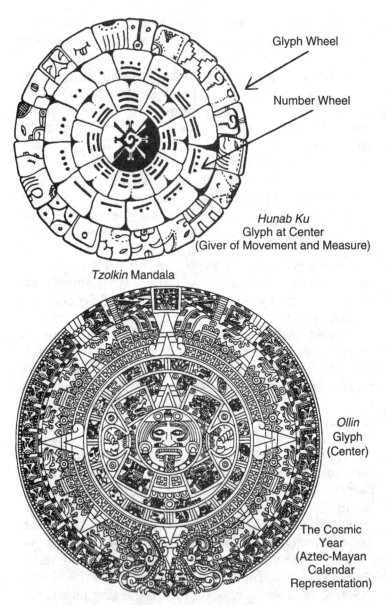

Glyph Wheel

Number Wheel

Hunab Ku
Glyph at Center
(Giver of Movement and Measure)

Tzolkin Mandala

Ollin
Glyph
(Center)

The Cosmic
Year
(Aztec-Mayan
Calendar
Representation)

Figure 3. The Mayan Calendar System

central glyph of the fifth Great Cycle.

According to the Mayan calendar, the current Cosmic Cycle began nearly 26,000 years ago. Interestingly, this time frame does coincide with the time of a major migration from Asia across the Bering Land Bridge into the North American continent, during which time the Maya's ancestors may have made their way to this land. Humankind is now in the Fifth World, an era which began on August 13, 3113 B.C., following the destruction of the Fourth World by flood. The Fifth World is now rapidly drawing to a close, with its final day being December 21, 2012.

The sun glyph for the Fifth World Great Cycle is the turtle or *ollin*. It is acknowledged by the Maya to represent a movement or shift, a meaning which traces back to the beginning of the world itself, which was created when the Great Mother Turtle turned over on her back to bring forth the earth. Mayan legends maintain that the Fifth World will end in a great upheaval of some kind, and that soon thereafter a new era will begin, marked by the return of the old gods, and the Mayan civilization. The Sixth World is described as a time when good will finally overcome evil, and man will enter a golden age of brotherhood, peace, and the remembrance of ancient spiritual knowledge. Today, descendants of a remnant of the Maya, who never submitted to the Spanish, called Lacandones, still make pilgrimages to the ruined pyramid-temples of Yaxchilan, offering incense and prayers to the ancient gods to hasten the coming of that day.

Further complicating the Mayan calendar was the cycle of the Thirteen Heavens and Nine Hells, which was superimposed upon the sacred year. Incidently, the beginning of the most recent cycle of Nine Hells began on April 21, 1519, the same day that the Spaniard, Cortez, landed at Vera Cruz and began the conquest of the Aztecs. The last day of the Nine Hells cycle was August 16,

1987, the same day as the Harmonic Convergence, a unique astrological alignment of planets, that was thought by many to herald the beginning of a "new age." Considering the accuracy and precision of the *Tzolkin*, the correspondence of the start of the last cycle of Nine Hells with the arrival of the Spanish in the New World, and the significance of the beginning of the Thirteen Heavens and the Harmonic Convergence, the Mayan calendar system must be considered as a significant prophetic source when analyzing predictions concerning the new millennium.

Divine Revelation

The Hopi Prophecies.   The Hopi are a Western Pueblo tribe of Native Americans, who today reside mainly in northern Arizona. They have inhabited this region for over a thousand years, tracing their ancestry back to the Anasazi (the "ancient ones"), who built the marvelous cliff palaces found at Mesa Verde and the great pueblo community of Chaco Canyon. Their rich cultural heritage made them the immediate focus of early anthropologists who sought to analyze their kinship, ceremonial rituals, and religious beliefs. Yet after seventy years of study, the descriptions of Hopi ceremonies reflected nothing more than surface descriptions of ritual paraphernalia and detailed accounts of their use in song, dance, and story. The esoteric meanings of Hopi religious tradition remained hidden, carefully guarded from disbelievers by those entrusted with its care.

Then, in the late 1950s, as a result of talks between Hopi elders and anthropologist Frederick H. Howell, the Hopi agreed (perhaps offered is a better word) to share the deepest meanings of their religious rituals and ceremonies, so that this knowledge might be preserved in writing for future generations. The consequent work was conducted by award-winning writer Frank Waters, who, after living with the Hopi for three years, published *Book of the Hopi*, designed to be an expression of the Hopi world- view as it was preserved through oral tradition for untold generations. "Its aim as a free narrative was to achieve the full spirit and pattern of Hopi belief, unrestricted by de- tailed documentation and argumentative proof."[3]

Book of the Hopi quickly became a classic study for anthropologists, theologians, psychologists, and a bestseller with the general public. It records the story, as told by thirty Hopi elders, of the Hopi creation myth, the successive creation and destruction of three previous worlds, and the people's "Emergence" from one world to the next, including their emergence into this Fourth World. The Hopi maintain that each previous world was destroyed when its people deviated from the divine plan of the Creator and pursued their own selfish, materialis- tic aims. Yet through each destruction, a small remnant who honored the divine plan survived to populate the next world. *Book of the Hopi* also tells of prehistoric clan migrations, the annual cycle of religious ceremonies, and gives an account of the historic period beginning with the first Spanish contact in 1540. Of interest here are the Hopi prophecies, told not only through oral tradition but depicted as pictographs on four sacred tab- lets, given to the Hopi clans at the time of their Emer- gence into the Fourth World. One tablet was given to the Fire clan by Masaw, Guardian Spirit of the Fourth World, and three tablets were given to the Bear clan, the leading clan of the Fourth World, by Soqohomna, the Bear clan deity. Today, the Fire clan tablet remains in that clan's possession. It was last displayed publicly in 1942. The Bear clan is said to retain possession of two of their origi- nal tablets, while the smallest of the three is said to have

passed to the Parrot clan in 1960. Frank Waters was permitted to examine this tablet during his research among
the Hopi.

The four tablets were given to the Hopi to guide their
way in the new Fourth World. They outlined the way in
which the Hopi clans were to make a migration through
the four directions before returning home to the center,
which was to be their permanent dwelling place. Those
who were strong and remained true to Hopi teachings
would one day return. Those who pursued evil ways
would forget their purpose and become lost, never finding the return path. The tablets also depicted where their
final home would be found—a place between two great
rivers (today Hopi land stretches between the Rio
Grande and Colorado Rivers), and also instructed the
Hopi on how to live upon returning to the center.

In addition to the information on these tablets, and
the oral mythology which surrounds them, Hopi knowledge of the ending of the Fourth World is based on interpretations of various petroglyphs found on "prophecy
rock" on the Hopi Black Mesa. Although photographs of
this rock are prohibited, oral interpretations of the
petroglyphs have been passed down for generations,
and the Hopi have diligently watched for three signs
which were to indicate that the final days of the Fourth
World were drawing near. The three signs inscribed upon
the rock were a swastika, the sun, and a red hat and
cloak. Each sign was to signal a time of purification,
when the Great Spirit would "shake the world," shakings
designed to get peoples' attention and remind them that
they are all children of one Father. The first shaking
would be with the right hand, the second with the left,
and the third would be with both hands. The events
these shakings would unleash would hasten the resolution of planetary karma. The last sign would precede the

final "Purification Day." If the people pay attention to these shakings, and return to the right way of living, they will enter the Fifth World, a world based on peace, brotherhood, and the teachings of the Great Spirit. If they do not heed the voice of the Great Spirit and unite as one people, the Fourth World will end in destruction.

Hopi legends also speak of other signs which would appear prior to the Day of Purification, including wagons chained together and led by something other than a horse, a bug moving on a black ribbon, paths in the sky, spider webs woven through the air, a gourd full of ashes which would fall upon the earth causing land to burn and rivers to boil, and the construction of a house in the sky. The picture of wagons chained together invokes the image of the railroad, a bug on a black ribbon is the automobile traveling down a highway, roads and spider webs in the sky are seen to be air routes and power lines, and the house in the sky is thought by many to have been Sky Lab. The Hopi believe that the gourd of ashes capable of burning land and rivers came true with the detonation of the atomic bomb at Hiroshima. Other signs mentioned include hot places which will become cold and cold places which will become hot, evidenced by changing weather patterns experienced in the last few years, land sinking into the sea as well as rising above it, and the appearance of a "blue" star. In 1987, astronomers did observe an unexpected celestial event when a blue star in the Greater Magellenic Cloud, a subgalaxy of the Milky Way, erupted into a brilliant supernova, the brightest supernova noted within the last four hundred years. Prior to this eruption, astronomers believed that only red dwarf and white supergiant stars were capable of going supernova, and this event caused a significant rethinking of astronomical theory.

With the advent of World War II, the Hopi recognized

the swastika as the symbol of Nazism, and the sun as the "rising sun" depicted on the Japanese flag. Concerned that the first two signs had already occurred, the Hopi spiritual elders decided that it was time to share their ancient teachings. Their decision was based in part on another prophecy which foretold of a great house built of mica (which resembles modern-day glass), to be built on "the far eastern shore," where leaders of the world would one day meet. The Hopi had been instructed to make three visits to this house of mica. If allowed to speak, much of the destruction of the final purification could be avoided. If denied a voice, they were to return home and await the end time.

The Hopi believed that the house of mica was fulfilled with the establishment of the United Nations in New York City. In 1948, they therefore decided to send a delegation to the General Assembly of the United Nations in an attempt to share their information with the other nations of the world. Unfortunately, they were denied an opportunity to speak. Shortly afterward, the Hopi began to release a number of their secret teachings so that those who understood would hear and know that the end time was at hand.

The Hopi's continued concern about the fulfillment of other signs in their prophecies led them to approach the United Nations again in 1973. They were again denied a chance to address the General Assembly. In 1976, however, the Hopi were invited to address a U.N.-sponsored Habitat Conference held in Canada. Whether this was the third attempt as foretold in their prophecies, or if they will send yet another delegation directly to the United Nations, remains to be seen.

The Hopi have continually awaited the appearance of the third sign of Prophecy Rock—the color red. There are those who speculate that the third sign represents Communist China, whose flag portrays the color red, and whose military uniforms bear a red insignia. Another interpretation, however, is that the "red hat" people represent not the Chinese, but the Buddhists, particularly the "Red Hat Sects" of the Tibetans. Perhaps not surprisingly, the Hopi were visited in 1979 by the head lama of the Red Hat Sect of Drepung Monastery in India. The Lama made the journey to fulfill an eighth-century prophecy of Padmasambhava, a master of the original Red Hat Sect, who said that "when the iron bird flies, and horses run on wheels, the Tibetan people will be scattered across the world. And the Dharma will come to the land of the red man."

Considering that Hopi prophecy states that the Fourth World can have one of two endings—a peaceful rebirth into the Fifth World or destructive annihilation, perhaps the two bearers of red can be thought of as representing those two possibilities. The Buddhists represent the positive aspect of red. If humankind heeds the call and manifests the spiritual attributes of the soul, the human species will have the opportunity to enter a new world characterized by peace, unity, and continued advancement. If, however, humankind ignores the warnings, and continues upon the materialistic path of self, the negative aspect of red will manifest, possibly as a hostile attack by Communist Chinese forces, which will once again plunge the world into a war of devastating destruction.

The Hopi prophecies have foretold many signs leading to the end of the Fourth World. Many signs have come already come to pass. Hopefully, the human species will heed the final warning of the third shaking, and make Purification Day a time of rejoicing for the new way of life which can be born, rather than a time of mourning for the destruction of the human race.

The Biblical Apocalypse. Apocalyptic literature consists of those parts of the Bible, as well as other Jewish and Christian books, which contain an apocalypse or symbolic vision of the future. These visions usually embody a final confrontation between good and evil, the appearance of a messianic figure, as well as the appearance of a figure of great evil, commonly called the "anti-Christ," the end of the present, corrupt world due to a catastrophe, and the creation of a new world in which the powers of evil have been eliminated. Old Testament apocalyptic books include Daniel and Ezekiel, as well as passages from Isaiah and Zechariah. New Testament writings include passages from Jesus' Sermon on the Mount, and the Book of Revelation. Other works include the Book of Enoch, Jubilees, and the Apocalypse of Baruch contained in the Jewish Pseudepigrapha, as well as the Apocalypse of Peter in the Apocryphal New Testament.

Biblical apocalyptic writings are cryptic, filled with metaphor, symbolism, and paradox, all of which contribute to making their interpretation difficult at best. Fundamentalists prefer literal interpretations while others apply a more symbolic meaning to the events described. No definite dates are given, and many generations have thought that these writings pertained to their own time. References to wars and rumors of war, famines and pestilence, earthquakes, and false prophets can have applicability at more than one point in historical time, just as the Archangel Gabriel indicated that Daniel's vision referred to both the "time of the end" and the "distant future." Add to this the fact that the Edgar Cayce readings maintain that the Book of Revelation speaks not of the physical world, but of the spiritualization of the human body, and the biblical prophecies become even more enigmatic. The readings equate the opening of the seven seals with the opening of the seven chakras and the overcoming of the physical self. The old world led by Satan equates to the ego of self, and the new heaven and earth born in Christ equates to the birth of the spiritual self.

The wide range of interpretation of biblical prophecies can be seen by considering a few examples offered to explain the better-known prophecies. Various sources have identified the antichrist as Hitler, the Ayatollah Khomeini, Saddam Hussein, Muammar Khadafi, and Mikhail Gorbachev, as well as the more esoteric interpretations of terrorism and materialism. The alliance of ten nations referred to in The Revelation has been interpreted to be the National Security Council of the United Nations, the North Atlantic Treaty Organization (NATO), the European Common Market, the Organization of Petroleum Exporting Countries (OPEC), and a yet to be formed alliance of Arab nations. The days of darkness referred to in Matthew, Luke, Revelation, Isaiah, Joel, and Zachariah, have been proposed to occur as a result of a nuclear detonation, a pole shift, the appearance of a comet within our solar system, and the ash thrown up by volcanic activity, as well as the more symbolic interpretation of darkness being the loss of spiritual knowledge.

Rather than debate the merits of such diverse points of view, the biblical predictions can be discussed in terms of "key events," which refer to a specific, defined circumstance, which is to happen prior to the end of the world. Two such prophecies have recently been fulfilled. They are the return of the Jewish people to their homeland (Ezekiel 34:13), and the preaching of the Gospel to all nations (Matthew 24:14). A third is the final Jubilee Year of Israel spoken of in the Dead Sea Scrolls.

The biblical prophecy of the return of the Jewish people to their homeland is one of the clearest prophecies as well as the easiest to date. History shows that following the destruction of the Temple of Jerusalem in 70

A.D., the Jewish people were scattered throughout the nations and left without a homeland. For nearly two thousand years they would wander and live in exile until the prophecy was fulfilled in 1948, with the establishment of the Jewish State of Israel. The fulfillment of this prophecy in this generation is the most concrete evidence available that the end times may be at hand.

In addition, this generation has also seen the realization of the prophecy which states that the Gospel will be preached "in all the world and then shall the end come." A reading given in 1943 indicated that this would be fulfilled by the end of 1944 when "there will be no part of the globe where man has not had the opportunity to hear, 'The Lord He is God.' "[4] Most experts agree that by the 1960s, the Bible was translated into hundreds of languages and distributed even in the most remote regions of the globe. Again, a second prophecy was fulfilled in this generation.

While the two key events discussed above have already occurred, many believe that the final Jubilee of Israel is rapidly approaching. Historically, the Jewish Jubilee year was the final year of a fifty-year period specified in the rabbinical laws of Leviticus (see Leviticus 25:8-12). It was to be a holy year in the manner of the Sabbath day, in which no crops were to be planted or harvested, no debts collected, and all captives released. The Dead Sea Scrolls speak of the final Jubilee of Israel as the time when the high priest Melchizedek (taken by many to mean Jesus) will reincarnate and lead the righteous in a final battle against the wicked. It doesn't take a mathematician to know that the Jubilee Year of the State of Israel will occur in 1998, fifty years after its founding. What remains to be seen is whether this will be the *final* Jubilee of Israel as described in the Dead Sea Scrolls.

Visions of the Seers

The Quatrains of Nostradamus. Michel De Nostre-dame, called Nostradamus, was born in 1503 to a well-educated and prosperous family of Jews who had converted to Christianity decades earlier. His two grand-fathers were personal physicians to King Rene of Prov-ençe, and they gave Nostradamus an excellent education in the classics, mathematics, science, and astrology. He attended the University of Montpellier where he earned a medical license. Shortly afterward, southern France was hit with an outbreak of a chronic form of bubonic plague. Nostradamus devised an unusual cure, com-prised of various herbs and rose hips, which contained extremely potent doses of Vitamin C. These "rose pills," combined with a prescription of clean water, fresh air, frequently washed bedding, and a low-fat diet, success-fully treated thousands of people. When Nostradamus returned home after his successful work throughout France, however, he found his own wife and children stricken with the plague. Unfortunately, the disease had progressed too far for his remedies to work, and the "healer of thousands" stood by and helplessly watched his own family die. Their deaths sent him into a terrible depres-sion, and drove him further into the study of magic and the "hidden" sciences. He left France to escape the watchful eyes of the Church Inquisitors and embarked upon a pilgrimage of self-discovery throughout Europe, during which time his prophetic powers awakened.

In 1544, France was hit with another bout of plague, and Nostradamus returned home, administering his rose pills throughout southern France. His intervention was attributed with saving the cities of Aix, Salon, and Lyons. When the outbreak subsided, he returned to the city of Salon where he lived out the rest of his life with his second wife and new family.

Nostradamus continued to have prophetic visions, and cautiously published an almanac on prophecy in 1550. Encouraged by its success among the upper classes and nobility, Nostradamus embarked on an ambitious project to write the ultimate book of prophecy which would describe all of the *possible* futures until the end of time. The book consisted of ten volumes called "Centuries," each containing one hundred "quatrains," or four-line poems. He began the work in 1554, publishing Centuries I through VII within two years. He completed the last three Centuries in 1558, although he decided against publishing them while he was still alive. Quatrains for Centuries XI and XII were planned but never finished.

Publication of *The Centuries* brought Nostradamus even greater notoriety. Medical colleagues called him an embarrassment. Philosophers both praised and cursed him. Some thought him an agent of Satan, and others thought him to be mad. The Parisian royal court, however, was enamored with his work, and his most devout fan was the French Queen Catherine de' Medici, who also became his champion and protector. He became a frequent visitor to the royal court, where he was received by both Catherine and King Henry II.

Rather than being the melancholy man many expected to see, Nostradamus was said to be cheerful and good-humored, which caused many to doubt the sincerity of his dire predictions. He responded that the potential for human cruelty he saw in the future made it even more important to practice positive, hopeful living. He died at his home in Salon in 1566, after a long and prosperous life, dying on the date he had earlier predicted.

The quatrains of Nostradamus continue to be avidly studied long after his death. Many of them seemed to be little more than confused ramblings which made little sense. It was usually hindsight, however, which revealed the uncanny accuracy of his predictions. Today it is acknowledged that Nostradamus not only accurately predicted historical events of the last 450 years, but that he also foresaw the development of modern inventions such as the light bulb, power lines, airplanes, automobiles, and the discoveries of Louis Pasteur: "The lost thing [germs], hidden for many centuries, is discovered. Pasteur will be honored as a demi-god." (Century 1/Quatrain 5)

The hundreds of accurate predictions contained in the quatrains could not possibly be recounted here. In addition to accounts of the rise and fall of numerous European royal families, Nostradamus also predicted the details of the death of Henry II, the demise of Mary Queen of Scots and the rise of Elizabeth I, the London Fire of 1666, the birth of the United States, the horrors of the French Revolution, the fortunes of Napoleon (called Neapolluon in Century 4/Quatrain 82), and the specifics of the Bolshevik Revolution. Predictions of the modern era include the names of battlefields of World War I, the rise of Hitler, Franco, Mussolini, de Gaulle, and Mao Tse Tung, World War II, the Holocaust, the detonation of the atomic bomb, the assassination of President John Kennedy and Senator Robert Kennedy, the moon landing, the mysterious death of John Paul I and warnings to John Paul II, the space shuttle Challenger disaster, conflict in the Middle East and the rise of terrorism, the friendship and subsequent breakdown in relations between the United States and Russia, and the advent of AIDS. A few examples of quatrains dealing with recent events are recounted here to give a sense of the accuracy of Nostradamus' predictions. All translations are taken from John Hogue's *Nostradamus and the Millennium*.[5]

The rise of Hitler:
   From the deepest part of Western Europe
   A young child will be born to poor people;
   Who by his speech will seduce a great multitude,
   His reputation will increase in the Kingdom of the
   East [Japan].
                                (Century 3/Quatrain 35)
   They are said to have come from the Rhine and
   from Hister [Hitler].
                                (Century 4/Quatrain 68)

The Holocaust:
   Human flesh through death is burned to ashes.
                                (Century 5/Quatrain 1)

Charles de Gaulle's three elections as president of France:
   For three times one surnamed de Gaulle will lead
   France.
                                (Century 9/Quatrain 33)

The assassination of John Kennedy and his brother Robert Kennedy (also, Jeane Dixon's predictions of these events, and the controversy as to whether Lee Harvey Oswald was the lone gunman):
   The great man will be struck down in the day by a
   thunderbolt [gunshot],
   The evil deed predicted by the bearer of a petition;
   [Jeane Dixon's prophecy]
   According to the prediction another falls at night.
                                (Century 1/Quatrain 26)

   The ancient work will be accomplished.
   And from the roof evil ruin will fall on the great man.
   Being dead, they will accuse an innocent of the
   deed.

The guilty one is hidden in the misty woods.
(Century 6/Quatrain 37)

Is "the guilty one" a possible reference to the blurred photograph of a man beneath the trees on the grassy knoll holding a long, metallic object?

The Apollo moon landing:
He will come to take himself to the corner of Luna [the moon]
Where he will be taken and placed on alien land.
(Century 9/Quatrain 65)

The space shuttle Challenger:
Nine will be set apart from the human flock,
Separated from judgement and counsel;
Their fate to be determined on departure.
The unripe fruit will be the source of great scandal [NASA]
Great blame, to the other great praise.
(Century 1/Quatrain 81)

The AIDS epidemic:
A great plague will come with a great scab.
Relief near but the remedies far away.
(Century 3/Quatrain 75)
In the feeble lists, great calamity through America
... plague.
(Century 2/Quatrain 65)

Considering the accuracy of Nostradamus' predictions over the last 450 years, it would seem an easy task to simply review the remaining quatrains to determine what the future holds. The quatrains noted above, however, are easy to interpret because they concern events which have already occurred. Hindsight helps us understand their meaning. For example, until the rise of Hitler, no one knew what "Hister" referred to. Until the assassination of President Kennedy, the quatrains about "the great man" remained unidentifiable. Quatrains about future events are still cryptic in nature, difficult to understand and subject to varying interpretation. There are, however, a number of quatrains about future events which lend themselves to a fairly consistent interpretation. An analysis of these quatrains reveals the following predictions for the coming years.

The end of the Roman Catholic papacy. Numerous quatrains refer to the demise of the Roman Catholic Church by the year 2000 A.D. There will be a great schism within the church, and a false pope name Clement will reign for seven months. Then the Vatican will be ransacked and plundered, as the last pope—St. Peter—will occupy the Holy See during the Vatican's final destruction.

The appearance of the "antichrist." Nostradamus predicted the appearance of three such figures in history. According to his quatrains, Napoleon and Hitler were the first and second antichrists, with the third to come from the Middle East. For twenty-seven years he will unleash a bloody war upon the world. Islamic fanatics will fan the flames of war and cause a reddened icy rain to cover the earth. Possible candidates for this figure include the now deceased Ayotollah Khomeini, Muammar Khaddafi, Saddam Hussein, and terrorist leaders Abu Nidal and Abu Abbas, who was responsible for a terrorist attack on the *Achille Lauro* cruise ship.

A number of scholars believe that the twenty-seven-year war referred to in the quatrain does not refer to a regional conflict, but to the war of terrorism which has been unleashed upon the world. Since the war is to end by the year 2000 A.D., it follows that it would have begun in 1973. That was the year of the Yom Kippur war between Egypt and Israel as well as the oil embargo by the OPEC nations, and it certainly coincides with the early stages of the terrorist threat posed by Arab extremists.

An Islamic nuclear attack on a naval fleet. One quatrain speaks of the "melting of a great fleet" in the Mediterranean, "because of a heat as great as the Sun's, the fish will be almost cooked." This description clearly brings to mind the intense heat felt in the aftermath of a nuclear attack.

A global war. A number of quatrains speak of a possible third world war, a holy war or jihad, brought about by the uniting of the Arab nations under a strong master of Islamic law. Iran will attack Macedonia (Greece), and Libya will attack Romulus (Italy), which will be destroyed by a great fire. The fighting will spread from Israel to Lake Geneva. Russia will enter the war on the side of the Arab nations, and launch an attack into Paris, as France is attacked on five sides. Russia will later switch sides and join forces with the European nations to push back the Moslem invasion.

Possible starting dates for this war were normally interpreted to be 1991 or 1993. Both dates have, of course, come and gone, without the appearance of the predicted conflict. With each passing day, the likelihood of this scenario decreases. Hopefully, the cooperative peace efforts of various nations have helped humankind avoid this global destruction.

A United States—Russian (Soviet) alliance. One quatrain predicts that the two great powers will become friends, which will be seen as an increase for all. Following this, the new land (America) will be at the height of her powers. Another quatrain, however, goes on to say that the alliance will last only thirteen years. Both powers will then "surrender to the barbare (sic) and Iranian leaders" after suffering a great loss.

In 1987, the United States and the Soviet Union did move toward a closer understanding and friendship. With the fall of Communism in 1989, the commitment of the United States to help the Russian people was even more firmly emphasized. Hopefully, the friendship between the two countries will continue to grow, and outlast the thirteen-year prediction.

Worldwide famine, droughts, and earthquakes. An increase in earthquakes was predicted to begin in 1986, with dire consequences for the world. A massive quake will hit India followed by a chain reaction of smaller quakes through Asia Minor, Greece, and the western coast of Europe. Greece will be decimated by flood and half of England will sink into the ocean. "Earth shaking fire from the center of the Earth will cause the towers [skyscrapers] around the New City [New York] to shake." (Century 1/Quatrain 87) Following a tremendous earthquake "the great theater filled with people will be ruined." A great maritime city, surrounded by crystal [glass] will be shaken by a terrible wind from winter solstice until spring.

A pole shift. In a letter written to King Henry II, Nostradamus described the final twenty-five years of this century as a time of great upheavals, culminating in a massive pole shift in the year 2000 A.D. He states that following omens in the spring, there will be "reversals of nations and mighty earthquakes." In October, there will be a "great movement of the Globe," of such magnitude that it will seem as if gravity has lost its pull, and the earth will be plunged into "the abyss of perpetual darkness." Unfortunately, these predictions of earth changes closely coincide with those of other prophecies, including Edgar Cayce's.

The quatrains of Nostradamus thus appear to describe a future world of war, famine, death, and destruction. Since they portray a world which no one welcomes, the question many people ask is whether the events depicted in these quatrains must come to pass. Are they inevitable?

In answering this question, it should be remembered that Nostradamus originally wrote his prophecies to indicate the *possible* futures of humankind, meaning that he believed that the future events he saw were subject to change based upon humanity's choices and actions. Indeed, there are a number of quatrains which indicate the possibility of two *different* outcomes of the same event, particularly if those involved in the event heeded the warning signs that were given.

In addition, there are dozens of quatrains which speak not of death and destruction but of the flowering of a new "religious consciousness" during the end of this century. Over sixty quatrains describe the birth of a religious movement and its spiritual teacher. The teachings seem to be based on Eastern beliefs which are taken to the Western world. The teacher will appear in Asia, but be at home in Europe, linked to the teachings of Hermes and the Caduceus Wand, a Western mystical symbol for enlightenment. The teacher will deliver a great people from voluntary slavery and subjection.

Further, the quatrains continue on to the year 3797 A.D., describing a future world of peace and wisdom, where a balance between science and religion is attained. The power over life is discovered, and humankind begins to travel to the stars. The "final conflagration" occurs in 3797 A.D., although humankind will not be destroyed, because, by then, it will possess the ability to leave the earth and live among the stars.

The quatrains of Nostradamus, therefore, do not necessarily indicate that the final years of this century must be a time of war and chaos. An alternate possibility exists as well. If this generation heeds the warning signs and people of vision work hard to bring about the peaceful resolution of conflict, humanity can choose the alternate path which will lead to the growth of a new religious consciousness and ensure that the promise of the next millennium as an era of great advancement and progress can come true.

The Edgar Cayce Readings. There is a significant amount of material in the readings regarding the last fifty years of this century and the beginning of the next millennium. Most of these readings were given over a period of twenty years, from the mid-1920s to 1944. The readings speak of topics already discussed, such as social, political, and economic change, the laws of karma, and spiritualization of the body. A mere seventeen readings provide additional information on earth changes, meaning geophysical upheavals that will change the face of the globe. This material was always presented in the context that these changes are a necessary part of humankind's evolutionary progress, and will herald the beginning of a spiritual transformation which will result in a new era of enlightenment for humankind. The transition from this age to the next was to begin in the period 1958 to 1998, "when this period has been accomplished, then the new era, the new age, is to begin."[6]

Considering that the readings number over 14,000, seventeen readings may not seem to represent a significant amount of material. Yet this relatively small source actually provides a wealth of information, because the readings provide such detailed answers in response to the questions which were asked of the sleeping Cayce. A summary of the major changes presented in the readings follows:[7]

The earth will be broken up in many places. The early portion ['58 to '98] will see a change in the physical aspect of the West Coast of America. There will be open waters to appear in the northern portions of Greenland. There will be new lands seen off the Caribbean Sea, and *dry* land will appear . . . South America shall be shaken from the uppermost portion to the end . . .

The greater change, as we will find, will be the North Atlantic Seaboard. Watch New York! Connecticut, and the like.

. . . many portions of the East Coast will be disturbed, as well as many portions of the West Coast . . . Even many of the battlefields of the present [1941] will be ocean, will be the seas, the bays, the lands over which the *new* order will carry on their trade . . .

Portions of the now East Coast of New York, or New York City itself, will in the main disappear. This will be another generation, though, here; while the southern portions of Carolina, Georgia—these will disappear.

The waters of the lakes [Great Lakes] will empty into the Gulf [of Mexico], rather than the waterway over which such discussions have been recently made [St. Lawrence Seaway].

Then the area where the entity is now located [Virginia Beach, Virginia] will be among the safety lands, as will be portions of what is now Ohio, Indiana and Illinois, and much of the southern portion of Canada and the eastern portion of Canada . . .

of Canada and the eastern portion of Canada ...

Los Angeles, San Francisco, most all of these will be among those that will be destroyed before New York even.

If [author's emphasis] there are the greater activities in the Vesuvius, or Pelée, then the southern coast of California—and the areas between Salt Lake and the southern portions of Nevada—may expect within the three months following same, an inundation by the earthquakes. But these, as we find, are to be more in the southern than in the northern hemisphere.

... lands will appear in the Atlantic as well as in the Pacific ... Poseidia will be among the first portions of Atlantis to rise again. Expect it in sixty-eight and sixty-nine; not so far away!

The greater portion of Japan must go into the sea.

The upper portion of Europe will be changed as in the twinkling of an eye.

... there will be shifting then of the poles—so that where there has been those of a frigid or the semitropical will become the more tropical, and moss and fern will grow.

When there is a shifting of the poles. Or a new cycle begins. [This answer was given in response to the question, "What great change or the beginning of what change, if any, is to take place in the earth in the year 2000 to 2001 A.D.?]

In recent years the readings on earth changes have come under a great deal of scrutiny by advocates of Edgar Cayce's work. One reason is that the most dire predictions did not come from Cayce's usual source—his higher self accessing the Universal Consciousness—but from an entity which identified itself as the Archangel Halaliel. This type of interruption in the source of the readings rarely occurred, although on several occasions the Archangel Michael did speak through the sleeping Cayce. Michael's messages, however, occurred only a few times within a forty-year period and consisted mainly of admonitions to listen to the message being given, while Halaliel's appearance continued for several consecutive months in 1934. After much debate, the A.R.E. Study Group for which the readings were being given decided, although not unanimously, to reject any further assistance from Halaliel and rely strictly on Cayce's own contact with the Universal Consciousness. Following that decision, Halaliel did not appear again.

There is disagreement as to whether the changes predicted will be sudden, cataclysmic reactions resulting in massive death and destruction, or gradual in nature, allowing time for preparation. Certain readings do seem to indicate that a more gradual scenario is possible, as evidenced by the opening sentence of the last earth change reading, 1152-11, given in 1941. "As to conditions in the geography of the world, of the country—changes here are *gradually* [author's emphasis] coming about." Further, some readings which have been interpreted to mean geophysical change may actually relate to political upheavals. A good example of this is reading 3976-15 which states that Europe may be changed in the twinkling of an eye. Many people now believe that this may refer to the drastic change in "the map of Europe," which was significantly altered following the collapse of the

Soviet Union, wherein over a dozen satellite territories have declared their newfound independence.

Another factor which must be considered is the fact that the readings themselves indicate that the choices and actions of humankind *can affect* predicted events. This is why most readings do not contain a specific date for an event; the future is fluid and can vary according to the decisions made. "Tendencies in the hearts and souls of men are such that these *may* [author's emphasis] be brought about."[8] Again, "As to the changes that are coming—as in the fulfilling of time and space . . . these will, as indicated, depend upon what individuals and groups do about that they know respecting His will, His purpose with man."[9]

Considering the profound accuracy of the thousands of other Cayce readings, the earth change readings must be considered a reliable source of information. Whether they are interpreted literally, symbolically, or looked upon as subject to modification, the readings certainly make it clear that the world will soon experience change on many fronts.

The events described in the readings are similar to those found in other prophecies, including the Hopi, the Mayan, the biblical apocalypse, and the Nostradamus quatrains, all of which show remarkable parallels. There is no doubt that each prophetic source points to this time in history as a time of transformation which will culminate in the birth of a new age of humanity.

Apparitional Phenomena: Voice of the Holy Mother

Since the thirteenth century, hundreds of people around the world have reported the sudden appearance or "apparition" of the Holy Mother Mary. She has appeared in England, the Pyrenees, Mexico, France, Portugal, Spain, the former Yugoslavia, Rwanda, and most recently, the United States. Common elements of these visions include the sudden appearance of an ethereal, nonphysical image surrounded by light which is suspended above the ground, and who speaks in the person's native language. Sometimes her appearance is preceded by lightning or the appearance of an angel, particularly the Archangel Michael.

One of the first reported incidents of the Marian apparitions occurred in Guadalupe, Mexico, in 1531, when she appeared to a Native American named Juan, who had recently converted to Christianity. The lady spoke in Juan's native language—Tolpetlac—and told him to have a church built on the spot where she appeared. She proclaimed her love for his people, and made no predictions other than that Juan's people would one day embrace the Christian faith.

One of the Holy Mother's appearances which would have far-reaching effects for years to come occurred in Lourdes, France, in 1858, when she appeared to a sick and hungry fourteen-year-old girl named Bernadette. During a three-week span, the Lady who identified herself as the Immaculate Conception made eighteen appearances. The Lady showed Bernadette a hidden grotto with a spring which she claimed had healing properties. Today, the Lourdes shrine is the site of millions of pilgrimages each year, and there are thousands who have claimed to have been cured of various illnesses after being touched by the water of the spring. While Bernadette claimed that the Lady told her secrets about the future, no record was kept of these prophecies.

Perhaps the most famous appearance of the Holy Mother occurred in Fatima, Portugal, in 1917, when the Holy Mother appeared to three young children, ages six to nine. The children saw the Lady and her angel companion several times before they told anyone what they had seen. When they did, they were beaten and told to recant their silly stories. They refused. A month later, the children, along with several villagers, returned to the site where the Lady had instructed them to meet. Although the villagers did not see the Lady, they did see lightning flashing in the noonday sky and heard a voice speaking to Lucy, the oldest girl. Lucy's mother and the local priest still did not believe her, however, and tried to convince her that the devil was making her see these things.

The next month, hundreds of people flocked to Fatima to keep vigil with the children for the Lady of Light. Yet even these witnesses, who again saw a ball of light and heard a buzzing sound, were not enough to convince the children's families and others in Fatima. The children continued to be subjected to physical abuse and emotional torment. During the Lady's next appearance, Lucy asked her to perform a miracle to prove that she was real, hoping that this would stop their torment. The Lady agreed, saying that she would do so when she appeared the following month. Much to the children's dismay, however, their abuse only intensified, and their families received death threats from those who thought the children messengers of Satan.

During the Lady's next appearance, she identified herself as the "Lady of the Rosary," and made the following prophecies: World War I, the war to end all wars, would end within one year, and would be followed by an even greater war beginning in the reign of a pope named Pius XI. A great battle for the heart of Russia had already begun. The Russian prophecy stated that unless Russia consecrated herself to the Immaculate Heart, her errors would spread through the world, bringing war, persecution, and the end of nations. The Fatima prophecies, as given by the Lady in 1917, of course came true, and are today considered evidence of the miraculous by the Roman Catholic Church.

Lucy has since become a nun in the Catholic Church, and there is discussion that she has revealed additional prophecies to the Vatican as told to her by the Lady. The Vatican, however, has chosen not to make this knowledge public, and speculation continues as to why the Church has chosen to keep these prophecies secret.

Another significant series of Marian appearances occurred in 1961 at Garabandal, Spain, when the Holy Mother appeared to Maria Concépcion Gonzalez, nicknamed Conchita, and three other children. During a span of four years, the Lady made a series of appearances. Conchita and the other children faced the usual skepticism, questioning, and testing by the Catholic Church. Hundreds of observers were also drawn to the site of the apparitions.

Throughout these appearances, the Lady spoke of terrible "warnings" and "chastisements." One chastisement would be worse than being burned by fire. This chastisement was conditional, however. It can be avoided if humankind heeds the messages of the Lady, and returns to a life of prayer, fasting, and service. The Lady also spoke of a warning so severe that people would prefer death to experiencing its effects. This warning will catch the attention of those who do evil, she said, and cause the good to draw even closer to God. Finally, the Lady spoke of a miracle which would follow the warning. This miracle will be in conjunction with an event in the Church and the feast of a saint, occurring at eight-thirty on a Thursday evening. It will be the greatest miracle ever performed by Christ, and the world will not doubt its authenticity. A lasting sign of the miracle, which can be captured on film, will remain at the Pines of Garabandal. Although Conchita was shown the content of this miracle, she was forbidden to reveal any more details. She will, however, be allowed to announce its date eight days before it will occur. Another prediction reportedly made by the Lady was that there would be only two popes following Paul VI. If true, this means that the current Pope, John Paul II, would be the last Pope.

Marian apparitions also occurred in Medjugorje (in the former Yugoslavia), in 1981, as the Lady appeared to two boys and four girls, ages ten to seventeen. During these apparitions the Lady gave the children a series of ten "secrets," containing chastisements, warnings, and a miraculous sign. The seventh secret originally told of a chastisement, although the eighth secret stated that it had been averted due to the efforts of world prayer. Details on these events are sketchy, but the means of mitigating the chastisements are clear. Prayer, fasting, and meditation are the keys to avoiding these catastrophes, as well as the acceptance and recognition of the warnings and the miraculous sign when they occur. The Lady also spoke of the need for humility and love, stating that the power of love makes all things possible.

The Holy Mother also appeared in Betania, Venezuela, in 1976, to a young woman named Maria Esperansa. She appeared to seven young people, ages sixteen to twenty-one, in Rwanda in 1981, 1982, and 1989. Appearances in the United States were reported in Georgia in 1994. The messages given during these appearances were similar to previous ones, as the Lady spoke of the necessity for love and prayer as the means to bring about peace.

Although not an apparition, per se, an American woman named Annie Kirkwood claims to be in contact with Mary through telepathy, after which Annie records the messages by computer with the help of her husband

Byron. These messages from Mary are the subject of several books by Kirkwood,[10] and echo the themes of other Marian apparitions. They also recount additional information on the mission and training of Jesus, their life together, and coming earth changes which signal the beginning of a new era. Again, love and prayer are cited as the means to survive the coming years.

That these apparitions have only appeared to Catholics, with the exception of Annie Kirkwood (although not of the Catholic faith, Annie was raised in a Roman Catholic culture), is not surprising. There is a saying in anthropology that "tiger gods do not exist where there are no tigers," meaning that people tend to process and interpret data according to their beliefs, values, and attitudes (paradigms). If a person is going to have an encounter with the divine, it is going to occur within their own cultural frame of reference.

There are those who believe that the Marian apparitions are truly visitations by the Holy Mother. Others, however, see them as nothing more than figments of active imaginations, which perhaps occur to those who feel trapped by mundane lives of poverty and deprivation. One theory holds that they may be manifestations of the "feminine divine" aspect of God, represented by Mary, whose appearance always precedes that of the "masculine divine," namely Jesus. Or, perhaps these apparitions are actually aspects of the mystic experience, occurring to people who have begun to manifest the seventh sensory ability.

How a person views the Marian apparitions no doubt depends upon many factors, not the least of which is faith. Yet the accuracy of the Fatima prophecies cannot be discounted. It is also significant that these apparitions have actually been ongoing phenomena for over seven hundred years. Visions of the Holy Mother have occurred to people separated not only by distance and culture, but by centuries of time. Yet each apparition shares common elements and delivers a similar message of a return to prayer and love as the means of bringing about a new and better world. For that reason alone, their message, as well as their warnings, must be given serious consideration.

Common Prophetic Themes

Each of the prophecies discussed above provides a detailed description of events predicted to occur during the closing years of this millennium and the early years of the next. Some of the prophecies view these events as the next stage in a cyclic pattern extending back thousands of years. Others view the events to come as retribution for humankind's turning away from its spiritual source, and failure to observe the spiritual teachings given to it long ago. Still others view these conditions as the consequence of choices and actions which were contrary to universal laws, and maintain that humankind is merely reaping the destructive seeds it has sown.

Yet despite differences in the details of these prophetic visions, all of the prophecies discussed above, both ancient and modern, share at least four common elements. First, each prophecy speaks of the ending of the current age, whether it be the Fourth World of the Hopi, the Fifth World of the Maya, the cosmic year, the turning of the Wheel Dharma, or the current epoch of modern history. Second, the prophecies all speak of the last decades of the twentieth century as a time of drastic social, political, and economic change, as well as a time of extensive earth upheavals which have the potential of bringing about great destruction. They paint a bleak picture of this generation as a time of "trial by fire" when the earth and its inhabitants will be shaken to the very roots of their foundations. Third, each prophecy contains predictions for the beginning of a new era in human history, an era where the expression of spiritual attributes will be the rule rather than the exception.

The fourth common element concerns the appearance of a "great spiritual teacher" prior to the end of this century. Each prophecy refers to this teacher in terms of its own cultural references. The Buddha called him Maitreya, a great teacher who would turn the Wheel Dharma and revitalize its truth teachings. Nostradamus tells of the rise of a spiritual teacher from the East, who will be responsible for the birth of a new religious consciousness. The Maya prophecies speak of the return of Kulkulcan, commonly known as Quetzalcoatl, the great god who established the current age of the Fifth Sun. Quetzalcoatl, portrayed in Mayan legend as a bearded white man, promised to return to his people at the end of this age. Upon his return "from the East," he will institute spiritual teachings throughout the land and bring about the establishment of the new order of the Sixth World. The Hopi prophecies tell of the return of the "True White Brother" who, along with two helpers, will bring stone tablets matching those given to the Hopi clans at the beginning of the Fourth World. His return will be marked by the shaking of the earth with both hands. Those who have remained true to the ancient teachings will survive this event and go on to populate the new earth, and live in harmony according to the laws of the Great Spirit. The biblical prophecies and the Edgar Cayce readings, steeped in the Judeo-Christian tradition, identify this teacher with the return of the Elder Brother, Jesus of Nazareth, popularly known as the "second coming."

Interpretations of the Second Coming

There are two main schools of thought regarding the second coming of Jesus Christ—literal (fundamentalist) and symbolic (metaphysical). Fundamentalist interpreters of scripture maintain that the "second coming" refers to the physical return of Jesus, in bodily form. They interpret biblical references to mean that Jesus of Nazareth will return in the same manner in which He left the earth plane and ascended into heaven, pointing out that in the Sermon on the Mount, Jesus Himself spoke of His return in this manner. "For as the lightning cometh out of the east, and shineth even unto the west; so shall also the coming of the Son of man be . . . And then shall appear the sign of the Son of man in heaven: and then shall all the tribes of the earth mourn, and they shall see the Son of man coming in the clouds of heaven with power and great glory." (Matthew 24:27 and 30) Following Jesus' Ascension, during which He was enveloped by a cloud, the disciples were told by two angels that "This same Jesus, which is taken up from you into heaven, shall so come in like manner as ye have seen him go into heaven." (Acts 1:11) In Revelation, they point to the allegorical depiction of Christ's return. "And I saw heaven opened, and behold a white horse; and he that sat upon him was called Faithful and True . . . and his name is called The Word of God. And the armies which were in heaven followed him upon white horses . . . " (Revelation 19:11, 13-14)

Fundamentalists point to these passages as evidence that Jesus will return to earth in the same manner as He ascended into heaven from the Mount of Olives, appearing in bodily form, surrounded by light, angels, and much fanfare. It is an event that will be witnessed simultaneously by all the inhabitants of earth. Upon His re-

turn, He will smite evil, and chain Satan in the bottom-
less pit for a thousand years, during which time Christ
and the faithful will rule the earth.

The metaphysical interpretation looks more to the
symbolic and esoteric meanings behind biblical passages, and views the second coming in terms of a worldwide awakening, in which the Christ Consciousness will
be activated in each soul on the earth plane. Christ will
return in that He will be found in the hearts and minds
of all people, who will seek to manifest their spiritual
selves as He did two thousand years ago.

The Cayce readings seem to lend support to *both* interpretations of Christ's return. The following two readings
certainly seem to indicate that Christ's return will be
physical. "Then again He may come in body to claim His
own."[11] "For He shall come as ye have seen Him go, in the
body He occupied in Galilee. The body that He formed,
that was crucified on the cross, that rose from the tomb,
that walked by the sea, that appeared to Simon, that appeared to Philip, that appeared to 'I, even John.' "[12]

Yet a section of this reading recognizes a very important fact which often tends to be overlooked—Christ's
body is different than the normal human body. This is a
body whose vibrational rate has been altered, a body
that completely conquered the physical laws of the flesh,
even overcoming death itself, and was resurrected as a
new, spiritualized body which Jesus could materialize
at will, as evidenced by His sudden appearances to
the disciples, particularly His sudden entrance into
the "upper room" through locked doors. The complete
spiritualization of Jesus' body was the reason He was
not initially recognized by His followers, and also the
reason He seemed to glow with a bright light for a short
time after He appeared. So although Christ may return
"in the body," this body may be very different from the

physical bodies humans now possess.

Other readings, including different sections of those cited above, indicate that the second coming will be the awakening of the Christ Consciousness on the part of individuals. "Hence not in a body in the earth, but may come at will to him who *wills* to be one with, and acts in love to make same possible."[13] ". . . for He will walk and talk with men of every clime, and those that are faithful and just in their reckoning shall be caught up with Him to rule and to do *judgment* for a thousand years!"[14] "As given, for a thousand years He will walk and talk with men of every clime. Then in groups, in masses, and then they shall reign of the first resurrection for a thousand years; for this will be when the changes materially come."[15] ". . . ye find them gathering in a body to *listen* to that as may be given them by one who is to be a forerunner of that influence in the earth known as the Christ Consciousness, the coming of that force or power into the earth that has been spoken of through the ages."[16] Note that this reading also mentions the appearance of a "forerunner" who will appear before the manifestation of the Christ Consciousness, just as John the Baptist appeared as the forerunner of Jesus Christ. From these readings it can be inferred that the second coming will be more of a spiritual awakening which begins on an individual scale, gradually growing in proportion until critical mass is reached, and the human species embraces the spiritual paradigms of unity as a part of human consciousness.

Despite their differences, it is possible to see that these two interpretations are not mutually exclusive. It's quite possible that as the soul is brought to consciousness awareness and memory of First Cause is awakened, we will be able to see and recognize the Christ soul much in the same manner that the disciples did during those forty days following the resurrection. Perhaps this ability coincides with the emergence of the new sensory abilities of the fully integrated human. As humans develop their nonphysical senses and become capable of perceiving different dimensions of reality, we will be able to perceive the world of spirit, and will no doubt come to understand that the Christ spirit has always been, and always will be, walking at our side.

Further, both interpretations agree that the revelation of Jesus as the Christ will be made apparent to individuals everywhere on earth, whether this is accomplished by His physical return in a globally televised event, or whether "He comes again in the hearts and souls and minds of those that seek to know His ways,"[17] as memory of the First Cause is awakened on a global scale. The second coming will thus herald the beginning of a new era in which the spiritual attributes of the soul, as manifested in the pattern set by Jesus of Nazareth, will be the guiding force for all human behavior. Finally, both agree that no one knows the exact hour, day, or time when this will occur, although certain signs given by God indicate that this day is rapidly approaching.

The Days of Darkness. There is one element of the biblical second coming which is particularly significant because it is also found in other prophecies as well. This is the belief that the second coming, whether of Christ or another great teacher, will be preceded by a darkening of the sun and moon followed by several days of darkness. These "days of darkness," often numbered at three, are mentioned in both Hopi and Mayan legends, and are described in great detail by Nostradamus and in the Cayce readings. The prophecies agree that, whatever the cause, the days of darkness will be a worldwide event which will catch the attention of every human being on the planet. Many believe that it will be the final chance for people everywhere to abandon their old ways of hatred and division and embrace instead the fruits of the spirit. Those who have already made the choice of spirit over self will understand what is happening, and through prayer and meditation, know what to do to survive. Those who refuse to change and again reject the spiritual path, will be overcome with fear and horror, and may not survive the events at hand. Yet whichever choice is made, each person upon the planet will understand that the hand of the divine is at work in this phenomenon. This realization will affect all of humanity, and may perhaps be the pivot point which initiates the principle of critical mass in terms of the cognitive shift in consciousness which has already begun within the human species.

The UFO Question

No discussion of the predictions surrounding the end of this millennium would be complete without consideration of an issue which has recently captured a great deal of attention, namely, the issue of alien life forms and the role they may or may not play in coming events.

The possibility of life on other planets has been a long-standing topic of fascination among humans. Once science revealed the true nature of the universe, it was only natural to look at the stars above and wonder if other life might exist outside this planet. The vastness of the universe has caused many a scientist to admit that although there is no proof as yet, probability indicates that life must exist in other solar systems besides ours.

The past fifty years has shown an increasing number of UFO sightings and reports of alien abductions. The media has no doubt played a significant role in raising awareness of the possibility of alien life, as it introduced us to "friendly" aliens such as the lovable E.T., the noble Chewbaca and valiant Ewoks of *Star Wars*, as well as a more menacing variety of alien life as portrayed in the movie *Predator*. For the past thirty years, four *Star Trek* television series have brought imaginary aliens into our living room, making Vulcans, Klingons, Ferengi, Bajorans, and even the mysterious "Q" common household words. The recent popularity of the television show *The X-Files* is not only proof of our fascination with the idea of aliens among us, but demonstrates that many people sub-scribe to the theory that the government has long been aware of an alien presence, and has gone to great lengths to hide this fact from the public.

UFO sightings are being recorded in many countries in record numbers, including a spectacular mass sight-ing in Mexico City in the summer of 1995. Thousands of people reported seeing dozens of UFOs freely roaming across the noonday sky. This phenomenon was captured on camera by several television film crews and newspa-per photographers. These films and photos were tele-vised throughout Mexico, and the story was picked up by international wire services around the world. For some reason, though, the American press chose to ig-nore this story, and was the only national media service not to broadcast coverage of this unusual event.

Reports of alien abductions have come from dozens of people from all walks of life, and yet tell of similar experiences. Hypnosis has revealed that these people believe that what they remember is true. Astronauts and pilots have reported unexplainable incidents and some have even reported sighting the presence of unidentified space craft. Such reports are too numerous to be ignored or dismissed as the hallucinatory ramblings of a few. They are evidence that "something" is going on out there.

Aliens and the Prophetic Literature. What is most revealing about the prophetic literature is its *lack of direct references* to alien beings or activities at this time in history, although possible accounts of UFO phenomena can be found in the writings of various cultures. For example, the Old Testament prophet Ezekiel's vision of creatures with wings, and the wheels which accompanied them, has often been taken to be a description of a "flying saucer" type of vehicle. Ezekiel describes "wheels within wheels," which shown like chrysolite, burned with fire, and made the sound of thunder when they rose above the earth (Ezekiel Chapter One). Certain Mayan glyphs and Hopi drawings have been interpreted as depicting alien life forms.

There are also indirect references in the prophetic literature which some people have interpreted as alluding to the fact that aliens will play a role in upcoming events. One such reference comes from a Cayce reading which addresses earth changes which will occur during the period 1958 to 1998. "And these will begin in those periods in '58 to '98, when these will be proclaimed as the periods when His light will be seen again in the clouds."[18] The reference to lights in the clouds has been interpreted by some to mean the UFO sightings occurring during this period. Some people maintain that the Mayan Kukulcan and the Hopi True White Brother are actually references to alien beings who visited these civilizations in past generations.

The lack of any specific reference to aliens, however, reveals far more than scattered passages which *might* indicate an alien presence. The prophecies are so specific and detailed on all other issues, that it could very easily be argued that the lack of such references means that aliens will play a minimal role, if any, in the events described.

The general consensus today among students of prophetic literature and metaphysical studies is that aliens do exist, have most likely visited ancient civilizations, and continue to visit this planet both now and in the future. The numerous UFO sightings and reports of alien contact are too abundant to dismiss or ignore. But the majority opinion is that those alien beings who are here at this time are primarily here as *observers*, who will not interfere in the events which are about to occur. It's further acknowledged that not all aliens are the same, nor are their motivations. The consensus is that there are three general categories into which the alien visitors fall—the wise, the curious, and the opportunistic.

The "wise ones" are not only more technologically advanced, but are more spiritually aware, being fully conscious of their relationship to the Creative Force. They are here to help humankind pass through this time of trial and testing, but they are wise enough to know that they cannot interfere in our development or choices. They have come to offer support and guidance primarily through the medium of prayer. The curious include those alien species who have come here to observe the events which are unfolding. They are aware that the inhabitants of this planet have a unique opportunity to take a giant step closer to unity with the spiritual source and they are curious as to how this will come about. They are benign for the most part, and bear us no ill will. They are simply here to learn. The opportunists, however, though more technologically advanced, do not possess the level of spiritual awareness that humans have attained. They have heard about the events occurring on this planet and have come to see how they might profit. Some are also intent upon studying the human species to learn more about its capability for emotion, particularly love, compassion, and empathy, emotions which they lack and do not understand. It is possible that this group is primarily responsible for the so-called negative abduction experiences.

So, while there may be aliens among us, they are here primarily to support and observe, and not to determine the path humanity will take. While there may be isolated incidents of alien intervention during the coming years, these will be the exception rather than the rule. The majority of them understand and honor the tenet of non-interference. The few who do not, and misguidedly interfere in human affairs, will, like any other beings, suffer the consequences of their actions.

The Tapestry of Prophecy

The richness of the imagery woven throughout the prophetic literature described in this chapter is extraordinary to say the least. The intricate weave of warp and woof told by each prophecy becomes all the more amazing when the parallels between tales are known. The words may be different, and the concepts depicted within diverse cultural milieu, but the ideas expressed are very much the same.

Reaction to the prophecies is as varied as the imagery itself. Some people totally reject these prophecies as being nothing more than fantasy, the product of foolish imagination. They continue to live out their lives as they always have, trying to "get ahead," investing in stocks and bonds, and worrying about the net worth of their portfolios. Others ignore them, choosing to believe that they will simply not occur. They so fear the prophecies that they feign disbelief. The fear, however, remains, and becomes the source of constant inner turmoil. Some people are so overcome with fear that they become paralyzed by the thought of the death and destruction the changes may bring. They see the situation as hopeless, and resign themselves to a situation they believe is futile. Other groups embrace these prophecies with a passion, believing that their acceptance of the prophecies somehow makes them "special," and more deserving of salvation than those who do not believe. Some groups are fervently preparing for the events to come by stockpiling food, water, and weapons, planning to retreat to a self-sufficient "fortress" when the cataclysms begin. Still others accept only certain predictions, such as the biblical prophecies, while rejecting the others, and plan to face the changes armed with the strong conviction that they are numbered with the righteous, and will therefore be saved.

The majority of people, however, view the prophecies with a sense of curiosity and concern. They understand the significance of the many parallels contained in such diverse sources of information, and consider the convergence of each prophetic time line as more than a coincidence. They also realize that many of the prophecies given have already come true, and marvel at the descriptions of trains, planes, and automobiles given in the Hopi prophecies, and the uncanny accuracy of Nostradamus' predictions.

It's certainly true that the cataclysms described in these prophecies have the potential to bring about great death and destruction. Too many people, however, focus only on the destructive aspects of the prophecies, and overlook the fact that no prophecy speaks of the destruction of humankind. Rather, they propose that the changes humankind will experience are the birth pains of a new epoch, a necessary part of our evolution which has the potential to provide opportunities for growth, learning, and the advancement of all humanity. It's possible that by forcing us to rely on our spiritual source, as well as one another, these changes may indeed provide the impetus necessary to leave behind the remaining vestiges of the old hatreds and biases so that we may move into a new era of human development characterized by the spiritual principle of unity.

Humanity did not come by the prophecies by accident or chance; they were given to us for a reason. They stand before us like a great multicolored tapestry, threads woven in and out, twisting, blending, braiding, unraveling. The tapestry shows us a picture of our future, but the tapestry itself is not that future, because the weaving of the tapestry is not yet complete. The design is set, but there are still threads yet to be stitched. It's up to us to stitch those threads and complete the design. Therefore, let us study the tapestry so that we might better understand the pattern with which it was woven, and the message it carries within.

From the sleep of a million starless dreams, the pulse of the planet quickens.

Restless, and deep within its being, a vision from the mists of consciousness awakes.

Through myth and symbol, an externalizing force uncoils as yawning synapses gently spark silent pre-dawn currents of new birth.

—Moira Timms,
Beyond Prophecies and Predictions

9

Understanding the Nature of Prophecy

Time present and time past
Are both perhaps present in time future,
And time future contained in time past.
                    —T.S. Elliot, *Four Quarters*

Evaluating Predictions of Change

WITH THE foregoing overview of some of the world's most important prophetic literature, we shall now see if it is possible to determine how and when the predicted events will occur. To aid in this process, there are four criteria against which the prophecies can be evaluated. First, are such predictions possible? Is there any evidence to indicate that the sort of changes described in the prophecies have occurred in the past? Second, is it possible to define a time line as to when predicted events will occur? Can prophecy be correlated with linear time? Third, does the prediction of these events mean that they must occur? Can prophecy be changed? Finally, are there any signs that the changes foretold in the prophecies may have already begun?

The prophecies regarding social, political, and economic change are certainly possible. Social change is an accepted fact, as human history traces the pattern of change from one civilization to the next. The changing winds of political fortune, the rise and fall of civilizations, and the adoption and abandonment of various economic systems are well documented. In addition, the idea of a new era characterized by cooperation, peace, and understanding, is an idea which would appeal to nearly everyone.

The idea of drastic, geophysical change, however, is much more difficult to accept because such cataclysmic upheavals would mean death and destruction, which no sane person would welcome. Further, until recently, the idea of cataclysmic events as shaping forces of history was thought to be untenable. This was mainly the result of a scientific controversy in the late nineteenth century which centered around two opposing theories of geologic change—catastrophism and uniformitarianism.

Catastrophism, championed by French naturalist Baron Georges Cuvier, proposed that the extinction of species was often caused by catastrophic events such as global flooding or volcanic eruptions. Although initially embraced, this theory was short-lived as geologists began to comprehend the true longevity of geological time. A gradualist view of geological history, called uniformitarianism, championed by James Hutton and Sir Charles Lyell, grew in favor. Uniformitarianism proposed that mountain ranges, land masses, and oceans were formed as a result of long-acting geological processes over great periods of time. Uniformitarianism gained nearly complete acceptance within the scientific community, and the idea of sudden, massive earth changes was discredited. Recently, however, evidence of "mass" extinctions in the fossil record has caused paleogeologists to take a second look at the idea of catastrophism.

Evidence of Cataclysmic Change

Modern research has demonstrated that the earth has a dynamic rather than static character. Studies on sea-floor spreading have combined with paleomagnetic studies to produce the theory of plate tectonics. This widely accepted theory proposes that there are moving plates in the earth's crust which are formed by volcanic activity at the oceanic ridges and destroyed in great sea-floor trenches located at the margins of the continents. The movement of these plates due to various pressures within the earth's core and mantle are responsible for volcanic activity and earthquakes.

Although most species extinctions can be explained through the natural process of competition within the environment, it has been proposed that several mass extinctions which saw the worldwide disappearance of numerous species, were more likely the result of sudden, geophysical changes on a global level. At the heart of this relatively new direction in thought is evidence that the mass extinction of the dinosaurs, along with the extinction of over 50 percent of marine invertebrates, which occurred about 65 million years ago in the late Cretaceous Period, was caused by a catastrophic event which may even have been of extraterrestrial origin!

Geochemical studies of the Cretaceous-Tertiary stratigraphic boundary in many parts of the world revealed a higher than normal iridium content than other crustal material, a level which resembles that found in meteorites. Based on this evidence, scientists Luis and Walter Alvares have theorized that the earth was hit by an asteroid or comet at the end of the Cretaceous Period. This "extraterrestrial visitor" was of a sufficient magnitude to have created enough dust in the atmosphere to have reduced solar radiation for months or years, dropped worldwide temperatures, and caused the extinction of plant species and temperature-sensitive animal species. The existence of a geological crater on Mexico's Yucatan Peninsula dates to this time and lends credence to the meteor theory. Another theory suggests that the iridium was caused by immense volcanic activity, which would have had a similar effect through the distribution of volcanic dust.

Based on fossil evidence, paleobiologists now recognize five such major extinctions. The first occurred during the Precambrian Period, 650 million years ago, when over 70 percent of all ocean algae became extinct. The second occurred at the end of the Cambrian Period, 500 million years ago, when large numbers of invertebrate marine life disappeared. The end of the Devonian Period, 345 million years ago, marked the worldwide extinction of many families of primitive fish, coral species, and the trilobites. The greatest mass extinction occurred at the end of the Permian Period, 225 million years ago, when more than 90 percent of all marine species disappeared. The dinosaur extinction at the end of the Cretaceous Period, is the fifth mass extinction recorded in the fossil record.

One must keep in mind that such mass extinctions are rare, however, and represent the exception rather than the rule. The normal evolutionary pattern of species development is one of generational, gradual adaptation and change in response to slowly changing environmental conditions. Yet, the fact that such mass extinctions have occurred does lend support to the theory that at times, catastrophic, worldwide changes such as those

noted in the prophecies have occurred and could therefore occur again.

The Evidence for Polar Wandering

In addition to geophysical upheavals such as earthquakes and volcanic activity, many of the prophecies
speak of cataclysmic change in terms of a pole shift. The
Hopi view this as the time the Great Spirit will "shake the
earth." The Mayan prophecies refer to it as a movement
shift, or the "turning of the Great Turtle." Nostradamus
calls it a "great movement of the Globe, when gravity itself will seem suspended." The Cayce readings, however,
use the modern terminology of "pole shift."

Today, science has verified the existence of such a
phenomenon, which it calls cyclic polar motion or polar
wandering. Science further recognizes two types of polar wandering—a change in position of the geomagnetic
poles of the earth and a change in the geographic poles
themselves.

According to British physicists W.M. Elasser and Sir
Edward Bullard, the earth's main geomagnetic field is
primarily created by the action of currents flowing inside its outer core and the conversion of this mechanical
energy into electromagnetic energy. A small percentage
of the geomagnetic field is caused by electrical current
moving within the earth's ionosphere, approximately
sixty miles above the surface. This "dynamo theory"
maintains that the geomagnetic field is maintained by
the self-sustaining dynamo action of the core which
flows in such a pattern that the electric current induced
by its motion through the magnetic field, sustains that
field. The movement of the core is induced by fluctua-
tions in tidal energy or heat.

Paleomagnetic research suggests that the convective

movement of fluid rock, principally iron, in the earth's outer core has resulted in irregular changes in the earth's geomagnetic field. Studies have shown that the intensity of the geomagnetic field itself has been decreasing by 6 percent every 100 years. In addition to the decreasing strength of the field, its regional positive and negative anomalies (poles) are also changing, drifting an average of 0.2 degrees west per year. The north geomagnetic pole has shifted 480 times to the northwest between 1933 and 1984, while the south geomagnetic pole is rapidly moving toward the Indian Ocean. One possible reason for these variations may be the changes in the earth's axial spin which is causing the rate of rotation to slow and the rotational axis to wobble. This wobble has been observed and measured since 1900, and appears to be correlated with periods of peak earthquake activity registering more than 7.5 on the Richter scale. It is unclear, however, whether this wobble is the cause or the result of the earthquakes. Another theory proposes that the geomagnetic field is affected by ionized particles generated by the solar wind.

Research has also revealed that there have been massive geomagnetic polar shifts as well as complete reversals of the geomagnetic field's polar distribution pattern. Charles Hapgood, Professor of Science at Keene College in New Hampshire, has theorized that three major pole shifts have occurred within the past one hundred thousand years. He suggests that the northern magnetic pole shifted from the Yukon to the Greenland Sea 82,000 B.P., and from there to Hudson Bay approximately 52,000 B.P. The last major pole shift occurred shortly before 12,000 B.P. when the pole shifted near to its present-day position. It is interesting to note that the date of 52,000 B.P. corresponds to a possible date given in the Cayce readings for the first destructive upheavals in Atlantis, while

the date of 12,000 B.P. corresponds to the continent's final destruction.

Scientists are also speculating that the most recent
pole reversals may have been caused by external factors
such as the passing of a comet or meteor through this
solar system. Such a cosmic body would definitely affect
the geomagnetism of the earth and could possibly in-
duce a pole reversal. It would also account for the
meteorite and tektite showers that appear to have accompanied some pole reversals.

Evidence regarding the shifting of the geographic or
rotational poles is less clear than that of magnetic pole
shifting. A geographic pole shift occurs when the earth's
crust slides over the magnetic core, causing a displace-
ment of land and oceans. Geographic pole shifts, therefore, would have far more devastating effects than the
shift of the geomagnetic field. Although there is some
evidence that such shifts have occurred, opinion is divided as to whether they occur simultaneously or independently from magnetic shifting.

The scientific evidence today thus makes it clear that
not only is cataclysmic change possible, but that pole
shifts can also occur. While isolated earthquakes and
volcanic activity may occur by themselves, it is almost
certain that a massive polar shift, particularly of the geographic poles, would be accompanied by a flurry of
earthquake and possibly volcanic activity. Like the inevi-
tability of social change, the cataclysmic events described in the prophetic literature are indeed viable
possibilities.

The Great Pyramid of Gizeh–
Chronogram of Human History

If we acknowledge that the events described in the

prophetic literature are possible, the next step is to explore the possibility of linking the sequence in which they will occur to a definite time line. Since many of the prophecies are cryptic, and references to dates absent or obscure, this might seem to be an impossible task. Yet this task was already accomplished for us by the builders of the Great Pyramid of Gizeh, who designed that monument to be more than a tribute to a pharaoh. The Great Pyramid was actually constructed to be a standing chronogram of human history.

According to the Cayce readings, construction on the Great Pyramid began in 10,490 B.C., and lasted one hundred years. Furthermore, the readings say that it was engineered by Atlanteans, the chief architect being Hermes, who was aided by a High Priest named Ra Ta. This, of course, runs contrary to traditional archeology which dates the Pyramid at 2,575 B.C. and contends that it was built as a tomb for the Pharaoh Khufu, or Cheops.

Recent support for the theory of the Great Pyramid being older than previously suspected comes from the work of Robert Bauval, a construction engineer who has spent over ten years studying both the pyramids and the *Pyramid Texts*, a collection of ancient Egyptian writings well-known to Egyptologists. His research mathematically correlates the location, orientation, and construction of the Gizeh pyramids to various star configurations, namely Orion, as they would have appeared in the sky in the year 10,500 B.C.! Further, he challenges the idea that the pyramids were used as tombs, pointing out that no mummies have ever been found in them. While Bauval's work is controversial, the soundness of his methods are causing many in the scientific world to take notice as evidenced by the following statement. "I am very much in agreement with your contention that the stars in Orion's Belt were an important element in the orientation of the Great Pyramid. I think you have made a very convincing case . . ." (I. H. S. Edwards, Keeper of Egyptian Antiquities, British Museum, 1954-1974.[1])

Rather than debate the age and purpose of the pyramids, it will prove helpful for our purposes to accept the information given in the Cayce readings as being correct. The readings go on to say that the Great Pyramid was built to be a lasting record of man's experiences of the current "root race," as well as a place of initiation where truth seekers could learn the ancient wisdom and knowledge recorded there. Both John the Baptist and Jesus of Nazareth, say the readings, underwent instruction in the pyramid prior to beginning their ministries. "In this same pyramid did the Great Initiate, the Master, take those last of the Brotherhood degrees with John, the forerunner of Him, at that place."[2] The readings go on to say that construction of the pyramid was designed to reflect events of human history "as related to the religious or the spiritual experiences of man."[3] Further, "the rise and fall of the nations were to be depicted in this same temple."[4]

The Great Pyramid remains a mystery of mathematical precision in both placement—latitude, longitude, and astronomical alignment—and design, which incorporates the relationship of pi and other mathematical concepts. Its accuracy continues to astound scientists today. Support for the theory of the Great Pyramid as a chronogram was found in research which revealed the significance of the "pyramid inch."[5] The geometric circle upon which the design of the pyramid is based equals 365.242 pyramid inches, which corresponds to the exact number of days in the solar year. By squaring the circle, the sum of the base's diagonals calculates to 25,826.53 pyramid inches, equivalent to the number of years in the precession of the equinoxes. The fact that the pyramid inch appears in different areas of the structure further emphasizes its significance to its builders.

In 1925, David Davidson, a structural engineer, conducted a twenty-four-year study of the pyramid's mathematical proportions, geometry, and astronomical alignment. He confirmed that a six-thousand-year time line, 3999 B.C. to 2001 A.D., is reflected in the structure of the pyramid. Further, factors such as the type of stone used, color and layering, and directional turns of passages, were found to enhance the timeline. During one particular reading, Cayce was asked to comment on the accuracy of Davidson's interpretations. This is the response he gave: "Many of these that have been taken as deductions are correct. Many are far overdrawn. Only an initiate may understand."[6]

What follows is a descriptive journey through the chambers of the Great Pyramid, as interpreted through the readings, and supported by Davidson's and Bauval's research. Cayce corrected two of Davidson's original dates for the King's Chamber and Chamber of Chaos from 1936-1953 to 1938-1958, and these are the dates given below. (Please refer to Figure 4, *The Great Pyramid of Gizeh.*)

The Descending Passage. Upon entering the Great Pyramid, you find yourself in the Descending Chamber, one of two main passageways within. Its beginning is marked by a scored line which represents the date of 2141 B.C. During the vernal equinox of that year the pole star of the Orion constellation last aligned with the pyramid's entrance, and shone down the Descending Chamber. By measuring backwards to the entrance itself, we calculate the date of 2623 B.C., the year of Pharaoh Khufu's death. The significance of this date is that it represents the time in which the meaningful teachings of the Great Pyramid were "rediscovered" and under-

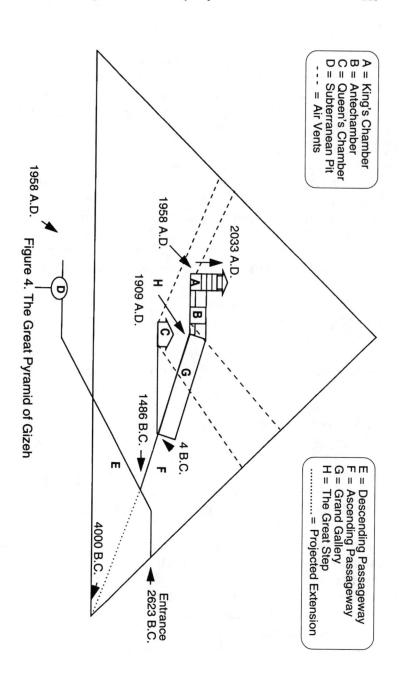

A = King's Chamber
B = Antechamber
C = Queen's Chamber
D = Subterranean Pit
- - - = Air Vents

E = Descending Passageway
F = Ascending Passageway
G = Grand Gallery
H = The Great Step
.... = Projected Extension

Figure 4. The Great Pyramid of Gizeh

stood by the Egyptian priesthood. With time, the purpose for which the pyramid was built had been forgotten by the generations of Egyptians who followed. It was not until the reign of the Pharaoh Khufu that its meaning was rediscovered and it once again became a center for teaching and initiation.

As you proceed down the Descending Passage you reach a junction where a second passage diverges upward at an angle identical to the slope of the Descending Passage. The corresponding date of this junction would be 1486 B.C., the time of the Exodus when Moses led Israel out of captivity. The Descending Passage continues downward past ground level and eventually ends in the Chamber of Chaos.

The Chamber of Chaos.   The Chamber of Chaos or Upside-Downness is little more than a subterranean pit, with a rocky floor and low ceiling. It has the effect of making a visitor so disoriented that you cannot tell which way is up. At the far end of this chamber is a small tunnel, so low that you can only crawl through it. The uninitiated mistake this tunnel for the way out, but soon find that it dead ends within fifty feet of its beginning. The beginning and ending of this tunnel date at 1938 and 1953 A.D., respectively.

The Descending Passage and the Chamber of Chaos represent the downward spiral of human development, the devolution of spirit into the material world, or the journey from light into darkness. If we had pursued this path, rather than turning upward at the junction mentioned above, we would have remained on the downward spiral, and eventually ended up in a dead end of chaos and destruction. The tunnel dates of 1938-1958 certainly represent a low point in human history as evidenced by Nazism, the Holocaust, World War II, detonation of the atomic bomb, and the arms race. Since the tunnel ends in 1958, it is possible that this path would have led to the destruction of the world in that year, quite possibly by nuclear annihilation. Fortunately, humankind made the right choice at the Exodus junction, and began to move upward along the Ascending Passage.

The Ascending Passage. Although there is no passage downward from the Exodus junction other than the Descending Passage, studies have extended the slope of the Ascending Passage through the junction point and downward to the outside face of the pyramid, which reflects a date of 4000 B.C. According to biblical genealogy, this date represents the creation of Adam and Eve.

When the Ascending Passage was first entered in modern times, they had to dig around a twenty-nine foot granite plug, which blocked the entryway. The first section of the Ascending Passage is called the Hall of Truth in Darkness, or, Israel under the "Yoke of the Law." It is the time when humanity considered obedience to the law as the means of finding salvation. Its starting point of 1486 B.C. represents the Exodus and symbolizes the release of humankind from the captivity of the material world as we choose spiritual freedom over material comfort and began the long journey to the Promised Land. The Hall of Truth in Darkness ends at the date of 4 B.C., the birth of Jesus of Nazareth. At this point the Ascending Passage continues upward into the Grand Gallery, while a secondary, horizontal passage leads to the Queen's Chamber.

The Queen's Chamber. This chamber is also called the Chamber of Second or New Birth. The downward step from the horizontal passage leading to this chamber represents the symbolic death of self and rebirth into the afterlife. This was the place of judgment, where the heart of the deceased or initiate was weighed against the feather of truth on the scales of judgment. The Queen's

Chamber ends in the year 1918, a date marking the signing of the Armistice which ended World War I, and the
beginning of the League of Nations. Although this political body folded, the principles for which it stood represented spiritual truth, and its very proposal marks a high
point in human history. The readings even indicate that
the Christ Spirit was present at the peace table with
Woodrow Wilson, who fought against heavy odds to establish this visionary body. " . . . He sat at the peace conference in Geneva, in the heart and soul of a man not
reckoned by many as an even unusually Godly man; yet
raised for a purpose, and he chose rather to be a channel
of His thought for the world."[7]

The return from the Queen's Chamber to the Ascending Passage is called the Path of the Coming Forth of the
Regenerated Soul, and symbolizes the spiritual rebirth
of the soul.

The Grand Gallery.   The first section of the Ascending Passage now expands in height and width into the
Grand Gallery, or the Hall of Truth in Light. The beginning point of this gallery, 4 B.C., is the year in which Jesus
of Nazareth was born, and the expansion in size is
thought to symbolize the expansion in consciousness
brought about by His teachings. The Elder Brother, the
Wayshower, had overcome the flesh, and by overcoming
death itself proved the reality of our spiritual being. The
law was thus fulfilled, and humankind could now walk
in "Truth in Light," understanding that salvation came
not from obedience to the law, but the overcoming of it.
On one side of the gallery marks the year 30 A.D. This is
the date of the Crucifixion and the Resurrection. The
other side of the Gallery indicates the year 1776, the year
of the American Revolution when our forefathers made
a written pact with God, guaranteeing "life, liberty and
the pursuit of happiness" for all. The Gallery ends at the

date 1914 A.D., just prior to World War I. Immediately outside the Grand Gallery is the Great Step, a thirty-five inch step that must be straddled or climbed.

The Great Step. The Great Step marks the date 1909 A.D., just prior to the start of World War I. It is also the point at which the measure of the time line changes as the scale of the pyramid inch now comes to represent one month rather than one year. It would seem that at this point the Great Pyramid is telling us that time has been accelerated. It is quite possible that this step represents the beginnings of the "times and halftimes," as mentioned in the Bible and the Cayce readings, when God speeds up the passing of time so that humankind might survive the horrors which will soon be unleashed. This idea is supported by a reading given by Cayce in 1933 which stated that the time and half times "has been and is being fulfilled."[8] The Great Step leads to the "first low passage" of the Antechamber.

The Antechamber. The first low passage of the Antechamber is so low that you must crawl through it. It marks the dates from 1914 to 1918, a low point in human history identified with World War I. The Antechamber itself represents a ten-year period, 1918-1928, the signing of the World War I Armistice and the beginning of the Great Depression, respectively. It is also called the Chamber of the Triple Veil, due to the triple sectioning of its granite walls. The limestone floor blocks previously encountered have given way to granite. Within the Antechamber stands a large stone slab known as the Granite Leaf, the center of which marks the end point of the geometrically projected line of the slope of the Ascending Chamber which begins at the outer edge of the pyramid, referred to above. The line's end point at the Granite Leaf's center is calculated to be September 17, 2001 A.D. A "second low passage" which leads out of the Ante-

chamber covers the years 1928 to 1938, a period characterized by the loss of spiritual values. This passage ends
at the entrance to the King's Chamber.

The King's Chamber.   The King's Chamber, or Chamber of the Open Tomb, is the final chamber within the
Great Pyramid. The entrance to this chamber dates at
1938 while the ending wall dates at 1958. These dates
coincide with the dates in the tunnel of the Chamber of
Chaos, reflecting the principle "as above, so below."
While Davidson ended the time line there, the readings
state that it actually continues up the far wall of the
chamber.

There are seven stones which rise above the King's
Chamber, which resemble the shape of a Japanese pagoda, five stones with intervening spaces forming the
pillar, and two stones angled to form a pointed apex. The
five lower stones are made of red granite while the upper
two are made of grey limestone. The intervening spaces
of this chamber are covered with quarry hieroglyphics,
one of which is believed to be the cartouche of Pharaoh
Khufu, and the reason that the pyramid is thought to be
his tomb.[9] Following the ground level date of 1958 upward, the timeline extends upward to the apex of the
pagoda which dates at 2033 A.D.

When the King's Chamber was opened, archeologists
found that it contained an empty sarcophagus made of
red granite. According to the readings, the purpose of the
empty sarcophagus was to make clear the interpretation
of death, meaning that although the physical body died,
the soul was eternal. This chamber was the place of the
final initiation, where initiates would come to experience this truth. An initiate was said to spend three days
in the sarcophagus in deep meditation, during which
time the soul left the body to travel in spiritual realms.
Upon the soul's return, the initiate understood that the

divine nature of the soul was the true self, and mastered the knowledge and powers of the soul's divine heritage. *Interpreting the Chronogram.* Although the readings indicate that the Great Pyramid time line is so specific as to indicate the year, day, hour, place, and individuals of various events, we have not yet learned to read these signs. As far as we can discern, the pyramid does not reveal specifics of future events, but rather outlines general trends and inclinations in the spiritual development of humankind. Important dates throughout human history are recorded in the Pyramid's architectural attributes such as the entrance and egress through passages, the front and back walls of chambers, the upward and downward slopes at junction points, the widening or narrowing of passages, the height of stones overhead, and the color and texture of the stones themselves. The two main passageways represent the two roads between which humankind was free to choose. The Descending Passage of materialism led downward into darkness and chaos, ending with the destruction of the world in 1958 A.D. The Ascending Passage of spirituality led upward into the light and truth, and leads to the final overcoming of death.

While the accuracy of the pyramid's time line is fascinating, of more interest are future dates as they are represented within the King's Chamber. We know that we have entered the King's Chamber and are now progressing up the stone formation on its far wall. Author Kirk Nelson makes an excellent case that the seven stones which rise above the King's Chamber represent the seven chakras, the five red (earth) granite stones being the lower chakras and the two grey (brain matter) limestones which form the apex being the pituitary and the pineal glands.[10] Further, based upon the architectural attributes of this wall, there are several years which can be pinpointed as having special significance.

The two-year period 1998-2000 A.D. is depicted by the boundaries of an intervening space between the second and third stones. These years correspond to a time which many prophecies say will be the time of great social change and geophysical upheaval, when the great spiritual teacher will reappear, and the pole shift will commence. The fact that these dates are given a position of prominence in the pyramid's architecture can be taken as evidence that this will be a momentous time in human history.

The most intriguing date, however, occurs not in the King's Chamber, but in the Antechamber, where the date September 17, 2001, is represented at the center of the Granite Leaf. Scholars have been hard pressed to explain the significance of this. The answer, however, may be found in the Egyptian name of the chamber, which translates to the "Chamber of the Triple Veil." Esoterically, a "veil" refers to the loss of spiritual awareness which occurred when the souls devolved into matter. The veil acts as a perceptual filter. While on earth the veil clouds our spiritual perception so that we see only the illusion of three-dimensional physical reality; we forget our spiritual nature and come to think of ourselves as physical rather than spiritual beings. The initiation within the Antechamber taught the initiate to see past the veils of illusion and to understand our spiritual nature and origins.

This veil is also symbolized by the great curtain in the Temple of Jerusalem which separated the inner altar from the outer sanctuary. It was this curtain that ripped at the time of Christ's death on the Cross, because, by overcoming death, He had overcome the final illusion, and demonstrated for all humankind that we were not the physical bodies we inhabit, but spiritual beings.

Considering this, since there are *three* veils represented in this chamber, perhaps there is a correlation to the "three days of darkness," foretold by so many prophecies. Perhaps the date of September 17, 2001, represents the date of this event, following which critical mass of the new cognitive shift will be reached so that the veil of the physical world (so readily represented by the events of 1928-1938) is finally lifted, as memory of the First Cause is brought to full awareness, and human consciousness is changed forever.

The date 2012 A.D. falls at the bottom of the fourth stone, a date which coincides with the end of the Mayan calendar, and the establishment of a new era. I propose that the year 2012 may possibly be the year when the Hall of Records, discussed in the following section, is discovered. I feel this is a more likely date for gaining entry into the records than earlier years such as 1998 or 2000 A.D. which have been proposed elsewhere. I base this upon a reading which states that the opening of the Hall of Records cannot occur until " . . . the *full* [author's emphasis] time has come for the breaking up of much that has been in the nature of selfish motives in the world."[11] I don't think the selfish motives of man will be dissolved by 1998 or even 2000. These years will be a time of great turmoil and fear for many people who will not understand the changes that are occurring. It will not be until after the days of darkness when humankind has a "mass revelation" so that the veils of physical illusion are finally torn down, that humankind as a whole will attain the shift in cognition. Although the days of darkness will initiate this shift in consciousness, it may take some years for it to reach full manifestation. Thus, the year 2012 A.D. may be the culmination of this shift which will set the conditions so that the Hall of Records may be opened.

The year 2020 A.D. depicted at the top of the fourth

stone, could also be a candidate for the year the records are discovered, although I feel that is a little too late in the overall time line. The final date in the Great Pyramid as reckoned by distance, 2033 A.D., located at the apex of the King's Chamber, most likely represents the closing of this age of humankind, when the influences of the Aquarian Age overtake the waning Piscean influences. It is here that the chronogram of this age of man ends, and where humankind will begin a new era in its evolutionary journey.

The Mystery of the Sphinx

No discussion of the Great Pyramid of Gizeh would be complete without mention of its silent companion and guardian, the Sphinx. For thousands of years, the Sphinx has maintained a silent vigil over the Gizeh Plateau, watching and waiting for the time when its secrets would be revealed. Until recently, it was covered up to its neck by sand. The excavation of the Sphinx, however, can be taken as a sign that the time for the revelation of its mysteries is drawing near.

According to the Edgar Cayce readings, a storehouse of records lies beneath the sands of Gizeh. This is the Hall of Records, which contains the history of Atlantis from its earliest beginnings when the soul first took material form, up through its final destruction, as well as the teachings of the Law of One. According to the readings, the Hall of Records will one day be entered from connecting chambers which extend from the Sphinx's right paw. While it has been assumed that this is the forepaw, the readings do not specify this clearly. The readings go on to say that the Hall of Records cannot be opened until there is a preparation by individuals and the "breaking up of much that has been in the nature of selfish

motives in the world."[12] Further, only the three individuals who sealed this chamber will be allowed to open it
once again. "Hept-Supht, El-ka, and Atlan. These will
appear."[13] The Hall of Records "may not be entered without an understanding, for those that were left as guards
may *not* be passed until after a period of their regenera-
tion in the Mount, or the fifth root race begins."[14]

The reference to "the Mount," is taken to be a reference to the Mount of Olives, the location where Jesus
ascended into heaven, and which certain biblical passages indicate will be the site of His return. From this, an
assumption can be drawn that the opening of the
Records will not occur until after an event of some sort
takes place on the Mount of Olives.

Further, the fact that this reading so specifically mentioned these three individuals by their Atlantean names
must hold some special significance. It may be a sign of
some sort, either to them or to those others who will help
in this endeavor. No doubt these three souls will incarnate into the earth plane with this as their main life mission and at some point come to a full understanding of
the task they are to accomplish. They will know when the
time is right, and they will meet again, at the appointed
moment, to undertake the task of reopening the vault
they sealed so many thousands of years ago.

Yet before Hept-Supht, El-ka, and Atlan enter the
vault, they will have to disarm the forces which were set
in place to guard the records, forces which can kill with a
single thought. There may also be other powers at work,
powers which would seek to hinder their efforts, prefer-
ring that humankind never know the light contained in
those chronicles. Fortunately, these three will not be left
alone to accomplish what may prove to be a difficult
undertaking. There will be others nearby who will help
them through prayer and strengthen them with love. If

these three remain true to their purpose, they will overcome all obstacles and accomplish their task. The Elder
Brother, as always, will walk at their side and show them
the way.

An interesting side note concerning these three individuals is the correlation which can be drawn between
them and the "three who will come from the East" spoken of in the Hopi prophecies. For the Hopi prophecies
also speak of three people, one of whom is the True
White Brother, who will travel to the Hopi from the East,
bearing stone tablets similar to those given to the Hopi
clans at the beginning of the Fifth World. Could they perhaps, be the same individuals? Could the stone tablets
of the Hopi prophecies refer to tablets which will be
found in the Hall of Records, tablets which resemble
those already in the Hopi's possession? Could it be that
the accuracy of the Hopi prophecies is due to the fact
that they were handed down to their ancestors by Atlanteans who, according to the readings, made their way to
North America? While this is only a speculative question,
it is an interesting one to ponder, and one to which we
may soon have the answer.

Edgar Cayce reading 5748-6 cited above contains one
of the few references to the term "root race," stating that
the records cannot be entered until the fifth root race
appears. We know from the readings that the present
human body, referred to as the "Adamic body," represents the fourth root race. If you refer back to Table 1,
you will see that the first three root races could correspond to the spirit form, the light body, and the thought
form, respectively. Since the current human species is
the fourth root race, the appearance of the fifth root race
must correspond to some sort of major change within
the human species. It's quite possible that this change
could refer to the biological development of the multi-

sensory perception of the fully integrated human, and the cognitive changes this will bring.

Perhaps one of the future dates in the pyramid time line, such as 2011 or 2020 A.D., represents the culmination of the developments which must first occur before the Hall of Records can be opened. Whatever the exact date will be, the time for this discovery is near at hand. When it occurs, it will no doubt be heralded as the most extraordinary discovery of all time. Not only will the existence of Atlantis be proven, but a record of the entire history of the soul's devolution into matter will be found, as will a written record of the laws of the One God. Humankind will finally know the answers to many of the questions which it has pondered for so long. For now, however, we can only purge the "selfish motives" from our own hearts and wait for others to do the same. Until then, the Sphinx will continue to keep its watchful vigil, and remain the silent sentinel of the Gizeh plain.

The Nineveh Factor:
How Prophecy Can Be Changed

The time line of the Great Pyramid substantiates the belief that many of the events described in the prophetic literature will be happening in the closing years of this century. Given the fact that many of the prophecies deal with destructive events of either natural or man-made causes, the question naturally arises as to whether these predictions must come to pass, or if there is some way they can be altered, or even avoided.

The answer to this question comes from an Old Testament story involving a man called Jonah. God came to Jonah and told him that the city of Nineveh was going to be destroyed in forty days because of the citizens' evil ways. God instructed Jonah to go to the city and warn the people so that they might change and be spared this destruction. Initially Jonah tried to avoid this task by setting sail in a ship going away from Nineveh. The ship met a violent storm at sea, however, and Jonah was cast overboard and swallowed by a whale. Jonah spent three days in the whale's stomach, during which time he had plenty of opportunity for meditation and reflection. Then, the whale disgorged him, and he washed up upon a beach. Realizing that he couldn't escape God's command, Jonah did go to Nineveh and warn the people. Unlike the people of Sodom and Gomorrah, however, the citizens of Nineveh heeded Jonah's words, changed their ways, and averted the predicted destruction. Jonah was actually upset that the city wasn't destroyed, and railed at God that he had been made to look like a fool because the prophecy didn't come true. God reminded him that it was *because of his warning* that the people changed their attitudes and behavior, thus *altering the state or condition of things* upon which the prophecy was based. By changing the conditions, they changed the prophecy.

The readings clearly support the validity of this idea, which I call the "Nineveh Factor." " . . . there are those conditions that in the activity of individuals, in line of thought and endeavor, keep oft many a city and many a land intact through their application of the spiritual laws in their associations with individuals . . . Tendencies in the hearts and souls of men are such that these upheavals *may* [author's emphasis] be brought about . . . it is not the world, the earth . . . that *rule* man. *Rather* does man—by *his compliance* with divine laws—bring order out of chaos; or, by his *disregard* of the associations and laws of divine influence, bring chaos and *destructive* forces into his experience."[15] Even Nostradamus stated that the purpose of his quatrains was to show all the possible futures open to humanity. Further, the time line of the Great Pyramid clearly shows that humankind has had the choice of different paths.

Prophecy or prediction, therefore, is dependent upon the current thoughts, beliefs, attitudes, and actions of a people which are in effect at the time the prophecy is made. If these remain constant over time, the prediction which is predicated upon their existence will manifest. If any of the conditions upon which the prophecy is based change significantly, the prediction will change as well. A prophecy can thus be postponed in time, so that people might be better prepared to deal with it, modified in some way so that the potential devastation is lessened, altered so that a change manifests in a different manner, or even avoided entirely. The Nineveh Factor is one reason that Jerry Lekstrom, a member of my A.R.E. Study Group, in Massachusetts, is fond of saying that "Prophecy is self-defeating."

Yet if this is true, why have so many prophecies, such as those of Nostradamus, come true? The answer may be that until recently, there has not been a significant enough change in people's attitudes and behaviors to alter the conditions upon which the prophecies were based, and so they did come to pass. As greater numbers of people experience biological and cognitive change, and become aware of the power of creative thought, more people have come to the realization that they *can* make a difference. They understand that if humankind seeks to express the attributes of the spirit, and forsakes the destructive way in which it has treated Mother Earth, then many of the changes spoken of in the prophecies can be altered, modified, and possibly avoided. They now understand that they can change the world by first changing themselves.

There has been significant progress in this regard in this generation. Environmental groups have made sincere efforts to right the wrongs previous generations have inflicted upon the earth. Some groups have spearheaded efforts to repair the environmental damage done to our planet, and to educate others so that such offenses against her and our fellow species are never again perpetrated in the name of progress. Social action groups have committed themselves to bringing about a better understanding among people of differing ethnic origins, religions, races, and creeds. Even governments have issued apologies and made reparations to the descendants of certain groups who were mistreated and wronged in earlier times. Still other groups such as Amnesty International perform a watchdog function, and seek to make inroads in bringing about the fair and humane treatment of all human beings.

The last twenty years has also seen a proliferation of prayer groups which have sprung up around the globe. Prayer groups and healing circles of many denominations have been actively praying for such things as an end to hatred and violence, world peace, the healing of Mother Earth, and a hastening of the spiritual awakening on the part of individuals everywhere. Earth Day, an international celebration held each April, and the Worldwide Day of Prayer for Peace held each New Year, are symbols of this movement which advocates the constructive use of the power of prayer. Not only has there been a great increase in prayer activity, but more importantly, this prayer has not been for self, but for others, and for our world. Since prayer is the most powerful force in the universe, it must surely have had an effect upon the potential futures available to humankind.

Indeed, that is exactly what appears to be happening today. Students of the prophecies are aware that a number of the predictions which were expected to occur in the early 1990s have not yet happened. There is a general consensus, although by no means a unanimous opinion, that this apparent delay is due to the worldwide prayer effort. It is a topic which has generated much discussion during the last several years.

There are several "schools of thought" regarding this issue. At one extreme are those who believe that the predictions must manifest as given. They believe that the time for these events has simply not yet occurred, although they anticipate that they will begin before the end of the century. A spokesperson for this line of thought is found in Gordon-Michael Scallion,[16] whose own psychic predictions show far more devastation than those of Nostradamus or Edgar Cayce. Others, however, have raised a question regarding the accuracy of Scallion's time line. They have suggested that his time line is out-of-synch in that he is perceiving the end result of gradual changes which will occur over the next several centuries, rather than within the next few years. At the other extreme lies a small minority who argue that the cataclysmic upheavals have already been averted because human consciousness has been raised to such a point that an alternate future now lies before us.

A more middle line of thinking, and perhaps the most reasonable, accepts that some of the predictions have been averted or modified, while others must still come to pass. Those that may have been averted include the worldwide drought and famines, and the global nuclear war predicted by Nostradamus. Based upon numbers of their quatrains, the drought and famine were to have begun in 1986 and reached their zenith by the early 1990s. Clearly this has not occurred on the scale indicated in the quatrains. Similarly, the years 1991 and 1993 were considered likely candidates for the start of a global (nuclear) war which has thankfully not happened. Further, predictions of earthshaking events in 1995, as given by certain of the Marian apparitions and a Native American visionary named Sun-Bear, now deceased, have not materialized.

Predictions which may have been modified or postponed include the twenty-seven-year war as described by Nostradamus, the changing face of Europe as described by Cayce, and numerous predictions of earthquakes in the western United States. It is possible that the twenty-seven-year war is manifesting as the war of terrorism rather than as a conventional war, which would have brought much greater destruction. Some people have also pointed to the demise of the Soviet Union and the rise of new, independent countries as fulfilling the reading which stated that Europe would be changed in the twinkling of an eye. Europe was changed, its map radically altered within a matter of days. But the prophecy manifested as a political rather than geophysical change.

Further, devastating earthquakes expected by many to hit the western United States in 1995 have not come to pass. While there have been two major earthquakes in recent years, they were not as severe as expected, particularly in terms of loss of life. It's possible that these quakes were given as warnings to allow people time to prepare or to leave before the major quake hits. They could also be examples of prophecy dealt with mercy. Can you imagine what the death toll might have been if the California quake of May, 1995, had occurred during the rush hour of a workday, rather than the early morning hours of a holiday? And what if the San Francisco quake of October 1989 had hit a few hours later when Candlestick Park was filled with thousands of people? Is it possible that this was the "great theater filled with people (that) will be ruined" by a tremendous earthquake as foretold by Nostradamus? There's no way to know what the structural damage may have been if the stadium had been occupied at full capacity (over 10 million pounds more weight) when the quake hit.

Yet while a number of the prophecies have been modified or altered, the middle line of thought also acknowledges that there are some predictions which must happen simply because humankind must reap the consequences (seeds) of the destruction and disharmony it has already enacted (sown). These include: the sinking of a great portion of Japan into the sea, the rising of land in the Atlantic and the subsequent shift in shoreline in North America and Europe, an increase in volcanic activity worldwide, earthquakes and a possible volcanic explosion in the western United States, and a pole shift around the years 2000-2001 A.D.. Whether or not these particular prophecies occur as predicted remains to be seen. It may still be possible to alter some of these events. The future is, after all, predicated upon the decisions and actions made in the present. Therefore let us use the present as best we can, and continue to act "with principle and vision" to bring about the dawn of the new era as foreseen in the prophecies.

Seeking Signs of Change

As the new millennium approaches, people are beginning to search for signs which indicate that the changes foretold in the prophecies are coming to pass. In terms of geophysical change, there are subtle signs which indicate the earth changes may be upon us. The last twenty years has seen an increasing level of earthquake activity worldwide. Volcanoes, dormant for thousands of years, have erupted with little warning. Weather patterns are changing so quickly that meteorologists can no longer provide accurate forecasts. Torrential rains have occurred, and areas which never before had a problem have been hit with massive flooding. Cold areas have experienced extreme hot temperatures and hot areas have experienced record cold. Snow has fallen in places where none has fallen before. Record high winds have been recorded in many areas and prolonged droughts have happened in once fertile regions. All of these are indications that many of the earth changes have already begun.

It is in the area of social change, however, that we find the greatest evidence of change already in progress. One does not have to be a historian to realize that the nations of the world no longer conduct business as they did even fifty years ago. The century-long trend of the collapse of colonial imperialism and the rise of independent nations culminated with the abolishment of apartheid in South Africa and the collapse of the Soviet Union. Ancient enemies have sat down together at peace tables in an effort to bring about a lasting peace in the Middle East. Today, most nations seek a diplomatic resolution to differences before they resort to armed conflict.

Within our own country, the concept of "Manifest Destiny" which was used as justification to take whatever we wished by force for over two hundred years, no longer holds popular appeal. In contrast, consider our last use of armed force against another nation during Operation Desert Storm. Our government did not act until asked to do so by Kuwait, and then sought the permission and approval of other nations before taking action. Once Kuwait was "liberated," we quickly withdrew our troops and returned home, not wanting to give the appearance of having a permanent presence in the area. Operation Desert Storm was, no doubt, the most polite military action this country has ever waged, and certainly signals the change in attitude apparent within this country. Today, our military personnel are perceived less as "warriors" and more as "peacekeepers," working side by side with the military of other countries which a short time ago were sworn adversaries, and carrying out humanitarian missions rather than armed conflict.

The world has also seen the criteria for dominance change from one of military might to one of economic power. Today world leaders seek to dominate through the world market rather than through conquest. It's the country with the soundest monetary system, be it dollar, yen, or mark, that becomes a world power, not the country with the strongest military force. Alliances today are based not on military coalitions but on economic alliances and trade agreements. Those nations which seek to threaten world security are sanctioned with economic restrictions and embargoes. It is becoming apparent that the lone, rogue nation cannot stand alone, and a country's success depends upon cooperation with other nations.

While some may argue that a world order based on economic competition is little better than a world based on military prowess, it is still evident that humankind is taking a step in the right direction toward the new era as described in the prophecies. As the importance of military might has decreased, the revenue which once went to support the military industrial complex can now be diverted to other areas, and hopefully result in a better standard of living for all. There is still a long way to go before economic competition is replaced by mutual cooperation, but we have certainly taken a major step toward achieving that end. If nations can put down their weapons, and move from their conflicts from the battlefield to the world trade market, perhaps it is not so inconceivable that one day they will reach out to one another in the spirit of mutual cooperation and harmony.

Prophecy as a Tool of Understanding

The prophecies were not given to make us fearful. Rather, they were given to us as tools of understanding, so that we might understand, accept, and prepare for the changes to come. That is why this information has been revealed through so many diverse channels. If we are aware of the transformation which is coming, we can begin to prepare for it, and perhaps even initiate action which will help lessen the severity of the changes when they occur.

Yet what kind of preparations can be made for the types of earthshaking events described in such dire predictions? The answer to this question lies in the prophecies themselves. Although the words used may vary, each prophecy emphatically states that survival depends not upon material resources, but upon attunement to the spiritual source—God—and the manifestation of the spiritual attributes of the soul.

The preparation then, must be spiritual. " . . . not then in the amount of moneys, lands, holdings, houses, cattles, or gold—but in that ability to serve thine brother lies strength, security . . . "[17] "Not in mighty deeds of valor, not in the exaltation of thy knowledge or thy power; but in the gentleness of the things of the spirit."[18]

As we prepare for whatever lies ahead, we must also remember that no one is here by chance; these events are not being arbitrarily imposed upon us but are the result of choices and actions made in times past. Each soul that is present on the earth plane is here because the choice was made to incarnate at this time. Some have come to correct past errors. Others have come to master lessons which can only be learned under these particular circumstances. Still others have returned to help those who will not understand what is going on around them. Each soul has its own reasons for being here, and has chosen to accept the consequences these changes may bring into its experience.

Facing the changes to come may not seem as frightening when we realize that we do not have to face them alone. We can call upon one another and trust in God's promise that He stands ever ready to support and sustain us in times of need. The best preparation we can make, therefore, is in terms of spiritual attunement with the Creative Force. If we do this, we can be assured that when the changes come, we will be where we are meant to be and doing that which we are meant to do, fulfilling the purpose for which we came with love, patience, and understanding. Our survival depends not on physical means, as presumed in times past, but on the acceptance of spiritual truths, the paradigm of the future.

> *He that dwelleth in the secret place of the most High*
> *shall abide under the shadow of the Almighty.*
> *I will say of the Lord, He is my refuge and my fortress:*
> *my God; in him will I trust.*
> *For he shall give his angels charge over thee, to keep*
> *thee in all thy ways.*
>
> —Psalm 91:1-2,11

Author's Postscript

We live in a time of great change, a time of a political and social paradigm shift.
We live in a critical period of human history.
The outcome of our thoughts and actions will determine the fate of life on our planet.
—Carlos Warter, M.D., Ph.D., *Recovery of the Sacred*

THIS BOOK is based upon the idea that as the new millennium approaches, the human species is standing at the threshold of a major transformation during which it will experience a biologic change in sensory perception and a cognitive shift in consciousness. It has also been suggested that as a parallel to the microcosmic evolution occurring within the human species, there will be macrocosmic evolution occurring in the world in the form of social and geophysical change. Further, by accepting the validity of the universal Law of Cause and Effect, the future is seen as being predicated upon the past, with future events being the result of choices and actions previously set in motion. It was therefore proposed that to truly understand the future we must first understand the past. We must first understand who we are and why we came to be, before we can comprehend where we are going.

By adopting an evolutionary perspective, we understand that the changes the new millennium will bring are the result of millions of years of preparation on the physical, mental, and spiritual levels of our being. We come to understand not only how, but why these changes must occur. We begin to see them not as calamity and misfortune, but as opportunities for learning and growth, stepping stones on the upward spiral of the spiritual path which leads us to a closer oneness with the Creative Force.

Lessons We Have Learned

By looking at the past, we learned of the soul's spiritual creation and the purpose for which we were created—to be companions and co-creators with God. We learned of the souls' devolution in consciousness whereby through an error in perception, we came to think of ourselves as separate from God, and began to use our creative abilities for selfish purposes. We also learned of our descent into matter, which was created as a means of escape for us, so that we might comprehend the error we had made. Once again, however, we misused our co-creative powers for self-gratification, and removed ourselves even further from God Consciousness.

Through the creation of the human body, however, humankind was presented with an opportunity to reverse the downward spiral of devolution, and begin its journey back to its original state of oneness with God. By applying the reasoning faculty of the mind in accordance with universal law, humankind slowly began to pull itself out of the earthy mire into which it had descended. Through the faculty of reason, we became self-aware, and began to see ourselves as distinct from our environment. As we developed our mental faculties we began to integrate the second component of ourselves—the mind—into our conscious being. We began to move away from paradigms based on physical sensation and toward paradigms based upon the reasoning faculty of the mind. The world around us became less a mystery and more a puzzle to which we were constantly adding more pieces.

By looking at world culture today, we saw what appears to be a paradox, a place of contrast between great evil and great good. We have learned that this paradox stems from the fact that the present time in human history is a time of testing, when each soul is being given an opportunity to make the ultimate choice between good and evil, the spirit and the material world. Not only is each soul being afforded the opportunity to balance the Law of Cause and Effect, but so are the nations, as each country must meet and answer the karma it has created.

We also learned that throughout history, humankind has continually questioned the why of its being, contemplated its nature and purpose, and pondered its destiny. Even today, with all our technological and scientific advances, we continue to long for something more, something greater than what we discern through our physical senses. This yearning can be attributed to the fact that memory of the First Cause, though repressed, still remains the driving force of our existence, ever reminding us of our true spiritual nature.

We further came to understand that the process of spiritualization is awakening the conscious memory of

the First Cause within the human species today. We
about to integrate the third component of ourselves
the soul—into our conscious being as we come to t
conscious awareness that we are spiritual beings. Th
development, along with the development of new sen
sory abilities, will prove to be a most important step in
our spiritual evolution, for it is the cornerstone upon
which the paradigm shift of the next millennium will be
based. In order to move away from the paradigms of divergence, we must first acknowledge our oneness as
spiritual beings, and understand that earthly differences, which up to now have kept us separate from one
another, do not represent our true spiritual being.

Humankind stands at a crossroads where it may
choose to continue with old behavior patterns based on
ancient hatreds, or move beyond such "divisional"
thinking and manifest instead the fruits of the spirit. As
in the Great Pyramid, one road leads to destruction and
a return to the illusions of the physical world, while the
other leads to the promise of a new future based on the
fully integrated human, where body, mind, and soul
work in unison. The fate of humankind thus lies in the
choice of this generation.

The Destiny of Humankind

It's quite possible that the differences between the
five-sensory human and the multisensory, fully integrated human of the future, may be significant enough
to warrant classification as a new subspecies, similar to,
yet different from present-day *Homo sapiens sapiens.*
This new subspecies may very well coincide with references in the Cayce readings to the appearance of the
"fifth root race," and be the reason so many prophecies
have designated this generation as a time of profound

...lso explain why the Great Pyramid
...a record of our current species' (fourth
...y, ends at the year 2033 A.D. Since the
...d human is capable of "knowing" at the
...of the soul, I propose that one name to
...this new subspecies might be *Homo sapiens*
...m the Latin *intueri*, which refers to the "fac-
...owing without the use of rational processes, or,
...ate cognition," such as that which occurs when
...ul is brought to conscious awareness.

...s important to understand that there may not be
...ificant morphological[1] differences between our-
...ves and *Homo sapiens intueri*. In fact, much of human
...volution in the past half million years has depended
upon changes in brain size, structure, and function,
rather than on gross anatomical differences. Overall
physical differences between ourselves and the Neandertals, and even the later *Homo erectus* specimens, are
minimal. The primary difference may manifest as physiological changes in the brain's internal structure, function, and organization, much in the same way that
similar changes led to the development of language. This
time, however, these changes will lead to the development of new sensory abilities which will facilitate the
integration of the spiritual aspect of the soul.

As body, mind, and soul work in unison, *Homo sapiens intueri* will cease to identify with the three-dimensional world of physical matter and identify instead with
the spiritual landscape of the soul. Such humans will
know that they are spiritual beings, and actively demonstrate their spiritual attributes in their interactions with
one another. Further, we will recognize the power inherent in our being, and rediscover the truth of conscious
evolution. No longer will we see ourselves as victims of
impersonal laws which direct the course of history, but

as active participants in the creative process of life in Hopefully, the hard lessons we have learned during tribulations on earth will have taught us to use our discovered powers wisely.

In terms of social change, *Homo sapiens intueri* will bring about the spiritualization of culture, and establish a new order based on paradigms of unity. All of the idealistic, utopian views of a future world as proposed by the visionaries throughout history could become a reality. All of the energy humans have previously devoted to competition, arguments, disputes, conflict, and war, can be redirected to the positive pursuit of cooperation, service, harmonic accord, and mutual assistance. The possibilities of such a combined effort of all humanity are staggering. Only our imagination will limit our achievements.

Yet more significant than the establishment of a new social order, will be the contribution *Homo sapiens intueri* will make to the progress of our spiritual evolution. By applying a spiritual paradigm to the physical world, these humans will take the first step in righting what the soul failed to do those many eons ago, when it first chose the physical over the spiritual. Through conscious evolution, the soul will have the opportunity to once again manifest its co-creative abilities in harmony with universal law, and master the first lesson necessary to overcome the bonds of the flesh which have held us for so long. We will thus move a little bit closer to taking our rightful place in the celestial heavens as heir and companion of the Creator.

It may take hundreds of generations for the human species to learn the lessons necessary to achieve the complete state of union with the Creative-Force as demonstrated by the man called Jesus of Nazareth, yet achieve it we will. It is our birthright given to us by God,

self.
our
e-
l

...r destiny.

...lications of this reading: " . . . though

...ds, many universes, even much as to

...reater than our own . . . Yet the soul of

...encompasses *all* in this solar system or in

...ce we were created to be companions to

...als encompass not only all that exists within

but all that exists throughout all creation! The

...ennium will present an opportunity for us to

...at destiny. We need only make the choice to put

self in order to do so.

The Light That Dispels the Darkness

Skeptics would say that this vision of the new millennium is an idea which will never come to fruition. Humankind, they argue, is too riddled with prejudice and self-interest to ever attain a "utopian" world based on spiritual principles. The integration of body, mind, and soul is an impossible task, or one which is generations away in the future.

I disagree with this position, and maintain that fully integrated humans are a reality today. They may not yet outnumber the five-sensory human, but we are rapidly approaching the pivot point of this development in our evolution. In answer to the skeptics, I would like to share with you an excerpt taken from the diary of a young woman who possessed an extraordinary ability to see with the soul, even in the most dire of material conditions.

You know, if you don't have the inner strength while you're here to understand that all outer appearances are a passing show, as nothing beside the great splendor (I can't think of a better word right now) inside us—then things can look very black here indeed. The misery here is quite terrible and yet late at night when the day has slunk away into the depths behind me, I often walk with a spring in my step along the barbed wire and then time and again it soars straight from my heart—I can't help it, that's just the way it is, like some elementary force—the feeling that life is glorious and magnificent, and that one day we shall be building a whole new world.[3]

This excerpt, which has been described as "a testimony of faith, hope, and love, written in hell," was taken from the diary of Etty Hillesum, a native of Holland, who died in the Holocaust at the age of twenty-nine. It was written shortly before her death at Auschwitz, the most notorious of Nazi concentration camps.

Somehow, Etty was able to look beyond the physical atrocities which surrounded her and see through to the reality of spirit. Even in the depths of the most brutal conditions known to man, Etty was able to raise her vision upward to catch a glimpse of our true potential as spiritual beings. Etty was truly a light shining in the darkness, a light that will never be extinguished but will exist for all eternity, etched upon the skein of space and time. Her courage and insight remain an inspiration for all, and should impel us to try to make her vision a reality.

Still, there are those who would say that exceptional times call for exceptional measures, and maintain that the Ettys of this world are far and few between. They doubt that such insight would occur under the weight of everyday existence which wears us down so insidiously that we do not even see the depths to which we have fallen. In answer to those critics, I will share another story of an improbable accomplishment, namely the growing of a garden in Cabrini Green.

Cabrini Green, in Chicago, Illinois, was one of the first low-income housing projects to be built in this country. Originally intended as a solution to inner city problems, it was designed as a self-sufficient community, offering not only affordable, decent housing but a school, church, playground, and recreational areas. Within a few years it became apparent that this American dream was not working out as planned. Petty crime plagued the residents, and it wasn't long before gangs and drug dealers moved in, destroying any hope for a decent way of life. Ten years after its inception, Cabrini was one of the worst crime- and drug-ridden areas of the city. Destruction of property ran rampant, and many of the buildings were left in shambles. Even the police could not enter the area safely, and special teams were assigned to try to contain the chaos. Drug deals and shootings became a way of life. Gangs actively recruited new members from among the younger children in full view of parental authorities who were helpless to stop it. Children going to school walked over dried blood from drug deals gone bad, and thought nothing of falling to the ground at the first sound of gunfire. The school itself instituted a policy so that when gunfire erupted outside, teachers were advised over the public address system to close windows and doors, for fear a stray bullet would enter.

Then, five years ago, a man named Jack Davis happened to have his shoes shined by some boys who lived in Cabrini Green. At first Jack was surprised to hear the youngsters were from Cabrini because of its well-known reputation for crime. Here, he thought, were two boys who were trying to make an honest dollar. He wondered if there were any other children who might be interested in doing the same. An unconventional idea formed in Jack's mind as he asked the boys if there were any vacant fields near the project. Hearing that there were several, Jack acted upon his most unusual idea.

He approached the Cabrini Green Residents' Committee and proposed to start a garden in Cabrini Green. He would provide the initial capital to purchase seeds and equipment so that he could start a vegetable garden in one of the vacant lots. With the help of interested children who lived there, he would supervise the care of the garden and share the profits with them following the fall harvest. Although the committee was skeptical that the idea of this "white" gentleman from southern Illinois would succeed, they agreed to let him try.

Jack did find several children who were interested in his idea and committed themselves to working that summer in return for a share of the fall profits. The first year was not an easy one, as Jack and the children were harassed, and residents stole the tomatoes and peppers prior to harvest. Still, they were able to make a small profit and Jack vowed to return the following spring.

The start of the second year did not prove to be any easier. Jack saw that he would need neighborhood support to make the garden a success. A devout Christian, Jack sought help through the local church. With the help of Pastor Thomas Murdock, he connected with Dan Underwood, a Cabrini resident known for being a "community shaker and mover." When Dan first went to meet Jack, he found him and the children lying on the ground, taking cover from nearby gunfire. Convinced that Jack was committed to making the garden a success, he agreed to help.

Dan began to recruit more children and muster neighborhood support. As the garden grew, Jack sought outside assistance, and secured the financial and advisory support of the Burpee Seed Company. By the third year, the project had grown to include three garden plots as well as a field in Elburn, Illinois, whose use was donated by Burpee. Jack's simple garden project became "Cabrini Greens," and they now sold produce to local restaurants and grocers. By the fifth year, they were growing special order vegetables for four-star restaurants in the Chicago area, and expanded their sales to a local farmer's market. Twenty-seven children worked on Cabrini Greens last year, taking in a net profit of over $6,000.

More important, however, are the personal stories which have sprung from the success of this unconventional idea. One teenage girl who worked in the gardens for several years recently received a full college scholarship in horticulture. A boy was taken on as an apprentice chef by a world-renowned restaurant, which will sponsor him at a Parisian cooking school at the completion of his training.

When I first heard this story, I couldn't believe this was the same Cabrini Green I was familiar with. As a native of Chicago, I knew too well the horror stories which surrounded that place. That such an idea could succeed in the midst of despair and turmoil caught me totally by surprise. Then I realized that this story is but one more example of the transformation which is enveloping the human species. Jack, Dan, Pastor Murdock, and the children who volunteered to work in the dirt of the earth, refused to see things as others perceived them, and instead looked beyond to how they knew things could be. And so a garden of hope now grows in Cabrini Green, and I know that if a garden can grow there, it can grow anywhere. That garden is more than a success story, it is the promise of our future.

The Journey Home

Since the moment we had the erroneous thought of

separation from God, we have been seeking the way back to a state of oneness with the Creative Force. Our entire history has been the saga of that journey. Our travels up to this point have been arduous and slow. At times it seemed that for each step forward, we were thrown two steps back. Yet we have persevered, as Edgar Cayce said, "line upon line, precept upon precept, here a little, there a little."

Today, with the development of multisensory perception, we are ready to bring memory of the First Cause to conscious awareness. With this comes the realization that as co-creators with God, we possess the power within to direct the course our future evolution will take. We can hasten our journey homeward on the upward spiral of spiritual evolution simply by making the conscious choice to do so.

This is our birthright and our destiny. This was the hope of Etty Hillesum's visions as well. This was the hope of Jack Davis and the children of Cabrini Green when they planted those first seeds. We owe it to them and to the countless others who died for the belief that we are more than we appear to be, to ensure that those beliefs become reality. Each person possesses the power to change the world by first changing him- or herself. You need only look deeply within and remember your spiritual origins and the purpose for which you were created. To seek anything else is to deny a portion of yourself.

The critical year of 1998 is rapidly approaching. The time of the prophecies is upon us. The time of change is now. Let each one of us do everything possible to become one of the lights shining through the darkness, loudly proclaiming that we are more than we appear to be, proudly declaring our kinship with God. By allowing your spiritual attributes to manifest in this material world, you will truly become a blessing to others, for

God's love and light will shine through, illuminating all you touch. As you do so, you make the choice of conscious evolution and raise not only yourself, but all of humanity, a little bit closer to the goal which we all seek to attain—a return to our original state of oneness as co-creators and companions with God.

> *The journey to God is merely the reawakening of the knowledge of where you are always, and that you are forever.*
>   *It is a journey without distance to a goal that has never changed.*
>   —*A Course in Miracles*

p168 - Refer to the Buddhist "Maytreya"...
Are you familiar with a character who calls himself that in (Maryland)...
Who seems to appear to crowds, etc
I read a book about that—and did not know what to make of it

The references to an emergence of an anti-Christ—seem to correspond somewhat with the coming into the world scene of Obama:—

p230 — Reference to a most intriguing date
Sept 17, 2001 — Any connection to 9/11?
" loss of spiritual awareness..."

Notes

Foreword

1. Metaphysics is defined as "the esoteric branch of philosophy which deals with first principles and ultimate grounds, causation, and the relation of universals to particulars." (*The Random House Dictionary of the English Language*, 2nd edition, unabridged, *sub verbo* "metaphysics," p. 1208).

2. *A Course in Miracles* is inspired writing that was received by Helen Schucman. In 1965, Helen, then a professor of medical psychology at Columbia University's College of Physicians and Surgeons, began to receive information through a voice which identified itself as "the Christ Spirit." This continued for seven years and resulted in a set of three books which comprise the *Course*. Its primary teaching is the undoing of guilt through love and forgiveness of others.

3. The concept of the Universal Consciousness, also called the Universal Mind or "collective consciousness," is centuries old and found in many cultures. It is based on the premise that all knowledge and understanding that has ever been and will be, exists as a collective whole which is everywhere present, existing independently of time and space.

4. Refer to *There Is a River*, Thomas Sugrue, A.R.E. Press, 1942.

5. Bernie S. Siegel, M.D., *Love, Medicine, and Miracles*, p. 6.

6. Fritjof Capra, "Modern Physics and Eastern Mysticism," *The Journal of Transpersonal Psychology*, 1976, vol. 8, no. 1, p. 20.

Preface
A New Millennium

1. For a complete discussion of this concept, refer to *The Seat of the Soul*, Gary Zukov.

2. Meave Leakey, "New Roots for Our Family Tree," *The Washington Post*, August 17, 1995, p. A-4.

3. For a detailed treatise of the mystical experience, consult *A Most Surprising Song*, Louann Stahl.

4. Albert Einstein, "The Religious Spirit of Science," *Ideas and Opinions*, p. 40.

5. Reading 2823-3.

Chapter One
Our Spiritual Origins: Creation of the Soul

1. The word "man" is used in this book in the scientific, generic sense, and refers to the human species, containing both the male and the female genders. It is not intended to be sexist in connotation or exclude the female of the species. The terms *humanity* and *humankind* are used where possible, yet there are times when I consider their use to be cumbersome and unwieldy, and detrimental to the flow of the thought being expressed. In these cases, I have used the generic term "man."

2. I wish to credit author John Van Auken for his lucid explanation of this concept in his many writings and lectures.

3. Edgar Cayce reading ("Reading") 5753-1.

4. Reading 262-52.

5. Reading 5246-1.

6. Reading 1567-2.

7. Reading 263-13.

8. Reading 5755-2.

9. Reading 1549-1.

10. Reading 5367-1.

11. Reading 262-56.

12. *A Search for God*, Book II, "Spirit," pp. 120-121.

13. Refer to *A Course in Miracles*, Foundation for Inner Peace, p. 351.

14. *A Search for God*, Book II, "Spirit," p. 121.

15. Ibid.

16. Science operates from the paradigm or framework of physical verification. In order to be considered as a valid observation, an event must be repeatedly observable and measurable by independent physical means. Religion, of course, accepts as evidence that which cannot be detected by the physical senses. It operates from a nonphysical frame of reference.

17. Those desiring more information on scientific cosmology should refer to *The Left Hand of Creation* by John Barrow

and Joseph Silk, and *The Omega Point* by John Gribbin.

18. For a more complete discussion of the Edgar Cayce readings' description of this period in earth's history, refer to *The Creation Trilogy*, Eula Allen.

19. Reading 364-7.

20. I wish to express my thanks to Jerry Lekstrom and Deirdre Aragon, for their intuitive insights regarding the three soul groups who entered the earth plane during these times.

21. Some scholars identify this group of 144,000 souls with the "elect" referred to in the Bible. While the readings indicate that these individuals have repeatedly incarnated into the earth plane as a group, to help raise the consciousness of humankind, they also make it clear that this is not an exclusive gathering. Any individual who makes the commitment to manifest the Truth in daily life becomes one of the "elect," the true Israel, the true seeker.

22. Reading 294-8.

23. Reading 364-8.

24. Reading 364-3.

25. The Eastern concepts of *yin* and *yang* perhaps best describe these two aspects, which relate to the two polarities of the soul. All force has a positive or negative charge, and the soul, being energy, possesses this characteristic as well. *Yang* refers to the positive polarity, that which is outward, present, and active, called the masculine. *Yin* refers to the negative polarity, that which is inner, hidden, and receptive, called the feminine. Our original soul nature consists of both these aspects. Upon entry into the body, however, the soul chooses which aspect to project, thus determining which sex will manifest.

26. Reading 364-7.

27. Reading 364-3.

28. Reading 1968-2.

Chapter Two
Our Physical Heritage: Creation of the Human Body

1. Reading 900-24.

2. Reading 2454-3.

3. Reading 2156-2.
4. Reading 364-7.
5. Reading 262-63.
6. Reading Reports 294-202.
7. "The Coming of Man," Hugh Lynn Cayce, *A.R.E. Bulletin*, December, 1932, p. 1.
8. Reading 900-227.
9. The Edgar Cayce readings present a great deal of material on the "lost continent of Atlantis." Refer to *Edgar Cayce on Atlantis*, Edgar Evans Cayce.
10. Reading 900-70.
11. Reading 5753-2.
12. Reading 281-63.
13. Refer to reading 2067-7. Question: "When did the knowledge come to Jesus that He was to be the Savior of the world?" Answer: "When He fell in Eden."
14. Reading 5749-3.
15. Reading 3744-5.
16. Reading Reports 364-13.
17. "The Meaning of Edgar Cayce," Thomas Sugrue, *A.R.E. Bulletin*, June, 1947, page unknown.
18. According to the Cayce readings, the glands of the endocrine system are the spiritual centers of the soul within the body. This concept is discussed in depth in Chapter Four.
19. Sugrue, op. cit., page unknown.
20. Reading 900-70.
21. Reading 364-3.
22. Reading 5056-1.
23. Reading 364-11.
24. Reading 3744-5.
25. Ibid.

Chapter Three
Our Mental Legacy: The Evolution of Human Consciousness
1. Reading 3744-5.
2. Reading 262-81.
3. Reading 262-56.
4. Quotation attributed to Charles Fillmore, co-founder of

the Unity School of Christianity.

5. For further information refer to *Creative Visualization,* Shakti Gwain.

6. A paradigm filters information received and rejects stimuli which do not fit into its framework. Paradigms thus establish the boundaries for belief systems. Studies have shown that a researcher will disregard or even alter data which does not fit into his or her accepted paradigm.

7. Helen Keller, *The Story of My Life,* p. 36.

8. The discussion on culture does not include any of the information on the development of Atlantis as given in the Edgar Cayce readings. The reason for this is that culture, as addressed here, refers to universal human culture, and not the particular development of one group of people. The readings make it clear that the activities in Atlantis were specific to that area and people; they are not representative of human history on a global scale. *"These, then, able to use in their gradual development all the forces as were manifest in their individual surroundings . . . these became much speedier in this particular portion of the globe than in others . . . "* (Reading 364-3)

9. Carol R. Ember and Melvin Ember, *Cultural Anthropology,* p. 384.

Chapter Four
Three in One: Body, Mind, and Soul

1. Wilder Penfield, *The Mystery of the Mind: A Critical Study of Consciousness and the Human Brain,* as quoted in *Closer to the Light: Learning from the Near-Death Experiences of Children,* Melvin Morse, p. 101.

2. Edgar Cayce, *Auras,* p. 5.

3. Refer to *Auras,* Edgar Cayce.

4. Reading 319-2.

5. Rosemary Ellen Guilen, editor, *Harper's Encyclopedia of Mystical and Paranormal Experience,* "Chakras," p. 86.

6. Reading 262-20.

7. Those desiring more in-depth information on the chakras can consult *Color and Crystals: A Journey Through the Chakras,* Joy Gardner; *The Chakras,* C.W. Leadbeater;

or *Healing Hands*, Eileen Brennan.

8. Joy Gardner, *Color and Crystals: A Journey Through the Chakras*, p. 73.

9. Refer to Matthew 7:13-14: "Enter by the narrow gate; for the gate is wide and the way is easy, that leads to destruction, and those who enter by it are many. For the gate is narrow and the way is hard that leads to life, and those who find it are few." (RSV)

10. Reading 262-20.

11. Refer to Psalm 24:7: "Lift up your heads, O gates! and be lifted up, O ancient doors! that the King of glory may come in." (RSV)

12. Reading 262-20.

13. Reading 281-31.

Chapter Five
World Culture Today

1. Bruce McArthur, *Your Life: Why It Is the Way It Is and What You Can Do About It*, p. 5.

2. Reincarnation, as defined in the readings, does not include the Hindu concept of transmigration, which is the belief that the soul also enters animal bodies. The entry of souls into animal forms during the early part of earth history is considered an aberrant manifestation, not intended as a natural path of soul development, and one that has not occurred since. The readings make it clear that transmigration of the soul into animal bodies for purposes of reincarnation does not occur.

3. Reading 1554-3.

4. Reading 3976-29.

5. Reading 2800-2.

6. Reading 3976-15.

7. Reading 416-17.

8. Reading 3976-18.

9. Refer to *A Search for God*, Book II, "Day and Night," p. 154.

Chapter Six

Biological Evolution: Emergence of the Multisensory Human

1. A number of the following excerpts were originally compiled in *A Most Surprising Song: Exploring the Mystical Experience*, Louann Stahl. The original source of the quotations are noted in the following endnotes. Anyone wishing to explore the mystic experience in greater depth is encouraged to refer to this most excellent source book.

2. Nona Coxhead, *The Relevance of Bliss*, p. 44.

3. Arthur Koestler, *The Invisible Writing*, 1984, p. 427.

4. Jonathan Star, *Two Suns Rising: A Collection of Sacred Writings*, p. 181.

5. F. C. Happold, *Mysticism*, p. 34.

6. Arthur M. Abell, *Talks with Great Composers*, p. 6.

7. Coxhead, op. cit., p. 30.

8. Dante, *The Divine Comedy*, p. 605.

9. Raynor C. Johnson, *Watcher on the Hills*, p. 23.

10. Star, op. cit., p. 135.

11. As quoted in *The Protestant Mystics*, Little, Brown & Company, Boston, 1964, p. 320.

12. Paul Mendes-Flohr, editor, collected and introduced by Martin Buber, *Ecstatic Confessions*, p. 81.

13. Anwar Sadat, *In Search of Identity: An Autobiography*, Harper & Row, New York, 1977, p. 73.

14. In most cultures, shaman are male, although cases of female shaman have been identified.

15. Carlos Warter, M.D., Ph.D., *Recovery of the Sacred*, p. 23.

16. Richard Maurice Bucke, M.D., *Cosmic Consciousness*, p. 77.

17. Happold, op. cit., p. 34.

18. "New Thought" religions include the Church of the Christian Scientist, and the Unity School of Christianity, both of which emphasize a metaphysical approach to the study and practice of Christ's teachings.

Chapter Seven

Cognitive Evolution: Perception and Human Consciousness

1. David Layzer, *Cosmogenesis: The Growth of Order in the Universe*, p. 239.

2. Serge King, *Shaman's Path*, "Seeing Is Believing: The Four Worlds of a Shaman," p. 44.

3. As quoted in *A Most Surprising Song: Exploring the Mystical Experience*, Louann Stahl, p. 64.

4. Gary Zukav, *Seat of the Soul*, p. 12.

5. For more information on this theory refer to *A New Science of Life: The Hypothesis of Formative Causation*, Rupert Sheldrake.

6. *The Celestine Prophecy: An Experiential Guide*, James Redfield and Carol Adrienne, p. 27.

7. Zukav, op. cit., p. 27.

8. Carlos Warter, *Recovery of the Sacred*, p. xix.

9. Ibid., p. xiv.

Chapter Eight
Ancient Prophecies, Modern Visions:
Predictions for a Changing World

1. *The New Grolier Multimedia Encyclopedia*, Release 6, 1993, "precession of the equinoxes."

2. Those interested in learning more about the mathematical correlations of the Mayan calendar as reflective of a galactic harmonic beam which affects our evolution and planetary existence, can refer to *The Mayan Factor*, Jose Arguelles.

3. Frank Waters, *Book of the Hopi*, p. xiv.

4. Reading 2780-3.

5. John Hogue, *Nostradamus and the Millennium*, 1987.

6. Reading 2780-3.

7. See readings 3976-15, 1152-11, 311-8, 958-3, 270-35, and 826-8.

8. Reading 416-7.

9. Reading 1602-6.

10. Refer to *Mary's Message to the World* and *Messages to Our Family*, both by Annie Kirkwood.

11. Reading 5749-5.

12. Reading 5749-4.

13. Reading 5749-4.

14. Reading 364-7.

15. Reading 364-8.

16. Reading 5749-5.
17. Reading 5749-5.
18. Reading 3976-15.

Chapter Nine
Understanding the Nature of Prophecy

1. For a complete discussion of Bauval's theories, refer to *The Orion Mystery: Unlocking the Secrets of the Pyramids*, Robert Bauval and Adrian Gilbert.
2. Reading 5748-5.
3. Reading 5748-6.
4. Reading 294-151.
5. John Van Auken, *Ancient Egyptian Mysticism*, p. 38.
6. Reading 5748-5.
7. Reading 364-8.
8. Reading 262-49.
9. David Davidson and H. Aldersmith, *The Great Pyramid and Its Divine Message*, p. 117.
10. Refer to *The Second Coming*, Kirk Nelson.
11. Reading 2329-3.
12. Ibid.
13. Reading 378-16.
14. Reading 5748-6.
15. Readings 311-10 and 416-7.
16. For more information on these predictions refer to *The Earth Changes Report*, Gordon-Michael Scallion, editor, Matrix Institute Inc., various issues.
17. Reading 900-370.
18. Reading 849-11.

Author's Postscript

1. Morphology refers to the body's gross anatomical structure, such as bone, muscle, tissues, and organs. Physiology refers to the body's functions or processes in terms of chemistry and physics.
2. Reading 5755-2.
3. Etty Hillesum, *An Interrupted Life*, pp. 247 and 253.

Selected References

Allen, Eula. *The Creation Trilogy.* Virginia Beach, Virginia: A.R.E. Press, 1966.

Arguelles, Jose. *The Mayan Factor.* Santa Fe, New Mexico: Bear & Company, 1987.

Barrow, John, and Joseph Silk. *The Left Hand of Creation.* New York: Basic Books, Inc., Publishers, 1983.

Bauval, Robert, and Adrian Gilbert. *The Orion Mystery: Unlocking the Secrets of the Pyramids.* New York: Crown Publishers, Inc., 1994.

Cayce, Edgar. *Auras.* Virginia Beach, Virginia: A.R.E. Press, 1945.

Cayce, Edgar Evans. *Edgar Cayce on Atlantis.* New York: Warner Books, 1968.

Course in Miracles, A. Tiburon, California: Foundation for Inner Peace, 1975.

Davidson, David, and H. Aldersmith. *The Great Pyramid and Its Divine Message.* London: Williams & Norgate, Ltd., 1948.

Gardner, Joy. *Color and Crystals: A Journey Through the Chakras.* Freedom, California: The Crossing Press, 1988.

Gribbin, John. *The Omega Point.* New York: Bantam Books, 1988.

Gwain, Shakti. *Creative Visualization.* San Rafael, California: New World Library, 1978.

Hogue, John. *Nostradamus and the Millennium.* Garden City, New York: Doubleday & Company, Inc., 1987.

Keller, Helen, *The Story of My Life.* New York: Dell, 1902.

Keyes, Ken, Jr. *The Hundredth Monkey.* St. Mary, Kentucky: Vision Books, 1981.

King, Serge. "Seeing Is Believing: The Four Worlds of a Shaman," *Shaman's Path*, Gary Doore, editor. Boston: Shambala, 1988.

Kirkwood, Annie. *Mary's Message to the World*. California: Blue Dolphin, 1995.

Lambert, David. *The Field Guide to Early Man*. New York: Facts on File, 1987.

Layzer, David. *Cosmogenesis: The Growth of Order in the Universe*. New York: Oxford University Press, 1990.

Leakey, Richard, and Lewin, Roger. *Origins: The Emergence and Evolution of Our Species and Its Possible Future*. New York: E. P. Dutton, Inc., 1982.

McArthur, Bruce. *Your Life: Why It Is the Way It Is and What You Can Do About It*. Virginia Beach, Virginia: A.R.E. Press, 1993.

Nelson, Kirk. *The Second Coming*. Virginia Beach, Virginia: Wright Publishing Company, 1986.

Redfield, James. *The Celestine Prophecy*. Hoover, Alabama: Satori Publishing, 1992.

Robinson, Lytle. *Edgar Cayce's Story of the Origin and Destiny of Man*. New York: Berkley Publishing Corp., 1972.

Search for God, Books I and II. Virginia Beach, Virginia: A.R.E. Press, 1992 (anniversary edition).

Stahl, Louann. *A Most Surprising Song: Exploring the Mystical Experience*. Unity Village, Missouri: Unity School of Christianity, 1992.

Star, Jonathan. *Two Suns Rising: A Collection of Sacred Writings*. New York: Bantam Books, 1991.

Sugrue, Thomas. *There Is a River: The Story of Edgar Cayce*. Virginia Beach, Virginia: A.R.E. Press, 1973.

Timms, Moira. *Beyond Prophecies and Predictions*. New York: Ballantine Books, 1994.

Warter, Carlos, M.D., Ph.D. *Recovery of the Sacred.* Florida: Health Communications, Inc., 1994.

Waters, Frank. *The Book of the Hopi.* New York: Penguin Books, 1963.

Zukav, Gary. *The Seat of the Soul.* New York: Simon & Schuster, Inc., 1989.

About the Author

Kathy L. Callahan, Ph.D., was born in Chicago, Illinois. She received a bachelor's degree from the University of Illinois at Chicago Circle, and a Master of Science degree from Purdue University. As a graduate student, she traveled to Tucson, Arizona, where she completed an assessment study of alcoholism treatment modalities for urban Papago Indians, for which she earned a Ph.D., also from Purdue University. She was commissioned as an officer in the U.S. Navy in 1982, and has served on active duty since that time.

A longtime member of the Association for Research and Enlightenment, Inc., she strives to actively apply the principles found in the Edgar Cayce readings in her daily life. Her first book, *Unseen Hands and Unknown Hearts: A Miracle of Healing Created Through Prayer,* is based on her personal experience of a miraculous healing, aided by a nationwide prayer network, that occurred when her daughter contracted a life-threatening disease in 1991. Following the publication of *Unseen Hands and Unknown Hearts,* she wrote for *Miracles Magazine* and was interviewed by *Family Circle Magazine.* She was also featured on the syndicated television show *Sightings,* and on a segment of the Arts & Entertainment cable television show *Unexplained.*

She resides in Fairfax, Virginia, with her husband, Tino Aragon, their daughter, Deirdre, and their family dog, Spirit.

A.R.E. PRESS

The A.R.E. Press publishes quality books, videos, and audiotapes meant to improve the quality of our readers' lives—personally, professionally, and spiritually. We hope our products support your endeavors to realize your career potential, to enhance your relationships, to improve your health, and to encourage you to make the changes necessary to live a loving, joyful, and fulfilling life.

For more information or to receive a free catalog, call

1-800-723-1112

Or write

A.R.E. Press
215 67th Street
Virginia Beach, VA 23451-2061

DISCOVER HOW THE EDGAR CAYCE MATERIAL CAN HELP YOU!

The Association for Research and Enlightenment, Inc. (A.R.E.®), was founded in 1931 by Edgar Cayce. Its international headquarters are in Virginia Beach, Virginia, where thousands of visitors come year round. Many more are helped and inspired by A.R.E.'s local activities in their own hometowns or by contact via mail (and now the Internet!) with A.R.E. headquarters.

People from all walks of life, all around the world, have discovered meaningful and life-transforming insights in the A.R.E. programs and materials, which focus on such areas as holistic health, dreams, family life, finding your best vocation, reincarnation, ESP, meditation, personal spirituality, and soul growth in small-group settings. Call us today on our toll-free number

1-800-333-4499

or

Explore our electronic visitor's center on the
INTERNET: **http://www.are-cayce.com**
We'll be happy to tell you more about how the work of the A.R.E. can help you!

A.R.E.
215 67th Street
Virginia Beach, VA 23451-2061